God and the Natural World

For Gene,
in celebration of our friendship
and
in appreciation of your encouragement
of my work,

Walt

God and the Natural World

Religion and Science
in Antebellum America

Walter H. Conser, Jr.

UNIVERSITY OF SOUTH CAROLINA PRESS

Published in Columbia, South Carolina, by the
University of South Carolina Press

Manufactured in the United States of America

Library of Congress Cataloging-in-Publication Data

Conser, Walter H.
   God and the natural world : religion and science in antebellum
America / Walter H. Conser, Jr.
     p. cm.
   Includes bibliographical references and index.
   ISBN 0–87249–893–X (hardcover : alk. paper)
   1. Theology, Doctrinal—Southern States—History—19th century.
2. Faith and reason—Christianity—History of doctrines—19th
century. 3. Religion and science—Southern States—1800–1859.
4. Southern States—Intellectual life—19th century. I. Title.
BT30.U6C66   1993
261.5′5′097509034—dc20   93-1422

TO JANET

Contents

Acknowledgments

In 1983, during the commemoration of the five hundredth anniversary of Martin Luther's birth and the centennial observation of Karl Marx's death, I began my archival research on the *Vermittlungstheologie* in the (then) German Democratic Republic. In the no less auspicious year of 1990, as East and West Germany reunited, I concluded that research. I wish to thank the staff of the Katechetisches Oberseminar, the custodians of the August Tholuck Papers, for their hospitality during my stay in 1983. I also wish to give particular thanks to the faculty and staff of the John F. Kennedy Institute for North American Studies in the Free University Berlin for inviting me to spend the winter semester of 1990–91 as a visiting professor in the stimulating atmosphere of that institute and university.

Several institutions have generously given me permission to quote from collections in their holdings:

Princeton University Library
   Charles Hodge Papers
Speer Library of the Princeton Theological Seminary
   Charles Hodge Papers
South Caroliniana Library of the University of South Carolina
   James Henley Thornwell Papers
Evangelical and Reformed Historical Society and Lancaster
      Theological Seminary
   Philip Schaff Papers
Divinity School Library of Yale University
   Horace Bushnell Papers
Special Collections Department of the Robert Scott Small Library
      of the College of Charleston
   James Warley Miles Papers
Special Collections of Duke University
   James Warley Miles Papers
   Robert Gourdin Papers
Huntington Library, San Marino, California
   Francis Lieber Papers

Southern Historical Collection of the Library of the University of
    North Carolina at Chapel Hill
  Pettigrew Family Papers
  William Porcher Miles Papers
Katechetisches Oberseminar, Naumburg, Germany
  August Tholuck Papers
During the years I have worked on the topic of this book I have
come into the debt of many people. My colleagues in the Department
of Philosophy and Religion in the University of North Carolina at
Wilmington have been a frequent source of encouragement for me.
Outside this university other friends, including Professors Knud
Krakau, Ronald McCarthy, Keith Nelson, and Sumner Twiss, as well
as Dr. William C. Simpson, Jr., have all given me the benefit of their
insight and advice. Once again I owe a special measure of thanks to
Professor William G. McLoughlin for reading the entire manuscript
and saving me from several blunders. Emily Conser and David and
Megan Redmond likewise saved me from other no less important
mistakes, and I thank them too. Finally, I dedicate this book to Janet in
appreciation for all the energy, enthusiasm, and affection she has
shared with me.

God and the Natural World

Prologue

Controversies concerning science and religion have been much in the news of late. Newspaper editorials, television talk shows, and public forums have all discussed issues such as the appropriateness of teaching creationism versus evolution in public school curriculums, the beginning of human life as adjudicated by the courts, and the possibility of planetary destruction in a nuclear or ecological holocaust. While the urgency and seriousness of these contemporary deliberations are evident, one is also struck by the fact that reflection on the religious implications of scientific findings or, more generally, the nature of the relationship of science and religion can be traced in different forms in Western thought back through the Renaissance to the Middle Ages.

Beyond that many of the specific lines of argumentation, if not the individual issues themselves, appearing in these late-twentieth-century considerations have their roots in the antebellum American assessment of the engagement of science and religion. Deliberations, for example, over the nature of scientific method, the origin and nature of biological life, and the implications of technological innovations all took place in early-nineteenth-century America.

Historiographical interpretation of this relationship has usually depicted it in terms of conflict and, more specifically, the warfare of benighted religious forces with those of enlightened science. Here one found obligatory references to the condemnation of Galileo or, within the American context, the conviction of John Scopes in the famous Tennessee "Monkey Trial" of 1925. Similarly, the canonical texts of this approach, John William Draper's *History of the Conflict between Religion and Science* (1874) and Andrew Dickson White's *History of the Warfare of Science with Theology in Christendom* (1896), were often invoked to provide the standard themes of this interpretation.

Recently, this conventional evaluation has been revised, and a number of studies have recast the relationship of science and religion if not in terms of harmony then in terms of diverse interactions, specific divergences, and numerous instances of mutual support. A major result of this revisionist examination has been to remind scholars that science and religion are not monolithic entities but, rather, traditions

1

that have had complicated histories and whose organizational and conceptual boundaries have often overlapped with each other and with other groups.[1]

This book contributes to this revisionist approach by examining the relation of science and religion in the antebellum era and especially the interpretive strategies that a diverse group of mediational Protestant theologians in America employed to demonstrate to their age their commitment to the reconciliation of science and religion. Attention is concentrated on the Protestant tradition, for here was the locus of the antebellum discussion. Moreover, American Catholics and Jews in this era had other more pressing issues on their agenda. These theologians included Horace Bushnell, Charles Hodge, James Marsh, James Warley Miles, Edward Robinson, Philip Schaff, W. G. T. Shedd, Henry Boynton Smith, and James Henley Thornwell. I have called them "mediational theologians" for three reasons. First, individually and biographically they were influenced at many points by the mediational theology (*Vermittlungstheologie*) of nineteenth-century Germany. Second, they paralleled the European theological movement that included the mediational theologians of Germany but also the Broad Church movement in England and H. L. Martensen in Denmark and sought a reconciliation between Christian faith and modern science and culture, thereby hoping to bridge the historic division between supernaturalism and rationalism. Finally, many of the American controversies over the meaning and authority of science and religion have their roots in the antebellum era, and the mediational theologians responded to the tumult within their own profession and society at large with specific recommendations designed to resolve this dislocation of authority within American society.

Taken together, these American mediational theologians represent a remarkable and influential ensemble. Each of them received accolades and honors during his lifetime as well as enjoyed both national and international reputations. While their literary works ranged from tomes of systematic theology to journalistic forays into the more ephemeral issues of the day, all of these men had achieved prominence within the ranks of antebellum American society and had established ready audiences willing and eager to listen to their opinions, reflections, and advice. Charles Hodge, for example, was for several decades the lodestar of Princeton Seminary as well as a leader of the Old School wing within the Presbyterian church. James Henley Thornwell guided Southern Presbyterians throughout the controversies of the antebellum era and ultimately into the formation of their own Southern Presbyterian church. The challenges, rewards, and disappointments of academic theology were shared by others of the mediational theologians, as Edward Robinson, Philip Schaff, W. G. T. Shedd, and Henry Boynton Smith were all faculty members of Union Theological Seminary in New York City at one time or another in their careers, and together they influenced generations of students. Similarly, James Marsh, as president of the University of Vermont, left his mark on students and colleagues alike, having reformed the curriculum and introduced the writings of Samuel Taylor Coleridge to receptive readers in America. Finally, both Horace Bushnell and James Warley Miles, while serving most of their lives as parish ministers, established wider renown through their books and essays as well as public lectures. Combining access to pulpit and podium alike, then, these mediational theologians helped to define the issues, shape the strategies of discourse, and assess the meaning of the antebellum discussion of the relation of science and religion.

In American cultural studies and the historiography of modern science much attention has been given to the Darwinian controversy. By restricting itself to the antebellum era and, thus, to the deliberations in the decades immediately prior to Darwin's publication of his *Origin of Species* in 1859, this book provides new understanding and clarification of the specific historical relationship of science and religion in American culture.

Indeed, while this book focuses on the American context, roughly equivalent appraisals were taking place in England, France, and Germany. The geological explorations by James Hutton, the investigations in paleontology and comparative anatomy by Georges Cuvier, and the research in embryology by Karl Ernst von Baer, for example, were all examined in their respective countries for their religious implications as well as scientific consequences, and each elicited a wide range of responses by religious authorities. While scientific knowledge is not confined to nor an exclusive function of national boundaries, these scientific investigations in the decades before Darwin evoked spirited debates within their own countries at the same time that they contributed to a broader Euroamerican discussion and evaluation.[2]

Another theme that this book explores concerns the cultural meaning of science itself. For, while the post-Darwinian discussion of science and religion in America has largely focused on the implications of the findings of biology and geology, this volume demonstrates that the antebellum understanding of science was much broader, including anthropology, philology, and history as well as biology and geology. In the antebellum era the scientific field had not yet become so specialized in method and organization as would later become the case. Science in this earlier time period was thought of in general terms as entailing a principle of critical inquiry which could be widely applied rather than identifying a specific subject field.

Beyond exploring the comparatively neglected pre-Darwinian era this book also expands the intellectual context of the topic by identifying the specific avenues of appropriation of European thought and scholarship which these American mediational theologians drew on and utilized. The role of Scottish Common Sense philosophy and especially Baconianism in the antebellum era is well known. Much less attention has been given to the influence in America of Samuel Taylor Coleridge and virtually no consideration given to the German mediational school of theology. This is unfortunate, for, though Baconianism was significant, Coleridgean and other forms of romanticism played an important role in antebellum American reflection on science and religion. Beyond that the impact of German thought was diverse. It was certainly wider than Theodore Parker's assimilation of David Friedrich Strauss and was often drawn from specific schools of religious thought in Germany and thus was not the absorption of some free-floating amorphous Teutonic *Geist*. Consequently, attention to the specific intellectual backgrounds of these American Protestants is important and helps one more adequately understand the antebellum perspective on the engagement of science and religion.

Thomas Kuhn's well-known work on the structure of scientific revolutions has examined the role of paradigms in the history of science. Paradigms, at the very least, provide a community with a shared set of principles, beliefs, and values which help to order and explain the experience of a given community. Paradigms usually have a sufficient degree of flexibility built into them to encompass the flux of contingent experience; however, when radically innovative circumstances appear, paradigm shifts can occur, and communities can coalesce around new interpretations of experience.[3]

Antebellum American Protestants inherited if not a full-fledged paradigm, then at least a broad consensus regarding the relationship of science and religion. Scientific study of the Book of Nature, they believed, complemented pious examination of the books of the Bible.

Moreover, investigation of the natural world revealed the pattern of beneficent purposes for which God had created the world. Finally, it was argued that, in the biographical interests and professional careers of many scientists, one could see the reconciliation of scientific investigation and religious commitment.

During the first half of the nineteenth century this consensus came under attack for several reasons. Although scientific and religious traditions had provided models of authority and comprehensive understandings of the world for many centuries in the West, by the seventeenth century the Christian worldview was losing its explanatory franchise in the face of competing scientific findings. By the mid nineteenth century America was experiencing a widespread crisis of religious authority in which specific controversies over the age of the Earth, the unity of mankind, and the forms of biblical interpretation challenged older, more familiar Christian explanations. Added to these intellectual challenges were social ones. For by the antebellum era those broad processes of social transformation which historians call democratization were underway in American society, processes that contained wide-ranging implications for American Christianity. Taken together, then, these patterns of intellectual innovation and social transformation provide the context for the contributions of the mediational theologians in reworking the older consensus and responding to the fresh challenges of their day.

The responses of the mediational theologians to the crisis of religious authority in the antebellum era can be divided into three sorts of interpretive strategies. The first strategy focused on an appeal to history as a means of reconciling science and religion. In this view the physical world of nature and the historical world of mankind were linked together in dynamic and ultimately developmental patterns. Attention to these teleological arrangements could provide grounds for overcoming the persistent doubts facing American society.

The second strategy amounted to an affirmation of scientific method. Here the unity of scientific method, whether practiced in geology or theology, was insisted upon. Beyond that an emphasis on empiricism and the systematic presentation of the facts thus attained played a prominent role in this presentation.

The last strategy presented an analysis that asserted the dynamic nature of language and recognized the symbolic dimensions of all language. By clarifying the nature of language, one could illuminate and perhaps eliminate those controversies over the meanings of words which separated men and women. Thus, proper appreciation for the different levels upon which language operated would provide an avenue for the reconciliation of science and religion.

Finally, in addition to these interpretive strategies for mediating the claims of science and religion, these Protestant theologians proposed numerous answers to the social problems of their society. Slavery and the secession crisis were the two most pressing issues, and, while the recommendations of these churchmen were uniformly moralistic in tone and conservative in outlook, they were ultimately as divided among themselves as was the rest of the nation.

Political dates rarely mark correctly the contours of intellectual and cultural history. In the case of the mediational theologians, however, there is a serendipitous symmetry between the beginning of the Civil War and the publication of Darwin's *Origin of Species*. For, just as the shots at Fort Sumter brought the antebellum era to a close, so did Darwin's book, at least in the minds of the mediational theologians, represent an assault every bit as deadly as a cannon shot to their reconciliation of science and religion. Politics and culture, then, both contributed to a sense of crisis in the antebellum era of American history.

Historians of the post-Darwinian controversies in America have traditionally divided the religious response to Darwin between modernists and fundamentalists. It is a testimony to the significance of the mediational theologians that their work provided important resources for American Protestantism as it grappled with the implications of Darwinism and the profound shifts, which it seemed to entail. Thus, while the mediational theologians themselves were not sympathetic to Darwinian evolution, the work of Horace Bushnell, for example, with his efforts to redirect theology—by focusing on experience rather than dogmatic apprehension, by insisting on the fluid and symbolic nature of language, and by favorably evaluating the importance of science—provided modernists with the tools they needed to explore a new reconciliation between science and religion.

Similarly, in the work of Charles Hodge, with its claims concerning scientific method, fundamentalists found ammunition with which to attack Darwin, and, indeed, reverberations from that attack can still be heard today. The roots of Hodge's criticism could all be found in his antebellum writings and, as expressed in his extended essay *What Is Darwinism?* represent what one student of American fundamentalism has called the "classic formulation of the conservative position."[4]

The crisis of religious authority expressed in the polemics over science and religion and taking place in the last quarter of the nineteenth century in America has deep roots in the earlier antebellum era. The Darwinian controversy was more the catalyst for the debate within American Christianity than it was its originator. One cannot properly appreciate this fact unless one recognizes the nature and range of the discussion over science and religion which took place in the decades immediately preceding the publication of Darwin's volume. Thus, the mediational theologians were significant members of their nineteenth-century society, even if they have not loomed as large in its twentieth-century historiography. In their interpretive principles for the reconciliation of science and religion as well as in their social commentary, which derived from those principles, they made their mark on American society and their own distinctive contribution to nineteenth-century American Christianity.

Chapter One

The Crisis of Religious Authority

In 1859 Edward Hitchcock published an expanded edition of his book *The Religion of Geology and Its Connected Sciences*. In the history of the relation of science and religion the year 1859 has become better known for the publication of Charles Darwin's *Origin of Species;* nevertheless, the success of Hitchcock's popular first edition bolstered the confidence of the author and his publisher in bringing out this new edition. The purpose of Hitchcock's volume was straightforward—to demonstrate the reconciliation of science and religion. The argument over the compatibility of science and religion was an old one, dating back easily to the Renaissance; new discoveries in the eighteenth and nineteenth centuries, however, were putting renewed strains on older understandings and calling for fresh interpretations of the issues. In his book Hitchcock contended that science correctly understood and revelation rightly interpreted demonstrated no fundamental contradictions between themselves. Indeed, neither religion nor science had anything to fear from each other and ought to recognize the essential harmony and mutual corroboration that they shared.

Moreover, Hitchcock insisted that the supposed problems between science and religion were simply apparent discrepancies rather than real antagonisms. The general nature of scientific method was well established in the inductive examination of facts and the discovery of the laws by which the universe operated. Using this method the scientific community was, he argued, establishing "the settled and demonstrated principles of science." Thus, to understand science correctly was to examine this growing body of information. Likewise, other scholars were determining the meaning of the Scriptures through the use of the relevant rules of criticism and the clarification of the context and intention of the biblical authors. Once these procedures were properly employed, Hitchcock predicted, any seeming conflicts could be resolved. To be sure, he warned that one should not forget the true purpose of the Bible, which was, he contended, to teach the world religious truth. Scientific statements in the Scriptures, Hitchcock observed, were often couched in popular terms that were easily understood by the public and not in the precise and strict language of the modern scientist. Yet even differences in forms of expression could not hide the evidences of design and purpose which were so abundantly available in the researches of the physical sciences and which led one, Hitchcock confidently concluded, "almost necessarily to their divine Author."[1]

The invocation of induction, the examination of the uses of language, and the praise of design were familiar aspects of the antebellum discussion of the relation of science and religion. And Edward Hitchcock was a perfect choice to defend their harmony in these ways and others. Ordained as a Congregational minister, Hitchcock was also a trained geologist, who was responsible for state surveys in Massachusetts, New York, and Vermont and had additionally presided in 1840 as the first chairman of the Association of American Geologists. In 1825 he had joined the faculty of Amherst College and over the next several decades served there as professor of chemistry and natural history, then president of the college, and finally as professor of geology and natural theology. Hitchcock's portrait shows a stern man, smooth-shaven and dignified, with features that his era described as strong. Combining an engaging manner with his impressive professional background and institutional position, Hitchcock was equally at home on the lyceum circuit or the college rostrum, armed usually with a geologist's pick in one hand and a copy of the Bible in the other. Yet these pursuits entailed familiar hardships, as Hitchcock confessed that his popularity drew letters and inquiries about issues as diverse as the purchasing of fossils or a theory of continental drift to supplying a pulpit and the relation of geology to Noah and Moses.[2]

Still one theme remained constant in his work: "to illustrate, by the scientific facts which I taught, the principles of natural theology." In his inaugural address as president of Amherst College Hitchcock underscored this point when he observed, "every scientific truth becomes a religious truth, and nature is converted into one great temple." Concepts of divine purpose and design in nature again framed his interpretation and played an important role in his analysis particularly of his own specialty of geology. On an even broader level, though, Hitchcock averred that sound learning of all sorts and true religion were likewise linked in common goals and causes.[3]

Such a claim might hardly seem startling; however, in the context of early nineteenth-century American Protestantism, with its well-attended camp meetings and revivals, its popular suspicions of scriptural criticism, and its preference for immediate experience over received tradition, Hitchcock's appeal deserves note. Beyond that

Hitchcock's volume highlighted the questions of the meaning of science and the nature of the controversy between science and religion in the antebellum American scene. Finally, in his characteristic appeal to the very argument of design and purpose, which so many of his contemporaries found persuasive, Hitchcock irrevocably dated his book once the full impact of the Darwinian perspective became clear.

Science, Religion, and American Culture

Science in the antebellum era was practical and utilitarian in outlook. This understanding of science derived from that broader seventeenth-century reorientation and redefinition of science which shifted the prevailing conception of science from the inquisitive study of the medieval Scholastics to the instrumental exploration of Francis Bacon. In the scholastic perspective the universe was finite, hierarchical, and purposefully ordered. The natural order extended from the center of the earth to the distant stars. Science, within this context, consisted of the contemplation of this ordered world and the application of metaphysical principles to the phenomena of this world. Through the organization of these metaphysical truths into encyclopedic syllabi, compendia, and commentaries, the scholastic scientist strove for systematic presentation of all knowledge. The scientific revolution associated with Johannes Kepler, Galileo Galilei, William Harvey, Isaac Newton, and Francis Bacon, as one historian observed, replaced the cosmology of the closed world of the ancients with the open one of the moderns. In the place of a well-ordered and naturally stratified cosmos an infinite universe organized by mechanical laws emerged.[4]

Further implications, symbolized by the contributions of Francis Bacon, developed out of this reorientation. More as a philosopher than as a practitioner of science, Bacon epitomized four aspects of the new science. First, in a manner characteristic of the scientific revolution's concern with method, Bacon championed an experimentally based inductive method of analysis. Over and against the deductive categories of Aristotelian logic Bacon sought a new foundation for scientific procedure. Second, he hoped that on this basis scientific work would focus on the accumulation and classification of empirically derived information rather than the generation of deductive hypotheses. Third, just as this empirical method was available to anyone who properly understood its experimental procedures (a radically democratizing step in the context of the older scholastic adjudication of knowledge on the authority of received tradition, schools, and special learning), so too ideally was it useful for all. Bacon's repeated emphasis on the practicality of science and its potential for the increased control of nature by mankind was especially significant for the subsequent history of science. Finally, Bacon recognized the advantages of group research and the collective organization of scientists into bodies such as the Royal Society of London.[5]

Not surprisingly, this "new science" took on its own American coloring. During the colonial decades, for example, one of North America's claims for scientific recognition was the natural history collections that various colonists gathered and sent to Europe. With patrons in London and other major centers colonial Americans such as William Bartram, Cadwallader Colden, and Alexander Garden identified themselves as junior members of this larger European scientific community. After the American Revolution this patronage relationship, especially with the British, broke apart, and American scientists found themselves caught up in that broader flourishing of patriotic pride, which looked for new indigenous achievements (including scientific ones), by the newly independent Americans. Here the Enlightenment commitment to science as an instrument for advancing the happiness and material well-being of mankind reinforced the view of science as essentially a pursuit of utilitarian knowledge. The upshot of this view of science, at least in the Jacksonian era, was not only the emphasis upon the practicality of science but also the demand that it should be comprehensible to the common man. For it was the Jacksonian *Everyman* and not the professional scientist who ultimately should judge the worth of scientific endeavors.[6]

Another significant feature of antebellum science was its social location within American culture. Most striking was the distance of science in this period from that ideal of professionalization and research characteristic of its twentieth-century successor. Instead, science in the early Republic was still carried out by individuals who were usually self-taught or else educated in ancillary fields such as medicine. Distinctions between pure and applied research or science and technology were often blurred, in part due to the lack of specialization among the practitioners as much as to the predominance of "useful knowledge" as the all-encompassing banner under which all such work was practiced. Thus, even by the 1850s, with the appearance of better-educated individuals, such as Alexander Bache, James Dwight Dana, or Joseph Henry, as well as more specialized theoretical investigations, American science was more often than not equated with such technological inventions as the reaper and the sewing machine or the applied explorations of Charles Wilkes or the surveying and building of the transcontinental railroad.[7]

Developments in the biological and physical sciences (the two areas emblematically accepted by later generations as "science") demonstrate this inchoate blend between theoretical and applied science. Benjamin S. Barton and Henry Muhlenberg's early botanical researches provided a foundation for the work of Samuel Mitchell and Nathaniel Chapman in descriptive botany and *materia medica*. Similarly in zoology, Alexander Wilson's ornithological volumes, complete with colored plates, matched the later work in mammal studies by John Godman and Richard Harlan as contributions toward picturing and classifying the abundance of animal species in North America.[8]

In the physical sciences the success of Andrew Ellicott in collaborating with Jean-Baptiste Delambre in observing the satellites of Jupiter or that of Nathaniel Bowditch in refining latitude and longitude calculations as well as his work in celestial mechanics was noteworthy. Research undertaken by Alexander Bache on terrestrial magnetism and experiments by Joseph Henry on electromagnetic induction provide examples of endeavors that a later generation would incorporate under the rubric of physics. If Bowditch, Bache, and Henry's investigations represented the theoretical side of the physical sciences, Robert Hare's invention of the oxyhydrogen blowpipe, the calorimotor (a model for a galvanic battery), and the deflagrator (a generator for high electrical currents) pointed in the direction of technological application.[9]

In the aftermath of the revolution in the nomenclature and methodology of chemistry associated with Antoine Lavoisier American chemists adopted and soon revised the Frenchman's system. The great attraction of this new approach was that it construed chemistry as the study of the table of chemical elements, which could be linked, detached, and recombined in various forms, rather than understanding the practice of chemistry as the proto-alchemical recapitulation of first principles or metaphysical elements, as in Aristotle's enumeration of air, earth, fire, and water. Here again the line between pure and applied science was not always sharp, as shown by John P. Norton's research in agricultural chemistry and especially soil analysis and Benjamin Silliman's lectures on chemistry and his editorship of the important *American Journal of Science and Arts.*[10]

A final characteristic of antebellum science was its essentially voluntaristic and decentralized institutional context. Although there had been discussion at the time of the founding of the Republic about federally funded support for the sciences, and particularly a national academy or university, by the inauguration of Andrew Jackson, the situation was one of the "almost complete bankruptcy of science in the government." Divisions over the nature of the role of the federal government were largely responsible for the demise of federal support for scientific projects. In its place local and regional academies, lyceum networks, and occasional examples of state-funded undertakings occurred. The two best-known scientific societies were the American Philosophical Society located in Philadelphia and the American Academy of Arts and Science, with its headquarters in Boston. Less prestigious but more prolific were the municipal and state societies dedicated to natural history, botany, and minerals. Beyond these groups the development in the Jacksonian era of public lecture circuits provided another venue for the popularization of scientific information. Emerging in the 1830s, these public lectures grew in number, becoming important avenues for the dissemination of science or at least for the satisfaction of the craving for useful knowledge within some commonly understood framework of reference. State legislatures also supported scientific projects, especially when there was a demonstrable local advantage to be gained by the information. Edward Hitchcock's geological investigation of Massachusetts was matched by similar projects in North and South Carolina and several other states. In various ways, then, scientific research found encouragement in the antebellum era, though often this backing was indirect, and the price was the demand for proof of the utility of the results.[11]

The relationship of science and religion in antebellum America was an intimate and convoluted one. Much of the intensity of the engagement derived from the previous rich history of exchange between the participants. Theological interpretations of the natural world had dominated through the Middle Ages, but slowly climates of opinion were changing, and by the 1600s the growing prestige of the natural sciences indicated that orthodox Christianity would not only have to contend with new information about the natural world but also with the alternative accounts of that world presented by the scientist. In

short, by the seventeenth century familiar patterns of religious authority and explanation were changing, while various strategies of reinterpretation and reconciliation were emerging. Yet just as important as
the strategies themselves was the fact, as one historian has put it, that
the need for reconciliation between science and religion "meant some
change from the pattern of traditional Christianity. With the growing
prestige of science . . . its reconciliation with Christianity came more
and more to mean the adjustment of Christian beliefs to conform to
the conclusions of science."[12]

If in hindsight such a generalization provides an accurate indication
of the direction of the development of Western culture, it still blurs
important contours during the eighteenth- and nineteenth-century
discussion of the issue in American experience. During the era of the
early Republic, for example, many Federalists feared science for its
connection with the Enlightenment in general and the French Revolution in particular. In individuals such as Thomas Jefferson, Joseph
Priestley, David Rittenhouse, and Benjamin Rush, Federalists saw
science, religious radicalism, and political revolution complementing
one another. Ironically, during the same time period many Democrats
were suspicious of science for its elitist connotations and the resent-
ment of some of its practitioners when obliged to justify their efforts
exclusively in terms of publicly useful results.[13]

Such social and political suspicions did not directly dictate the nature of the relation of science and religion; they did, however, condition their broader process of engagement. Religious believers, for
instance, were more apprehensive about the implications of biblical
criticism or about the naturalist challenge to the very legitimacy of
supernatural agency, what one nineteenth-century American theologian called "the source of the infidelity of modern science." Thus,
within a context of social and religious distrust promoters of scientific
investigation in early American culture found themselves facing a
formidable task, one in which many of them consciously praised science's compatibility with Christian religion, democratic values, and
practical results as a way to garner greater public interest in and support for scientific inquiry. In other words, confidence in science was
not complete, and belief in religious authority, though slipping, had
not eroded completely.[14]

Consequently, in eighteenth- and early nineteenth-century America there were good reasons for religious believers and scientists alike
to seek to illustrate the harmony between science and religion, and in

this task they could use a variety of general arguments to illustrate their point. One of the simplest was the argument from biography. If one examines the lives of many accomplished and renowned scientists, proponents of this argument contended, one will see that they were religious men. This, of course, was the point demonstrated by such nineteenth-century American scientists as Edward Hitchcock, James Dwight Dana, Benjamin Silliman, or Joseph LeConte. Popular writers, however, more often invoked the name of Francis Bacon and, above all, Isaac Newton to make their cases. As one essayist put it, "when we consider what an influence one great man has upon the world, it is startling to think what the consequences might have been had Newton begun and ended his course without paying the reverence which he did to religion. . . . By imagining the evil he might have done as an irreligious man, we may estimate the good he has done, and is still doing, by his example as a Christian." Indeed, organizations such as the Academy of Natural Sciences in Philadelphia even incorporated religious goals into their statements of purpose—for in the promotion of natural sciences, the association declared, members sought "to ascertain and understand the laws of God, exhibited in the living organization which exists on its surface." Such study, the statement continued, "enables us to derive from objects that everywhere present themselves in our rural walks, not only amusement and instruction, but the highest inducements to piety and virtue."[15]

Another line of argument insisted that the study of nature was the study of God's work. Scientific investigation in this view was a religious calling, or, as the secular *DeBow's Review* put it in the subtitle of an article on Georgia, the Bible was "a textbook in natural history." The author of this essay continued in familiar fashion to counsel his readers that in the study of nature one has the opportunity to "trace the workings of the hand of God in every quivering leaf, or flittering insect, or shapeless stone. No object would meet our eyes in all Nature's range but it would speak to us of the God we serve and tell some tale of His benevolence and love." In such a construction of the issue the revelation of nature reinforced the revelation of the Bible. Religious believers need not fear science but ought to support the efforts of scientists to unlock nature's secrets, for, as one minister wrote, "the works and word of God are but counterparts of each other and are designed to constitute one great revelation by which the glory of God shall be most conspicuously displayed." Christians should not oppose scientific inquiry but, rather, insist that it be properly carried out, for in the end, the good reverend intoned, science is not the agent of Satan but the "handmaid of Christianity."[16]

The concept of science as a handmaid to religion dates back to the Middle Ages, with expressions found as early as the first century. As set forth by Saint Bonaventure (1221–74), science should not be undertaken for its own sake but only for the assistance it could give in the interpretation of Scripture. Consequently, the goal of the scientist was not to produce new information nor to validate hypotheses about the world but, rather, to glorify God. As Bonaventure put it, it is the "fruit of all sciences, that in all, faith may be strengthened and God may be honored." As noted previously, this construction of the relationship of science and religion began to be questioned by the end of the Middle Ages as the prestige and independence of philosophy and the natural sciences grew. Nevertheless, despite challenges, the image of science as a handmaid to religion continued with power into the nineteenth century.[17]

Even among its proponents, however, a nagging question remained: If science was the helpmate of religion, then why did its conclusions so often seem at odds with the claims of historic Christianity? Here religious defenders of the study of nature as the study of divine activity invoked a series of similar answers. Timothy Dwight, a Congregational minister and president of Yale College, was not alone when he insisted that scientific theory and investigation were not anti-Christian by their nature but, rather, were made so by the attitude of the investigator. Dwight, for example, stated that the problem was the demand by the scientist to exclude biblical testimony as a relevant and credible source of information as well as an exaggerated estimate of the scope and powers of human reason. Scientific research was better carried out, Dwight countered, with an attitude of trust in God's word and humility before his creation.[18]

An alternative answer focused on scientific method and the need for scientists to stick to facts rather than conjecture, hypothesis, and ill-proven theory. Science, in this view, was concerned with accumulating facts and slowly and soberly developing generalizations out of these facts. Thus, controversy between interpretations of scientific evidence and religious traditions was misplaced. Return to the facts of science, the proponents of this position insisted, and one would find that the clearly established facts of science and the time-honored traditions of religion were still in harmony.[19] The upshot of these appeals to motivation and method was clear. Religious defenders of the study of nature as the study of God's work had so much at stake in the assumption of the harmony between science and religion that they concluded that any conflict must only be an apparent one. Energetic efforts to remedy these faults would once again display that the works and words of God are one.

A related and even more significant proposal for the reconciliation of science and religion was drawn from the familiar argument from design. William Paley (1743–1805) gave an important expression of this proof, one that influenced scores of American clergy and laity. Drawing attention to the intricate interrelation and purposeful coordination of parts in the anatomy of creatures as disparate as insects and human beings, Paley argued that there could be no such design in nature without a Designer. Using another famous image, Paley likened God to a great Watchmaker who had purposefully and carefully constructed the universe then stepped aside to allow his divine timepiece to operate. The usefulness of Paley's argument for reconciling science and religion became clear as the scientist's role was defined once again as studying the natural world, now in order to understand, explain, and illustrate the divine plan. Order, harmony, and the concurrence of means to ends, as one writer put it, were abundant in the natural world, and the demonstration and elucidation of these dimensions would provide the bridge between science and religion.[20]

Yet a problem with Paley's formulation was that this divine Designer appeared so remote and distant from his creation, so unlike that image of superintending pastoral care to which American Protestants had become so accustomed. The argument from divine design was an important means for linking science and religion, but by the nineteenth century American Protestants were busy reinforcing it with the aid of the doctrine of divine Providence. The doctrine of divine Providence focused on the continuation of God's supervising presence after he had finished the Creation. The doctrine divided into two parts—general Providence, or the ongoing activity of divine sustenance, and special Providence, or those unusual acts of intervention such as miracles—and together these themes were used to remedy the deficiencies of Paley's argument at the same time in which they played an important interpretive role in the wider popular culture.[21]

The addition of the doctrine of divine Providence to that of design also enlarged the role of science in the investigation of the natural world. For, as a writer in one religious periodical stated, "true science, as it penetrates his works, discovers fresh tokens of his nearness to man. Astronomy, weighing the planets, and adding to their catalogue; geology, reading a new revelation in the great book of stone; chemistry, decomposing and recomposing all the elements of nature—may find at every turn some new proof of the Omnipresent One." Time and again writers would point out how a loving God had crafted the natural world not simply with a sense of purpose but, indeed, with an eye to human contentment. Even an author in *Scientific American*, for example, could not help but conclude that "the wisdom and beneficence of the Deity are strikingly displayed in the economy of moonlight, as distributed to our globe during various seasons of the year. The remarkable phenomenon of the harvest moon is familiar to everyone. . . . By these means, an immediate supply of light is obtained after sunset, so beneficial for gathering in the fruits of the season."[22]

With praise for the latest discoveries by the telescope and microscope of previously unseen worlds writers and journalists rhapsodized about the adaptation of the cosmos to human needs. And even in those cases, such as with certain types of insects, in which the utility to mankind was not yet apparent, "yet, in a more advanced state of human knowledge, when the naturalist shall be able to take a more comprehensive survey of creation and to see more clearly how all the parts are related to one grand design, then no doubt he will see what useful part swarms of caterpillars, that now seem designed merely as a scourge of man, bear in the economy of nature." Thus, even if it was through a glass darkly, American Protestants saw "illustrative tokens of the Divine goodness" in the content of the natural world. Sometimes these symbols signified spiritual goodness, other times material usefulness; nevertheless, even when their purposes were not fully known, an abiding trust that they were intentional parts of the divine plan undergirded the worldview of American Protestants. Beyond that the study of the natural world was necessary and proper, for science and religion in the view of the majority of these same Protestants were not at odds but, rather, were united in a common calling.[23]

Issues and Controversies

These were some of the representative arguments for the reconciliation of science and religion, and their statement and restatement could be heard in America in different forms throughout the first half of the nineteenth century. Yet, as one historian has written, "the 1840s and 1850s were a critical period in the relations of science and

Christianity."[24] Spelling out the contours, responses, and meanings of this crisis is the task of this volume as a whole; in a more immediate context, however, it is possible to identify some of the indicators that provide the background to the specific turbulence of the antebellum engagement between science and religion. In 1835, for example, David Friedrich Strauss published *Das Leben Jesu*, and in 1836 Ralph Waldo Emerson's *Nature* appeared. Between 1830 and 1833 Charles Lyell published his *Principles of Geology*, which was to have significance in America far outside its scientific field. In 1831 William Lloyd Garrison began his editorship of *The Liberator*, and in 1833 the state of Massachusetts disestablished the Congregational church, thus completing the process of legal separation of church and state which had begun decades earlier. Finally, in 1835 Charles Grandison Finney brought out his *Lectures on Revivalism* and thereby marked a watershed in American Protestant experience. In these ways and others the landscape of American Protestantism was changing, and with those changes came a new set of challenges to older understandings of traditional religious authority.

Among this welter of events, books, and persons three sets of issues—biblical chronology, the unity of mankind, and the forms of biblical criticism—appeared particularly troubling for antebellum American Protestants. The topic of biblical chronology emerged most forcefully within the fledgling field of geology and the debate over the age of the Earth. The traditional view of the question was well represented by Archbishop James Ussher, who in the seventeenth century, on the basis of biblical and calendrical calculations, had proposed that the Creation began on 23 October 4004 B.C., with preparatory measures commencing the previous evening at 6 P.M. Ussher's dating was not the first of its kind (the Huguenot scholar, Joseph Scaliger, for example, had earlier made similar chronological computations), yet, when Ussher's listing of biblical dates was printed into the marginalia of various standard editions of the Bible, Ussher's position as a spokesman for tradition was secured. Ussher achieved this remarkable precision by adding up the ages of the biblical patriarchs, computing the various astronomical revolutions and cycles, and establishing a framework of reference dates from which to return back to the very beginning of time itself.[25]

A recent and fixed date derived from biblical genealogy for the age of the Earth was not the only component of this traditional view of biblical chronology. In addition, the assumption of a static and hier-

archical organization of life shaped Christian orthodoxy. Again drawing its essential form from the biblical account, and especially as later
strengthened by a strong dose of Greek philosophy, this notion emphasized that God had made all the world—plants, animals, and
humans—once and for all during the six days of Creation. In this view
change within organic life—say the development of a new species or
the extinction of an older one—could not take place, for God and not
the life form itself was responsible for the creative process. Stasis, then,
was one ruling principle, and hierarchical order was another. The
structure of life was arranged with the flora and fauna ranked below
mankind and the angels and God Almighty above. This chain of being
represented a fixed plan of creation as well as a cosmological hierarchy.
For, up through the Middle Ages at least, this ranking of the natural
order of creation with mankind at its zenith paralleled the special place
given to Earth as the pivot around which the universe rotated.[26]

New findings beginning with the scientific revolution through the
nineteenth century challenged this traditional view. Copernicus, for
example, displaced the Earth from the center of the planetary stage
and pushed it out to the celestial periphery. On another level the
discovery of new forms of plant and animal life in the seventeenth
century ruptured existing taxonomies and required new systems of
classification such as that of Carl Linnaeus. Some of this new information could be assimilated within the framework of past orthodoxy, but
soon it became clear that the cumulative quantity and novel nature of
these discoveries amounted to a frontal assault on the older assumptions of stability and hierarchical order which grounded the traditional
worldview.[27]

Further damage occurred in the nineteenth-century debate about
fossils and their meaning. Whether one looked to the fossil specimens
exposed by the mining, dredging, and building by the captains of
European capitalism during the industrial revolution or to the American samples unearthed in the digging of the Erie Canal or the charting
of the Louisiana Purchase, ample supplies of fossils became available
and with them perplexing problems. For, once fossils were accepted as
the remains of living organisms that were petrified within various rock
strata, two salient issues emerged. First, the question of the origin,
growth, and development of biological life took precedence over that
of simple taxonomic ordering. Fossil remains represented an extended
sequential historical record, one that could be used to establish a
temporal continuum. Beyond that fossil locations indicated that areas

that were now dry land must once have been submerged under the sea and that certain species must evidently have disappeared for they were no longer known. Second, with this growth in historical consciousness, particularly as it was expressed in the development of techniques of stratigraphic measurement, the recognition of change over time demanded a radical expansion of the time frame for that change to have taken place. Instead of a geological and biological world built on stability and permanence, one of mutability and perhaps even caprice had emerged. No longer were cosmological origins fixed and recent, but, rather, in the ominous words of the geologist James Hutton, there was "no vestige of a beginning—no prospect of an end."[28]

The response to these new discoveries accounts for the tremendous productivity in geology during the nineteenth century. Once geological change was accepted controversies ranged between proponents of vulcanism and neptunism, between advocates of catastrophism and uniformitarianism, and between patrons of progress and prophets of decline. Beneath the tangle of these complicated but by now fairly familiar issues lies, according to Stephen Jay Gould, a set of fundamental metaphors that gave shape to this early nineteenth-century debate. One set of metaphors, Gould argues, depicted change as continuous, uniform, slow, and steady, while another represented it as discontinuous, episodic, liable to sudden interruptions, which could either speed up or slow down the process of change. Both versions represented a revision of the traditional static view of the world, for they both accepted change. Yet the proponents of discontinuity could more easily reconcile their science to the scriptural story of a cataclysmic flood than could the supporters of continuity, whose Huttonian picture of terrestrial creation extended indefinitely forward and backward in time raised considerable objections.[29]

A second set of metaphors, Gould points out, saw creation as existing fundamentally in a steady-state condition in which lands rose and fell but the world remained essentially unchanged versus a view that claimed that conditions cumulatively change over time toward progressive or regressive ends. Uniformitarians such as James Hutton and Charles Lyell championed the first position, while their catastrophist antagonists, such as Georges Cuvier or Louis Agassiz, argued for the second. Significantly, the catastrophists were progressivists in the sense that, while the Earth had suffered a series of cataclysms, often in the form of volcanic eruptions or tidal waves on a scale far beyond anything known today, each new episode of life marked an improvement over its predecessor. For the catastrophists this process culminated in mankind and the modern era, and its potential agreement with and support for biblical accounts again did not go unnoticed by those outside the scientific community.

Questions of serial catastrophes and the possibility of multiple creations were deeply embedded in another major controversy of the nineteenth century—the debate over the unity of mankind. The traditional Christian view spelled out in Genesis insisted on one creation with all human species descended from Adam. Yet, by the sixteenth century and continuing into the nineteenth, the discovery of other peoples and cultures as a result of European expansion in the Americas, Africa, Asia, and Oceania raised several puzzling questions. First, who were these strange non-European peoples, where did they originate, and how did they fit into the biblical account of creation? Could they be the descendants of a pre-Adamic race, or had there been, perhaps, a series of creations rather than simply one? Beyond that some cultures, such as the Indian and Chinese, claimed in their literatures that their civilizations were much older than the biblical account and, in fact, made no mention of Adam, Noah, or the patriarchs. How could these pagan authors be reconciled with those of the Christian Scriptures?

Another early expression of this challenge to biblical monogenesis appeared in the writings of the Frenchman Isaac La Peyrère (1596–1676). La Peyrère's *Prae-Adamitae* (1655) argued that God had fashioned two creations: the first created the Gentile race, which then spread throughout the world (including America), while the second created Adam, the forefather of the Jews. La Peyrère postulated that the deluge had not been worldwide but, rather, had only destroyed the Hebrews, leaving the descendants of the pre-Adamic creation in the New World, for example, untouched and unknown to the Old World until 1492.[30]

In 1774 Lord Kames had suggested a polygenetic explanation for racial differences, and in 1799 Charles White argued that black and white people were two different species. The most forceful arguments for polygenesis emerged, however, in the early nineteenth century with the so-called American School of Ethnography, associated with Samuel G. Morton, Josiah C. Nott, and Louis Agassiz. These men suggested that God had created not only a white Adam and Eve but also a yellow, brown, black, and red Adam and Eve not mentioned in Genesis. Samuel Morton, influenced in part by the new science of phrenology in the 1830s and even more by the measuring of human skulls Petrus Camper and others, launched a major debate over the multiple creation of the different types of mankind which raged through the 1840s and 1850s.[31]

Morton had abandoned monogenesis in 1844 as a result of work he had done measuring the skulls of the different races. He concluded that the skulls were clearly too different for too many centuries for them to be descended from one common source. Morton's pupil, Josiah C. Nott, became well known for his own attacks upon biblical monogenesis. "We have now on the earth," Nott observed, "an extraordinary diversity of types of mankind, which cannot be accounted for" by the Genesis story. Nott took particular delight in ridiculing some of the current presentations of the Genesis reckoning, such as that by the Reverend George Howe, who claimed that Adam and Eve were the progenitors of the human race and that they had personally produced over 200,000 descendants in the course of 130 years. "Yes, simple reader," Nott retorted, "200,000 descendants from a single pair in 130 years. . . . Did anybody ever hear of four mothers in 80 years producing 1000 souls, much less of 200,000 from a pair in 130 years. . . . And then, to embellish the picture we must imagine the most horrible incest of fathers, mothers, brothers, sisters, etc., mingled together in violation of the laws of God, laws of humanity and laws of nature."[32]

Polygenesis represented a powerful alternative to monogenesis in the early nineteenth century. It combined an appeal to current science together with moral outrage at the implications of descent from a single pair. Its contention that the flood was localized agreed with common sense, for accepting the flood as universal provided too little time, in the minds of many, to account for subsequent developments in history. Finally, in an age when the definition of what it meant to be "an American" was increasingly being identified with the white Anglo-Saxon race, this approach could be used to firm up the claim of the inferiority of nonwhite peoples.[33]

Nevertheless, most American Christians (as well as most American scientists) rejected polygenesis. In the first place its repudiation of Scripture marked it as far too heretical for most American churchgoers. The fact that other peoples and cultures were different from white Americans was due to environment, many still believed, and, if pagan chronologies were at odds with familiar biblical ones, then these antagonistic ones could simply be dismissed as the untrustworthy legends of superstitious people. Finally, the majority who rejected polygenesis found sufficient evidence to establish racial hierarchies in the Bible. The basis of the biblical argument for the inferiority of the dark-skinned races was commonly traced to the sons of Noah. In defining the racial differences among red, white, and black Americans, many monogenesists insisted that God had providentially differentiated Caucasians, Indians, and Africans by altering the color of Noah's sons Ham and Japheth. Shem, the progenitor of the red race, was the red or tawny color of his father, Noah. God altered Ham in the womb, and he emerged black; Japheth emerged white. Thus, from their birth God had ordained the distinctions between the three races, though, of course, Adam and Eve were their common ancestors. After the flood Shem's descendants remained in the Middle East, though some went further east as far as Siberia and across the land bridge to the New World; the descendants of Japheth went north and west to people Europe; the descendants of Ham went to Africa. Moreover, these interpreters contended that, while Noah cursed Ham and his descendants, Shem and Japheth were blessed by him. Thus, as many American Christians insisted, the servitude of blacks found ample justification in the Scriptures. There was no need to stray from the Bible.[34]

Anthropology as easily as geology, then, could challenge Christian orthodoxy. Where the Copernican revolution of the natural sciences dislodged mankind from the center of the cosmos, the nineteenth-century revolution in the human sciences impugned the view that all human history shared a common origin in Adam and a common destiny in a divine plan of salvation. Beyond that it challenged the very authenticity of the biblical story in its suggestion that there was a human history prior to or at least alternative to that presented in Genesis.

Biblical interpretation was a key point in the controversies concerning geology and anthropology, and debates over biblical criticism played an important role more generally in the antebellum American discussion of the relation of science and religion. The antebellum era inherited the rich legacy of scholarship and controversy over proper biblical analysis developed during the late eighteenth and early nineteenth centuries. In Enlightenment critics such as Matthew Tindal, Voltaire, or John Toland one found a clear expression of a vital interest in the Scriptures. These Enlightenment figures examined the Scriptures from a rationalist standpoint, and in their accounting problems of logical contradiction and moral credibility emerged. How, for example, could there be a morning and evening on the first day, if the sun was not created until the fourth day? How many animals was Noah commanded to take on the ark? Two of each kind or seven pairs of all clean animals? How could Moses be the author of the first five books of the Bible, as tradition claimed, when the book of Deuteronomy contained a full account of Moses' own death and burial? Other passages appeared morally questionable, if not outright mockeries. For instance, the slaughter of all living things in Jericho (Joshua 6), the revenge called down on one's enemies (Psalm 109), or the sexual escapades of King David (II Samuel 11) all drew critical remarks from Enlightenment rationalists for their incompatibility with traditional Christian morality.[35]

An even deeper challenge to biblical authority than that of the Enlightenment arose in the late eighteenth- and early nineteenth-century application of a historical perspective to scriptural texts. This new historical consciousness is associated, above all, with the emergence of romanticism. Obviously, historical thinking as such did not begin with the Romantics, for the Enlightenment had made use of historical knowledge. Rather, it was the new direction of this historical approach, symbolized by the organic metaphor and the categories associated with it, which marked the change. Under the Romantics' influence the image of Newtonian mechanics gave way to those of animate life. Models of the universe as a growing dynamic entity replaced those of a machine finished and complete.[36]

The implications of this historical consciousness for biblical interpretation were revolutionary indeed. Where earlier interpreters universally assumed that the Holy Spirit had been the real author of the Scriptures in their entirety, during the early nineteenth century new voices claimed that different and even contradictory elements coexisted in the Scriptures. Beyond the issue of uniform authorship the earlier precritical view construed the biblical text in strongly realistic terms. The biblical account from this perspective accurately described specific events in human history at the same time that it described a universal human history. Since it was a universal history embracing the whole of human reality, it was immediately relevant to any reader in any era of that history. Once again during the nineteenth century commentators contended that the Scriptures were intimately bound up with a particular author's intentions, with a specific time and place, and even with particular literary assumptions and conventions. In short, the Scriptures became historical texts, and new exegetical methods of reconstruction were needed to disclose their meaning and significance. Here was the context, then, finally, for the development of the so-called lower and higher biblical criticism. Lower criticism was that which was designed to establish the original text of Scripture, free from grammatical errors, mistranslations, and the like. The higher criticism took as its task the analysis of the various books of the Bible, their historical background, sources, authorship, and literary characteristics. Through the development of these methods biblical interpretation in the nineteenth century grew into a new period of creativity and maturity.[37]

This era of biblical criticism was especially productive in Germany, where debate over hermeneutical methods became quite heated in the late eighteenth and early nineteenth centuries and ranged from the conservative biblicism of Gottfried Menken through the historical-mythical analysis of D. F. Strauss. Biblical exegesis in nineteenth-century America, though generally slanted toward the conservative viewpoint, nonetheless reflected a similar range of interpretive options, for in important ways American biblical scholarship derived from European models, and nineteenth-century American Protestants took over biblical scholarship in modes ranging from the grammaticohistorical through the new Romantic and Idealist interpretive frameworks.

A fundamental question for nineteenth-century commentators concerned the doctrine of inspiration. Were the biblical writers inspired, and, if so, in what manner and to what degree? Beyond that were the Scriptures the Word of God per se, or did they only contain the Word much as a vase contains water but is clearly separable from it? Earlier eras might hardly have raised such questions or else quickly settled for familiar answers. By the nineteenth century, however, even conservative biblical scholars could not afford to pretend ignorance of the new lines of biblical criticism in Germany and elsewhere.

Once again there existed among antebellum American Protestants a discernible range of answers to these questions. While reference occasionally was made to the original autographs or manuscripts of the biblical books, since no one could produce them for examination, their relevance for resolution of the inspiration question was rather limited. A more widely held position was that of plenary inspiration. Among early and mid-nineteenth-century American Protestants this doctrine took two forms. The first mode emphasized the verbal dictation of the Scriptures by God. "The words of the sacred Text," as one writer put it, "are the words of God. . . . The original text consists of words which had been audibly spoken by the Revealer to the writer." Here not simply the message generally but the specific words themselves were selected by God and communicated to the biblical writer. This doctrine of verbal dictation within Protestantism dated back to the seventeenth century, during which time it had even been extended to cover the very punctuation of the text. Yet by the nineteenth century discrepancies between scriptural texts demonstrated by sincere and pious biblical critics raised serious problems with this view. Beyond that, in the minds of many, verbal dictation reduced inspiration to a kind of divine ventriloquism and was therefore unsatisfactory.[38]

The second doctrinal formulation insisted that God had superintended and watched over the biblical authors as they wrote but "did not supersede or set aside the natural powers" of the authors, for they "were not used as mere machines" but, instead, "were left in full use of their own natural capacities and tastes." This view still maintained that the Bible was the word of God rather than simply the words of human authors; it gave up, however, the insistence on the mechanical act of divine inspiration and conceded that the manner by which the biblical authors received this inspiration remained mysterious.[39]

Moses Stuart, professor of sacred literature at Andover Seminary in Massachusetts, gained a wide following within antebellum Protestant circles not only for his defense of plenary inspiration but also for his biblical scholarship. Given Stuart's prominence within evangelical American Protestantism, it is somewhat surprising how familiar and sympathetic he was with German biblical criticism. Across a wide spectrum of American Protestantism German theological efforts were dismissed as destructive of faith. That perception was wrong, of course, for within the range of German theological and biblical studies there were conservative confessionalists and moderate exegetes as well as radical critics. Nevertheless, American suspicions remained.

Two scholars in particular, Johann G. Eichhorn and Johann A. Ernesti, played especially formative roles in Stuart's thinking. Eichhorn taught at Jena and Göttingen and in his book *Introduction to the Old Testament* called for the further development of higher criticism of the Scriptures. In accomplishing this task, Eichhorn reaffirmed that one must explain the Scriptures according to the time, place, and circumstances of their authors. In so doing the biblical scholar could defend the integrity of the text and its meaningfulness against ridicule and objections from detractors, Eichhorn insisted. Such an approach to and explanation of the task of biblical scholarship was immensely appealing to Moses Stuart.[40]

Eichhorn's charter for biblical criticism also had important implications for Stuart's broader understanding of biblical interpretation in general. Stuart was an advocate of the grammaticohistorical method in biblical hermeneutics, an approach that he had taken over in large part from the eighteenth-century Leipzig professor of theology, Johann A. Ernesti. In Stuart's hands the grammaticohistorical approach meant that "everything belonging to grammar, rhetoric, and history . . . be considered in giving an interpretation to any passage." The approach "comprehends all, which strictly speaking, is a matter of scientifical, philological research." In seeking to explicate the grammatical meaning of a passage, Stuart insisted that one should interpret it according to the customary sense of the words and thereby examine etymology, context, parallel passages, and dialects. In revealing the historical dimension of a passage, Stuart put forward two questions as fundamental for any understanding. First, who is the audience to which the writings were initially addressed, and second, what can we know regarding the author? Thus, in line with much nineteenth-century biblical criticism Stuart underscored the specificity of authorial circumstance and context versus the disregard of an earlier generation of interpreters for such questions.[41]

In articulating his hermeneutical vision Stuart built on a set of assumptions widely held within antebellum American Protestantism. Foremost among these was the belief that, in all things necessary for salvation, the Bible was perspicacious, and any normally intelligent reader could understand its general meaning. Consequently, while Stuart devoted his life to producing lexicons, grammars, and commentaries all designed to aid in the correct understanding of biblical passages, he still believed, as did most Americans, that a simple and pious reader could grasp the most salient biblical truths. Beyond that Stuart believed that truth as such was immutable and, thus, not fundamentally derived from or changed by culture and circumstance.[42]

The upshot of these assumptions was that the Bible could be read by anyone. Neither scholarly training nor individual revelation was finally necessary, just common sense and religious receptivity. Stuart opposed the suggestion that a reader needed divine inspiration in order to understand Scripture, for "of what use is a written revelation to the world, which is unintelligible without new miracles, in every case where it is understood. And where is the guilt of those, who do not see, what cannot be seen, without a miraculous interposition on the part of heaven." Yet, despite his tolerance for unaided reading, it is clear that Stuart believed a fuller and more correct reading would be attained by those familiar with the results of the grammaticohistorical approach to Scripture.[43]

Further, given the emphasis of this approach, it is no wonder that Stuart often criticized those who attempted anachronistically to read contemporary issues or current modes of thought back into the biblical authors. The attempts to make John express himself in the "metaphysics and philosophy of the present day . . . as though he really had in his eye, the disputes on these subjects by which our times are agitated" was senseless. Significantly, Stuart conceded that such exegetical work occasionally produced discrepancies between versions of the biblical texts. "In the Hebrew Mss. that have been examined," Stuart noted, "some 800,000 various readings actually occur, as to the Hebrew consonants. How many as to the vowel-points and accents, no man knows. And the like to this is true of the New Testament." And, if philology raised textual questions, historical examination of the context and circumstances of the biblical authors highlighted the salient differences between their society and nineteenth-century America.[44]

Yet these critical findings did not fundamentally trouble Stuart. He dismissed the textual variations as nothing more significant than differences in spelling, such as *centre* or *center, honour* or *honor*. As for differences of time and place, Stuart insisted that concern with these discrepancies was ultimately misplaced, for the Scriptures were essentially about religious truth, not cultural fashion or scientific theory. And religious truth, in Stuart's view, unlike these other forms of expression, always remained stable and constant. Do not look to the Scriptures for science but, rather, for religious truth—this was Stuart's basic view. For, as he put it,

> divine revelation was not designed to teach geography or physics, or astronomy, or chemistry. . . . When men learn, that a revelation from God respects religion, not the sciences, then they will be content to ascribe to every writer the opinions of his time which do not pertain to the subject of religion, and to interpret him in a manner that accords with this. . . . Let every writer be

placed in his own age, and if possible, transfer yourself back there, with him. View him in writing the Sacred Scriptures as teaching religion, not science, and then you are disembarrassed, in a moment, of a thousand perplexities. . . . What can be more unreasonable, than to demand, that because a writer is inspired to teach religion, therefore he is inspired to have a perfect knowledge of all the arts and sciences? The difficulties attending such a supposition are insuperable. And after all, what matters it to me, whether David understood the Newtonian Philosophy; or John the metaphysics of Locke, or Kant? If David or John have undertaken to give instruction on the subjects, this is one thing; but if they have not, but have merely touched them in the popular way (as we speak at the present moment of the sun's rising and setting), then that is another.[45]

Stuart often claimed that, once the grammaticohistorical findings had been established, the Bible could be interpreted as any other book. In saying this he meant to underscore the universality of the relevant rules of interpretation for both sacred and secular literature. Beyond that, however, Stuart never failed to emphasize that the Bible was "a revelation from God," and the power and integrity of its message and the fullness of its truth were safeguarded by the plenary supervision of God. Thus, in the end there was a continuing tension in Stuart's hermeneutics and theology between the authority of the Bible as a divinely inspired Gospel and the authority of human reason to interpret, explain, and understand that revelation.[46]

Moses Stuart's biblical criticism fluctuated between recognition of the need for scholarship and the demand for evangelical orthodoxy. His program for scriptural exegesis encouraged textual analysis at the same time that it championed the credibility of the text and the authenticity of the message. Theodore Parker, the New England Unitarian minister and scholar, developed a divergent position from Stuart regarding biblical criticism. Where Stuart, for example, along with much of American Protestantism, excoriated D. F. Strauss's *Das Leben Jesu*, Parker wrote a review that took issue with Strauss on certain textual interpretations but was basically sympathetic to Strauss's project. Thus, if verbal dictation represented the conservative end of the spectrum of biblical criticism in antebellum America, then Theodore Parker represented its liberal antipode.[47]

The differences over Strauss were symbolic of a wider split between

Stuart and Parker, and this could be seen nowhere more clearly than in their respective interpretations of the doctrine of biblical inspiration. Where Stuart held to a version of the plenary or full inspiration (and ultimate infallibility) of the biblical authors, Parker would only recognize a partial inspiration. For Parker the authors of the Bible were undoubtedly sincere and genuine in their beliefs—indeed, in his view they were religious geniuses—they were, however, not completely inspired. Parker derived this conclusion from contemporary European and American biblical scholarship, for, as he stated,

> modern Criticism is fast breaking to pieces this idol which men have made out of the Scriptures. It has shown that here are the most different works thrown together. That their authors, wise as they sometimes were; pious as we feel often their spirit to have been, had only that inspiration which is common to other men equally pious and wise; that they were by no means infallible, but were mistaken in facts or in reasoning; uttered predictions which time has not fulfilled; men who in some measure partook of the darkness and limited notions of their age, and were not always above its mistakes or its corruptions.[48]

Though he never held an academic position, Parker was a legend in his time for the depth and breadth of his reading, his mastery of numerous foreign languages, and his familiarity with classical and contemporary biblical scholarship. Moreover, while he spent his life in parish churches and public lecture halls, he was fundamentally convinced that there, as much as in the university, the demand of the times was for a scientific exposition of the Scriptures. The opportunity in the contemporary situation, Parker wrote, "asks men to do consciously, and thoroughly what they have always done imperfectly and with no science but that of a pious heart; that is, to divide the Word rightly; separate mythology from history, fact from fiction, what is religious and of God, from what is earthly and not of God; to take the Bible for what it is worth."[49]

Where Moses Stuart drew on Thomas Reid and Johann Ernesti, Theodore Parker was more indebted to the rich resources of European romanticism. In Parker's view all religions were based on two innate truths—a belief in the existence of God and a sense of dependence on Him. Thus, for Parker religion amounted to an impulse within the individual, yet one that could find many different expressions. Parker claimed to have derived these insights from the works of

Immanuel Kant and Friedrich Schleiermacher, though Parker's statements represent rather loose interpretations of the views of both Kant and Schleiermacher. Nevertheless, Parker's admission of intellectual pedigree was significant, even if in a manner typical of the Transcendentalist movement, his use of those sources was eclectic and personal.[50]

If all religion was the expression of a basic human impulse, still Parker contended that Christianity was the highest form of that expression. Yet he strongly separated what he called "the Christianity of the church" from "the Christianity of Christ." The former was contentious, power hungry, and transient, while the latter was "a simple thing; very simple. It is absolute, pure Morality; absolute pure Religion; the love of man; the love of God acting without let or hindrance." Beyond that Parker insisted that the truths exemplified by Jesus had nothing to do with his own personal authority any more than the truth of Euclidean geometry rested on the personal authority of Euclid. Rather, for Parker the significance of Jesus rested on the truth of his message, not that of the messenger.[51]

Theodore Parker had raised the question of dividing the Word rightly, and, of course, this was the basis of the controversy over the forms of biblical criticism. Philology as much as anthropology or geology had marked out a claim to the title of science, and in pursuit of this goal its contributions had made an impact on American Protestantism. The world of science in antebellum America was a complicated one. No longer simply identifiable with natural history and the physical sciences nor any longer the exclusive province of amateur researchers, American science had grown in methodological and intellectual sophistication and had expanded into new realms of knowledge.

Democratizing Challenges

Yet, while the controversies over the age of the Earth, the unity of mankind, and the forms of biblical criticism raised troubling questions for many antebellum American Protestants, another crisis at a different level was posing equally perplexing challenges for traditional conceptions of religious authority. American society itself was changing, and this process was nowhere more important than in the slow transformation of social authority from the patronage- and deference-based society of the colonial era to the more egalitarian one of the Age of Jackson. This democratizing impulse, as one historian has called it, reconstructed American Protestantism through its appeal to popular religious aspirations, which disregarded distinctions of class and education and inverted traditional forms of religious authority in the name of religious individualism and popular democracy.[52]

One result of this democratizing tendency was a new emphasis on the role of the laity and the appeal to popular support in ecclesiastical affairs. In a cultural context clamoring for religious disestablishment earlier colonial assumptions that derived the status and prestige of the ministry in part from the connection of church and state were no longer valid. Beyond that the rise of lay influence in church affairs was evident, not only presenting laypersons as partners but often as adversaries with the clergy for control of religious matters. Whether it was the stipulation of lay leadership in organizations such as the American Tract Society or the American Bible Society or the controversy over lay trustee control of property or lay involvement in the hiring and firing of ministers, the new prominence and power of laypersons in church affairs was striking.

The present implications and future significance of these changes were often noticed and commented upon. The Charleston preacher James Warley Miles pointed out in one sermon that too often congregations were unwilling to hear anything new, that they were uninterested in learning and study. Though such apathy was bad enough in itself, Miles lamented that congregational power had grown to the point that such laypersons "often have it in their power to make the pulpit what they like it to be, instead of its being an instrument of awakening . . . and of stirring up to a practical Christian life." Evidence of just such close attention to and active evaluation of the clergy is coincidentally demonstrated in the diary of one of Miles's own parishioners, Mitchell King. King was a prominent antebellum Charleston lawyer and widely read member of one of its literary societies. His diary reports his appreciation for Miles's preaching and ministry; other entries, however, show his deep dissatisfaction with several of Charleston's clergy.[53]

Whether or not King actually cashiered a clergyman for poor preaching, it is clear that a change in the view of the ministry was taking place in American Protestantism. Expectations of ministers were altered as the social order and public aspirations of Americans molted into new forms. Though, for example, the South remained dominated by a plantation culture and revivalist religion, historians have pointed to the persistence of a rational strain in theology, particularly among the emerging ranks of city and town dwellers, such as Mitchell King, who grew in numbers and prestige in the antebellum era. The demand for a religion that spoke to reason and the head as well as emotions and the heart was echoed by the New Englander James Marsh. Marsh, too, saw the need for persons who would proclaim a faith that could unite true religion and sound philosophy in such a way as to meet the changing circumstances of American society. The upshot of this transformation of the definition and understanding of the minister's role amounted to a change in the way the ministry was seen—as an office with authority rooted in the local community to a profession tied to a much larger and different social network.[54]

As the status and prestige of the minister changed, together with the wider transformations of social authority in America, other developments became apparent. Men who either had begun or might be expected to take up careers in the ministry, for example, were switching to the study of science. The ease with which such a career move could be accomplished underscores again the perceived congeniality between science and religion in the antebellum era. Here the person of Edward Hitchcock provides an apt symbol and illustration, for his abandonment of the ministry for a career as a science professor did not signal a renunciation on his part of a broader evangelical agenda. The same point has been made regarding men like James Dwight Dana, mineralogist and geologist; James Hadley, professor of Greek; Noah Porter, moral philosopher and psychologist; and William Dwight Whitney, philologist and Sanskrit scholar. Changing social conditions, which made the ministry less attractive, rather than dissatisfaction with religious truth account for these occupational shifts.[55]

The example of Edward Hitchcock also illustrates the broader meaning of personal opportunity and social dislocation as new careers open to talent and intellect emerged in early and mid-nineteenth-century America. In addition to the ministry new vocational choices as a journalist, political reformer, essayist, and lyceum speaker posed rewarding if unsettling possibilities. Ralph Waldo Emerson's own vocational odyssey from schoolteacher to self-described public ethicist to minister to writer and lyceum lecturer is well known. Of the individuals discussed in this volume Charles Grandison Finney, Moses Stuart, and James Warley Miles all began careers in law before turning to the ministry. James Marsh tried teaching and even manual labor on a farm before he decided to pursue ministerial studies. Finally, Horace

Bushnell, though he initially expected to go into the ministry, explored teaching, journalism, and legal studies before he returned to Yale University to attend seminary. The search for a calling, for a personally rewarding and socially recognized occupation, was hardly new; however, the context for its accomplishment in nineteenth-century America was more diverse and, thus, the process of resolution more perplexing than it had been previously.[56]

A final indication of the transformation of social authority in America is disclosed in the debate over the implications of establishing seminaries, particularly as these institutions symbolized the professionalization of the Protestant ministry in America. In the early colonial era candidates for the ministry typically would complete their college education, possibly take some postgraduate education in Europe or at their collegiate institution, then apprentice themselves out for further instruction and practice before receiving their own pulpits. This pattern continued into the 1700s, though, by the time of the First Great Awakening, with its emphasis on the necessity of a conversion experience, the earlier consensus on the need for a learned ministry was falling apart.[57]

In the first third of the nineteenth century, however, a movement to establish Protestant denominational seminaries emerged, with over a score beginning between 1807 and 1837. This seminary movement represented a crucial step forward in the process of the professionalization of the Protestant ministry. For in this context the seminary was an institution that acted to define the profession of the ministry. The concept of a profession, as several scholars have argued, assumes a situation sufficiently diverse that specialized knowledge and preparations are needed to cope with it. Moreover, it usually entails some organization or recognized body, which determines competence in the profession and which is responsible for licensing all candidates. In so doing the professional organization acts to protect the wider public against fraud and incompetence, while at the same time it elevates the status of itself and its own members by setting standards and restricting membership in the organization. In this way, through an appeal to properly credentialed expertise, status and the possibility of autonomous self-supervision can be enhanced.[58]

Further, as scholars have noted, membership in even a learned society can be a means to define one's status in a community, especially in times of social dislocation and cultural change. During the social turmoil of the first half of the nineteenth century organizations dedicated to the promotion of knowledge and groups gathered for the advancement of a profession both emerged and played important roles for intellectuals and professionals alike. Significantly, there were few parallel professional organizations beyond denominational associations within American Protestantism; thus, the seminary movement played an even more important role in providing a definition and identity for the concept of the minister.[59]

Nevertheless, though seminary requirements for entrance and graduation differed between denominations, the movement in the early 1800s to establish seminaries, as a whole, faced the criticism that, by establishing the prerequisites and defining the role of the minister, they were unfairly restricting entry into and monopolistically regulating the practice of the clergy. This was bad enough in a popular culture enamored with the rhetoric of opportunity for the common man; since the dominant forms of American Protestantism extolled the priesthood of all believers, however, it was even more suspicious. Thus, though the establishment of seminaries attests to the strength of forces interested in professionalizing the ministry within American Protestantism, residual fears of privileged aristocracies combined with the expansion of the American nation and its population accounts for the success of the less restrictive denominations such as the Baptists and Methodists. This also meant that the Protestant ministry during the early republic and antebellum eras never achieved professional coherence and, thus, never completely regained the prestige and security it once had enjoyed.[60]

Taking this transformation of social authority and the wider crisis of religious authority of which it was a part as its background, the following chapters examine the relation of science and religion in the antebellum era and especially the interpretive strategies that the mediational theologians employed to demonstrate their belief in the reconcilability of science and religion in their age. One of the most fascinating of these strategies was an appeal to history and the claim that a developmental and contextual approach contained the means for mediating the controversies between science and religion.

Chapter Two

History Revealed

An appeal to history provided an avenue for the possible reconciliation of science and religion in antebellum American culture. A renewed interest in history suffused the early nineteenth century, and especially the Romantic movement, in a far-ranging manner. Enlightenment historians such as Edward Gibbon or David Hume had earlier left their mark, but, in the volumes of Jules Michelet and Jacques Thierry or, on a different plane, in the philosophical analyses of G. W. F. Hegel or Johann Herder, a new and profoundly creative fascination with the contours, goals, and meaning of mankind's past became evident during the nineteenth century. And, if America had no Hegel or Herder, the public acclaim for the work of Francis Parkman, John Motley, William Prescott, and George Bancroft or the approval of the historical fiction of Walter Scott, James Fenimore Cooper, or Washington Irving all attested to the existence of corresponding popular American attitudes.

The extent of this historically minded consciousness ranged far wider than the tomes of these historians, novelists, and philosophers. For in an important sense the desire to trace phenomena back to their origins, or, conversely, to chart their development from their beginnings to the present, lay at the root of the new inquiries in biblical and linguistic as well as geological and institutional researches. Historical method, it seemed, could be efficaciously applied to rocks and texts, peoples, nations, and patterns of thought. Broader in scope than language, for even mute nature had its past, history for many observers held an analytical key that could unlock and reveal the true meaning of life. Beyond that, while a subsequent generation, under the aegis of a more positivist approach toward reality, sought to appropriate the mantle of science exclusively for its own work, several antebellum American thinkers stoutly asserted their own claim to the scientific imprimatur.

W. G. T. Shedd: History as the Comprehensive Science

W. G. T. Shedd, in his 1854 inaugural address as professor of church history at Andover Seminary, struck a representative note in his depiction of "historical science" as the most comprehensive of all branches of human knowledge. History, Shedd stated, was concerned with "all that man has thought, felt, and done," and the accomplished historian combined the talents of the philosopher, the theologian, and the poet in his efforts to capture the past. Indeed, in his desire to advance knowledge, to display truth, and to aid the human race, Shedd contended, the historian exemplified the best of the scientific spirit of the present age. Here in Shedd's pronouncement was the declaration of historical independence and the charter of its rights. For in enlarging the scope of the historian's territory from politics to include all human expression and actions, and in recognizing that the historian's task was at once literary, philosophical, and scientific, Shedd voiced the expectations made of historians for the next century.[1]

Despite the scope of Shedd's claims, during the nineteenth century the discipline of historical studies grew slowly in America. Within the theological seminaries the Congregational institution at Andover, founded in 1807, included ecclesiastical history within its list of courses; actual instruction, however, was sporadic until the mid-1820s. Princeton Seminary established the earliest professorship of church history with the appointment of Samuel Miller to that post in 1813. Yet Miller divided his time between lecturing in history and assisting ministerial candidates in honing their rhetorical and homiletic skills. At Harvard Divinity School and Union Theological Seminary in New York City the situation was even more slowly paced. There was no chair of ecclesiastical history at Union until 1850, and it took until the 1880s before Harvard paid real attention to historical studies. Within the secular universities the situation was no better, as professorships of history and seminars based on German models of scholarship waited until the 1870s and 1880s to appear in any force.[2]

Consequently, during the antebellum era in a general cultural context that slighted the past in its headlong rush into the future, prized the revivalist's experience of instant conversion over the pageant of ecclesiastical history, and acclaimed historical fiction as much for its sentimentality as for its accuracy, the power of appeals to history might seem limited. Nevertheless, a distinctive position, one infused with romantic categories and patterns of thought, was developed in the antebellum search for a means of reconciling science and religion.

This reconciliation built on two themes: first, that the physical world of nature and the historical world of mankind were linked together in one dynamic process, which, if correctly understood, would demonstrate the ultimate compatibility of these natural and human worlds and their methods of exploration; second, that these processes were developmental in nature—systems, in other words, in motion and directed toward recognizable ends. During the late eighteenth and early nineteenth centuries models of animate growth drawn from the biological sphere were replacing the Enlightenment's mechanistic paradigms as metaphors for understanding the universe. Mankind and the natural world were no longer fixed in a hierarchical and often antagonistic relationship but now were seen as blended flexibly, one with the other, as equal participants in a shared ecological communion. And even though, paradoxically, the expanded and improved technologies of steam and rail were outstripping the accomplishments of the previous century, early nineteenth-century Romantic poetry and philosophy championed spiritual and material integration and replaced images of human mastery over nature with icons of human coexistence and awe in nature's presence.

Writing in 1856, Shedd celebrated the union of the natural and historical sciences in their common exploration of the dynamic processes of life. Both pursuits had come to recognize human and natural history as "subject to a law of life and growth," and Shedd hoped that this insight would form the basis not only for their mutual progress but also for their mutual accommodation. The essential ingredient for such harmonious agreement lay in a proper understanding of the nature of historical development. In his inaugural address of 1854 as well as in the book *Lectures upon the Philosophy of History*, which he subsequently drew out of it, Shedd gave particular attention to the structure and significance of the developmental idea. This idea was simple enough, Shedd suggested, and he defined it as unfolding "from a given point, through several stadia, to a final terminus." As he expanded on the topic, Shedd drew on the wealth of concepts and terms that were the legacy of Romantic and post-Kantian thought to fashion an organically modeled version of development. Here was a system that irresistibly and ineluctably worked itself out, ceaselessly moving through a predesigned plan to its final culmination. Moreover, its components exhibited the interdependence of living tissues rather than the interchangeability of mechanical parts, while its patterns of meaning and significance could only be adequately understood by reference to the totality of its being and never by scrutiny of an individual element.[3]

Human history was essentially a tapestry of moral meanings in

Shedd's view. He applauded the moderating and conservative influences that history encouraged—first, by always interpreting a specific incident in terms of its whole context, and, second, by distrusting all innovations that departed from the grand continuity of human history. Indeed, his strongest criticisms were leveled at those who engaged in "atomic" and "pragmatic" analysis. The first refused to recognize connections between historical incidents and ages, while the latter conceded only that, if connections existed, they were of an external and superficial nature. Even in the interpretations of the smallest event, Shedd insisted that its wider connections in time and place be recognized. For the historical mind raises up a person or an episode only to plunge them back into the wide web of temporal, causal, and moral connections which gave them meaning and substance. Individuals can tell us very little, Shedd stated, for the "vastness of truth" can only be revealed through the total development of the whole.[4]

In an important illustration of his point Shedd praised the "productiveness and originality" of recent speculative philosophy in Germany, while he deprecated the works of the Scottish Common Sense philosophers, with their emphasis on an inductive examination of the self-evident facts of human experience. The German philosopher, he stated, first thoroughly grounds himself in the previous history of philosophy and seeks to make his system both the test and the fulfillment of that history. On Shedd's reading it was this lack of a historical sense that vitiated Scottish philosophy. Substituting appeals to common sense for a thorough historical grasp of the relevant issues, the Common Sense philosophers, in Shedd's view, failed to achieve their goal of establishing a firm basis for knowledge and defeating skepticism.[5]

In describing the nature of history as developmental Shedd marked out a central theme of Romantic philosophy. When he published his *History of Christian Doctrine* in 1863 he additionally contributed to a growing historiography, one stretching from Johann Herder through John Henry Newman and Theodor Kliefoth to Philip Schaff, a scholarly tradition that showcased the concept of development as the essential characteristic of church history. Beyond that Shedd wrestled in this work, as he had in his earlier reflections, on specifying the nature of this developmental process. Did a developmental concept justify whatever took place, as some commentators had earlier claimed the Calvinist doctrine of predestination excused any action on the part of a Puritan saint? What was the relation between aberrations or monsters and the normal course of events? Shedd never provided a full historical theodicy, yet he repeatedly insisted that his conception of development did not entail a normative idea of improvement. Rather, he asserted that development simply meant an expansion or unfolding and could go in either a progressive or regressive direction.

Important implications in Shedd's distinction between development and improvement could be seen in his further division of secular and sacred history. Operating within a conceptual framework that pictured nature as benign and sin and evil as the causal agents of error in the world, Shedd interpreted anomalies, mistakes, and catastrophes in the human and physical worlds as signs of mankind's recurrent choice of sin. Correspondingly, he further distinguished secular from sacred history on the basis of the availability of divine grace in the latter, guiding and directing its persons and institutions through revelation and Scripture to its promised goal. Shedd's framework of redemptive history shared a long pedigree in American and European religious traditions. Just because of its familiarity and the ease with which he could mold his developmental view of history to it, Shedd's historical reflections and studies illustrated the complementarity of Romantic philosophy and Christian theological apologetics.[6]

Palmetto Romanticism

Sitting in his study in Charleston, South Carolina, James Warley Miles also ruminated over the meaning of history. The results were a series of literary pieces which together propounded a historical metaphysics, one that analyzed the foundations of human knowledge and upon those grounds built a developmental framework encompassing the course and structures of human experience. Miles's fullest account of human knowledge was provided in his book *Philosophic Theology; or, Ultimate Grounds of All Religious Belief Based in Reason* (1849). Sympathetic to the post-Schleiermacher emphasis within Christian theology on human consciousness, Miles asserted that an examination of the nature of the individual's consciousness provided three results. First, such an inquiry discovered a feeling of dependence, deficiency, or incompleteness in human self-awareness. Second, through intuition, or the Coleridgean faculty of Reason, as Miles phrased it, one found the preexisting Idea of an independent first cause which was available to mankind and could correct this felt insufficiency of life. Finally, Miles stated that a sense of moral accountability or a discrimination between right and wrong could be detected in any thorough investigation of human consciousness.[7]

For Miles, then, not only were metaphysics and epistemology closely tied together, but fundamental questions about the origin of the world and the structure and meaning of human experience were answered by religion and the existence of an Absolute First Cause, or God. Miles considered his discussion a definite advance over eighteenth-century metaphysics and especially the argument from design put forward by William Paley and others. For to Miles his argument demonstrated the existence of the idea of God necessarily implanted in human consciousness as revealed through the intuitional powers of Reason. More than just a bow to Coleridgean epistemology, Miles's metaphysics marked the further American appropriation of a broad spectrum of European thought and highlighted the shift from arguments built upon ascending scaffolds of external evidences of the divine to ones appealing to the innermost murmurs of the heart.

Miles's presentation of the incomplete nature of human consciousness found its counterpart in his portrayal of religion as the search for "the true synthesis of the imperfect and the perfect . . . of man the microcosm of the universe, the crown of nature, and God the original of the finite type, the author and end of all existence." Thus, both the form and content of his analysis centered on that same desire for unity, reintegration, and harmony which lay at the very core of the Romantic movement and which so powerfully animated its literary, philosophical, and religious expressions.[8]

Out of this abstract foundation Miles constructed his framework of development. Already in *Philosophic Theology* he had sketched the necessary development of all life in organic terms. In subsequent statements he worked out the manner in which the Absolute Cause expressed itself through a series of necessary laws in history. In a lecture to an undergraduate society at the College of Charleston Miles pointed to the progressive development that underlies human life. The physical world, he stated, demonstrated a unified evolution from simple to more complex levels of organization and existence. Moreover, Miles contended that this same process continued into the human sphere and the development not only of physical systems but also moral consciousness within the human race. Miles's concept of "progressive evolution" not only linked the physical and human realms; it also contained a basically optimistic perspective on the future of the human race. In another address, delivered in Berlin Germany in 1855,

Miles drew out his views on the challenges of the future, and especially those facing the American nation. Whereas in the earlier Charleston address Miles had only generally observed that humanity faced obstacles to its advancement, now in 1855 he claimed that the Western world was in a "great transition epoch," one that was just then preparing for a "higher evolution of the social and political condition." In traditional and flourishing fashion Miles rhetorically invoked the example of the decline of Athens and warned against that amnesia that would forget the lessons of the past. For, while he lauded the intellectual prowess of the Greeks, he criticized the party factionalism that he saw in both the Athenian democracy and his own contemporary America. Nevertheless, Miles concluded by reassuring his audience that the mission of America was clear, and, though the standards to which the nation would be held were lofty and exacting, the available resources were ample to meet the task.[9]

Miles had consistently drawn analogies between the development of the individual and that of the nation and mankind in general. This approach to the meaning of human history had often been employed by the Romantics in their striving after a universal history that would match their quest for a universal poetic vision of human reintegration and unity. Likewise, Miles's optimistic view of history resonated with romanticism. He modeled his meliorative concept in organic terms— that is, slow evolutionary growth rather than accidental, revolutionary, or cataclysmic styles of change. Significantly, while the Romantic resources of Europe, to which Miles was so indebted, need not necessarily be conservative in their outlook and implications, Miles regularly drew politically and socially conservative conclusions from them.[10]

In 1863 Miles provided the fullest version of his speculative philosophy of history, and in so doing both built on and expanded beyond his earlier statements. Once again the progressive development of mankind was invoked. So too, in true Romantic fashion Miles characterized natural and physical phenomena as expressing themselves inexorably through laws that were themselves directed to ultimate ends and goals. Finally, Miles discussed the issue of national destiny, yet this time in a more comprehensive manner. For here Miles scanned the course of human history and drew a straight line of development. Miles's reflections on history had always contained an element of ineluctability, an emphasis on an inner dynamic that designated the direction of development. Like several other commentators, Miles

believed that the advance of human progress had invariably been west-
ward, out of the civilization of ancient India, through Persia, Egypt,
Greece, and Rome to Western Europe and then to the United States.
The result was that, while each specific nation possessed its own particular history, it simultaneously exhibited the "phase of that general
idea or plan which is realizing itself through the entire drama of
universal history." For Miles, in other words, human history was pur-
posive, and each society played a role on the stage of world history.[11]

Reviewing the course of human development in more conceptual
terms, Miles found five lines of development: first, the evolution of
language through its various stages to its present position; second, the
evolution of religion from a primitive self-awareness of incompleteness and finitude to the recognition of moral obligation and the revelation of superhuman powers; third, the evolution of political
organization from the family and tribe to modern nation-states; next,
the evolution of art as the expression of both the constructive and
imaginative capacities of mankind; and, finally, the evolution of
thought as manifested in the history of philosophy. Taken together,
Miles contended, these lines of development encompassed human
culture and society, they were the vehicles through which God expressed himself and fulfilled his plan for humanity, and they were the
manifestations of the common dynamic forces at work in the natural
and human realms.

Just as with W. G. T. Shedd, human history for James Warley Miles
was heavily weighted with moral meanings. Individuals suffered no
setbacks or advances, nations neither rose nor fell, without it being
part of the divine plan. Likewise, neither individuals nor societies
existed simply for themselves but were, rather, part of a larger design,
linked inexorably one to another within the human community and
the divine plan of redemption. And, finally, despite any appearances of
invariable progress, Miles admitted the variety, pertinacity, and com-
plexity of human history. While he believed his philosophy com-
prehended history's ultimate meaning, Miles recognized that struggle
and conflict, individual avarice and tragic loss, were visible throughout
the course of human affairs. Yet for Miles, together with the vast
majority of Christians in antebellum America, a residual belief in the
freedom of the will, undergirded by a wider cultural assumption of the
freedom and autonomy of the individual, provided a ready explanation
for both the heights and depths of individual human experience.[13]

Here, then, was Miles's philosophy of history, a philosophy infused with both the Romantic categories drawn from contemporary Europe and the faith in providential design drawn from the ancient Hebrew prophets, a philosophy built on a metaphysics informed by Coleridgean powers of intuition and post-Kantian laws of the development of the natural and human worlds through time, and a philosophy that sought to be rational without being mechanical, intelligent without being concessionary, and affirmative without being naive.

The critical response to Miles's work was mixed, and his own frustration with the reception that his ideas received is evident in a number of ways. Indeed, as the majority of Miles's addresses were delivered at ceremonial occasions such as college commencements and subsequently printed in small numbers and distributed mainly to colleagues and friends, it was only Miles's *Philosophic Theology* that received public review. One Charleston religious journal, for example, suggested that the book was designed to increase the skepticism of the religious public in America. Moreover, it noted Miles's familiarity with German thought and predicted that, if Miles's ideas found acceptance in America, then the nation would quickly follow that same path to infidelity and damnation as Germany itself was supposedly experiencing. If this journal denounced Miles for heeding Continental scholarship too much, another reviewer accused Miles of not paying close enough attention and confusing the categories presented by Kant and his successors.[14]

One set of comments, however, heartened Miles. In 1850 the German church historian, Johann August Neander, wrote a review that praised Miles's book as "an important publication in the field of Christian Philosophy, Theological and Apologetic." In January 1850 a young American friend of Miles had delivered a copy of the book to Neander in Berlin. This emissary was delighted with Neander, stating that he was "a perfect specimen of a German student—his eyes so failed that he uses an amanuensis, his room crowded with unbound books and musty pamphlets," but also warning that, "if Miles's book should be too abstract, he may receive [from Neander] a reprimand instead of a compliment." Happily for Miles, however, instead of reproach, the book made a sufficient impression on Neander that he had one of his assistants translate it into German for wider distribution in Central Europe.[15]

In his review Neander approvingly noted Miles's use of the ideas of Kant, Schleiermacher, Schelling, and Friedrich Jacobi. Another European, Fredrika Bremer, noted the close similarity between Miles's work and that of the Danish theologian Hans Martensen. Such European praise would not have surprised Miles, for he too felt that his work was in line with the mainstream of Protestant scholarship in Europe. Yet, if he was pleased by the European commentary, he remained frustrated and at times bitter over the lack of understanding for his work at home. In a revealing letter Miles expressed his chagrin at the American responses to his work. "The Presbyterians have branded me an infidel," he wrote, "the Baptists as the same, a Romanist reviewer pronounced me little short of an utter Deist, even the Jews have thought me on the brink of infidelity, the Episcopal high-churchman deem me a heretic of horrid dye, while his amiable low-church brother, who thinks *him* in a sad way and blind, yet cordially agrees with him in judging me a dangerous heretic, and moreover, adding his own opinion that I am unconverted." Still, Miles took solace in his European connections and defiantly concluded: "I would rather be called infidel in the noble company of Neander and [Thomas] Arnold, than be lauded for the narrow-minded *orthodoxy* of Thornwell—and anybody among the popular religionists of the day whom you choose to add."16

The mid-1850s were a time of trial and despair for Miles. Failing in health and feeling increasingly unappreciated, he searched about for an escape, informing one correspondent: "I am sick and tired of this life. I am breaking up and breaking down and you must not be surprised at any moment to hear that I have gone away to Greece, to Turkey, to Kamschatka." Yet neither the eastern Mediterranean nor the Siberian peninsula were to be his destination. Instead, in the spring of 1854 Miles sold his considerable library and left for Western Europe. In a short letter to Robert Gourdin, the brother of Mrs. Thomas Young and the associate of Miles's brother, William Porcher Miles, James Warley Miles indicated that he had arrived in Amsterdam after an agreeable sea voyage and would soon be leaving for Berlin, "to bury myself in study. Beyond that I have no plan, no hopes, no future." Little is known of Miles's life during the remainder of his European stay. The German emigré and family friend Francis Lieber wrote to Miles's brother, complaining of having received no letter from Miles since his departure for Europe. Lieber hoped the errant scholar's health was sound for "a Berlin winter must be pretty grim to a Carolinian," and together with other family friends and associates sought a suitable college position to entice Miles back. Finally, in 1856 Miles returned from his self-imposed exile and took the position of librarian at the College of Charleston.[17]

From Berlin to Andover: Henry Boynton Smith

James Warley Miles once lamented that one reason he was misunderstood by his contemporaries was that he was not a member of any of the factions in the current conflicts but, instead, sought a higher position above party strife. Those who would choose a mediating role, or a role outside of party identification, often run the risk of misunderstanding and calumny from partisans committed to one or another side. Henry Boynton Smith embraced the role of mediator, both in his theological writings and in his relation to ecclesiastical conflicts. And in both his capacities as professor and as churchman, a deep reverence for history suffused and grounded his efforts.

Smith blended a training in the classics of New England theology with a thorough familiarity with contemporary German religious and philosophical thought. His lectures in church history earned him the praise of Philip Schaff, dean of American church historians, and upon his death Continental theologians, such as Isaak Dorner, eulogized Smith in laudatory terms for his theological contributions. Beyond that Smith played a prominent role in the Presbyterian church, especially in its reunion after the Civil War. Smith was born in 1815 in Portsmouth, Maine. His merchant father was prosperous enough to send his son to nearby Bowdoin College, and the young Henry was talented enough to be encouraged and praised by his teachers. In 1834 Smith enrolled at Andover Theological Seminary, whose reputation for orthodoxy Moses Stuart and Leonard Woods now carried forward. Yet Smith soon became ill and had to return to Maine, where he finished out his theological education at Bangor Theological Seminary.[18]

Though schooled in New England Calvinist orthodoxy, Smith was exposed to the new currents of German theological scholarship through Stuart at Andover and, at greater length, through Leonard Woods, Jr., at Bangor. Woods had been an assistant to both Stuart and Edward Robinson at Andover before taking the professorship at Bangor, and, like his Andover mentors, he combined an evangelical fervor with a judicious assimilation of German scholarship. Smith's theological education reached a turning point in 1837, when he went to Germany to study. He spent the next two years in Germany, principally at the universities of Halle and Berlin. When he returned to America he was not only a learned expositor of German thought but also in a position uniquely qualified to synthesize his inherited New England orthodoxy with that particular combination of ecclesiastical history and Protestant theology characteristic of the German theology of mediation.

The theological traditions Smith immersed himself in were principally those of the mediation theologians. The mediating theology (*Vermittlungstheologie*) was a loose alliance of German Protestant theologians, whose ranks included Friedrich August Gottreu Tholuck, Johann August Neander, Carl Immanuel Nitzsch, Karl Ullmann, August Twesten, Julius Müller, and Isaak August Dorner. Outside of Germany, the Dane H. L. Martensen and the Swiss theologian Alexander Schweizer worked out parallel theological projects. Symbolically at least, the movement began in 1828 with the founding of the journal *Theologische Studien und Kritiken* by Ullmann and others. The mediating theologians exerted a significant influence through the decades of the 1860s; by the 1870s, however, with the rise to prominence of Albrecht Ritschl and his followers, the mediators' authority had declined.[19]

Two broad purposes were at the center of this movement, purposes that were elastic enough to encompass the variety of persons aligned with this theological movement, yet ones that still clearly identified the group within the context of German religious thought and politics. First, these theologians sought a reconciliation of the Christian faith and modern science and culture, thereby hoping to bridge the historic division from the previous century between supernaturalism and rationalism. Second, these churchmen sought to overcome historic confessional differences within Protestantism and, thus, were active supporters of the various proposals in the 1800s for a union of Lutheran and Reformed churches in Germany.

In both of these pursuits the mediating theology was heavily indebted to Friedrich Schleiermacher. Throughout his writings, from the early *Speeches* to his later *Christian Faith*, Schleiermacher had his eye on those cultural despisers of religion who dismissed Christianity as antithetical to the spirit of the modern world. He sought to establish a basis for theological work that was scientific in spirit and contemporary in results. That such results would differ in certain regards from those of the natural scientist was clear; Schleiermacher, however, was convinced of the necessity and the efficacy of his efforts. Beyond that Schleiermacher gave his whole-hearted support to the church union endeavor, and especially the Prussian Union of 1817. The proponents of church union desired to erase the age-old differences between Reformed and Lutheran believers and to unite them in one common evangelical Protestant church. Sources for this idea ranged from the neopietist revival, with its deemphasis of doctrinal belief through the new spirit of nationalist consensus engendered by the War of Liberation, and the tercentenary of the posting of Luther's Ninety-five Theses to the personality of the Prussian king, Friedrich Wilhelm III. And, if Prussia led the way in church union, it was not alone, as similar programs were inaugurated between 1817 and 1823 in Nassau, the Rhineland Palatinate, Waldek, Pyromont, Anhalt-Bernburg, Baden, and Württemberg. Opposition to the union plans developed among both Lutheran and Reformed confessionalists, and, thus, the issue for the mediational theologians was joined.[20]

A renewed emphasis upon Christology together with a stress upon biblical foundations provided the means by which this broad program of mediation was to be achieved. In Karl Ullmann's *The Essence of Christianity* (1849) one finds a concentration upon the unity of the divine and the human in the person of Jesus. In the present era, Ullmann maintained, the modern church had drawn on the theological contributions of previous centuries. Taken together, these contributions represented a development, or an evolution, as Ullmann called it, through the centuries, and it was the task of the modern theologian not only to explicate Christianity's relationship to world history and other religions but also to delineate the specific content of Christianity and to highlight its particular nature.[21]

Ullmann located the scientific character of his enterprise precisely in this analytical ordering of the history of Christianity and in the uncovering of its relation to human cultural affairs. Beyond that he emphasized that the distinguishing characteristic of Christianity was not its doctrines nor moral laws, nor even its redeeming power, but the unique religious meaning of its founder, Jesus, as a truly divine and truly human person. Such a revelation, Ullmann concluded, was a disclosure of the reconciliation of the human and the divine. It was the highest goal of the Christian church, as the organic and institutional embodiment of the faith, therefore, to strive for the fullest unity among all its believers and a true and organic union among its churches.[22]

Two further examples of the *Vermittlungstheologen*, and of persons especially significant for several of the Americans in this study, were Johann August Neander and Friedrich Tholuck. Both men had roots in the Awakening (*Erweckungsbewegung*), that neopietistic movement that reached its height in Germany during the first half of the nineteenth century. This movement had ties to its baroque predecessor, yet, unlike that earlier experience, this nineteenth-century pietism was marked by its encounter with romanticism and especially with the Romantics' fondness for a sense of the mysterious in human affairs and a predilection for representing life in organic and developmental rather than mechanical and static models. The Awakening took place throughout Germany but with regional variations. In many areas its emphasis on individual conversion experience, its dedication to biblically based theology, and its positive disposition toward feeling and a religion of the heart over doctrines and a religion of the head promoted a broad and nondogmatic faith. In such a context appeals to an "evangelical Christianity," free of confessional differences, were common, and such appeals fostered support for the plans for church union. In other areas, such as Silesia or Bavaria, however, the Awakening furthered new study of creeds such as the Augsburg Confession and thereby advanced the defense of confessional standards and integrity. Whichever of these results occurred, the Awakening inaugurated a broad revitalization of religious life in Germany and bequeathed an important legacy to the next generation.[23]

The man known as Neander was born David Mendel in 1789 and changed his name to Johann August Wilhelm Neander upon his Christian baptism in 1806. He pursued his theological education first with Schleiermacher at Halle then later with the Old Testament and Hebrew scholar Wilhelm Gesenius at Göttingen. It was, however, church history that was his true love, and in 1813 he was called to the newly formed University of Berlin as professor of church history and remained there until his death in 1850.[24]

Neander's great work was his multivolume *General History of the Christian Religion and Church* (1826–1852). As he elaborated upon the history of the church from its origins through the fifteenth century, three themes became apparent. First, Neander conceived of church history as disclosing an essential unity in the midst of all its historical variety. This principle of unity, according to Neander, was the divine power of redemption, manifested in Jesus and unfolding in an organic development through the Christian church. Second, to be understood properly Neander insisted that this principle be examined historically and scientifically. The "demands of science" must be answered, Neander instructed his readers, and such an injunction called for both grounding one's work in the primary sources and locating an issue or person in its specific historical context. Significantly, Neander distinguished between what he called "genuine, unprejudiced science" and that of a "particular philosophical and dogmatic school." This was in part a rejoinder to the criticisms of Neander's Hegelian colleagues. For, where the Hegelian methodology drew a synthesis out of dialectical oppositions and contradictions, Neander emphasized a unity in diversity, or the continuous disclosure of an inner principle developing through the multiplicity of historical experience. Here Neander likened the history of the church to a process of leavening, whereby the germinal message of Jesus expanded throughout the world, planting itself in foreign cultures and distant lands and growing finally into full maturity.[25]

If Neander's model of historical development and his image of the leavening process betrayed his indebtedness to romanticism, then his fascination with the individual revealed his third theme, the portrayal of Christianity as a lived experience and not simply a series of theological doctrines or systems of abstract speculation. In this context the influence of the Awakening on Neander was again evident. It was his biography of Julian the Apostate which first earned Neander his call to the theology faculty at Berlin, and his often extended biographical accounts and individualized tropes—for example, Petrine and Pauline patterns—formed the framework of his *General History* as well. The depiction of history from the standpoint of the individual nicely complemented Neander's desire to demonstrate the divine power of Christianity in individual lives. The emphasis on the renovation of lives through the agency of personal conversion was a hallmark of the Awakening, and in this testimony Neander found the purpose for his scholarly project.

Friedrich August Gottreu Tholuck was also a product of the Awakening. Indeed, it was due to the influence of Neander and the Berlin pietist Baron Ernst von Kottwitz that Tholuck undertook theological studies. Tholuck's area of specialization was Oriental philology and biblical exegesis. But it was his pietistic fervor and pastoral concern rather than any academic depth and systematic rigor which gained him his following. From 1820 to 1826 he taught at the University of Berlin, largely due to the backing of Kottwitz and Neander. In 1826 Tholuck transferred to the University of Halle and, despite some initial opposition from the faculty, remained there until his death in 1877.[26]

Much of Tholuck's work was apologetic and moralistic in outlook, oriented to the Bible and emphatic in its emphasis on the importance of spiritual rebirth as the answer to human iniquity. Philip Schaff credited Tholuck with turning student interest at Halle from rationalist theology toward what Schaff called an "evangelical faith." Yet Tholuck did acknowledge the validity of the claims of science in much the same way as his teacher, Neander. For Tholuck, too, would accept the need for a "genuine science," yet he meant by that a philologically based examination and not the "speculative" sort of investigation which he thought David Friedrich Strauss exemplified and which he dismissed as misguided and pseudoscientific. In the end, then, Tholuck's mediation was one that invoked the name of science yet was less interested in a rigorous and methodologically self-conscious investigation than in the theological proclamation of sin and the redemption to be found in Jesus.[27]

During his years in Germany Henry Boynton Smith attended the lectures of Tholuck at Halle and later, at Berlin, those of Neander and Twesten. Additionally, he heard Leopold Ranke and Ernst Hengstenberg, met Tholuck's mentor, Baron Kottwitz, as well as Hegel's widow, and crossed paths with several of his American compatriots such as Edward Robinson and George Prentiss. Yet for Smith, as would be the case with Charles Hodge and many other Americans, it was Tholuck, through his friendship, piety, and pastoral concern, who made the deepest personal impression. For, while Smith would return to America with his head full of the theological apparatus of Twesten, Neander, Ullmann, and the rest of the mediating theologians, it was Tholuck who had touched Smith's heart. "To you more than all," Smith wrote Tholuck at the conclusion of his first year of study as he was leaving Halle and continuing on to Berlin, "to you do I owe the most and the best in this progress of my thoughts and knowledge: to you, in all my intercourse with you, as Professor and as companion, am I the most indebted in this transition state in my life. If I live long, the effect of your teaching will ever inspire me—if I should die early I will still thank God that I have enjoyed such instructions."[28]

Nor should it be surprising that Smith and other American students like him would respond positively to the style and camaraderie offered by Tholuck. Familiar from their American context with a theology of experiential conversion, well-warned about the theological dangers

lurking in Germany, and separated from the intimacy of familial contexts, many Americans found Tholuck's blend of pietism and learning,
personal solicitude and visible spirituality, a comfortable answer to
their doubts and a powerful vindication of their decision to come to
Germany in the first place. Smith knew why he had come to study
among the Germans and was forthright in recognizing the superior
position of German philosophy in comparison with all other nations.
Yet he took great pains to assure himself and others that his stay in
Germany had not damaged "my simple reverence for the Scriptures
and my simple faith in experimental religion."[29]

It was this combination of faith and philosophy which Smith
brought back from Germany and which he expounded on in a memorable lecture given at Andover Seminary in 1849. Here was to be the
testimony to the importance of German scholarship as well as the
measure of Smith's appropriation of mediational theology. Invoking
the names of Schleiermacher and Ullmann and praising the efforts of
men such as Tholuck in combating rationalism, Smith boldly declared
that "Germany cannot give us faith," but it can "teach us what is the
real 'state of the controversy' in our age."[30]

Beyond defending German theological efforts to his American audience Smith highlighted three important themes. First, religion and
science are reconcilable, and to say otherwise is both false and bad
policy, for it misunderstands the true nature of faith and philosophy,
and it delivers the whole of modern culture into the hands of infidels as
being incapable of redemption. Systematic theology, according to
Smith, is itself a science, one of its chief responsibilities to demonstrate the compatibility of the scientific criteria of comprehensiveness,
consistency, and exactitude with religion. And, if intractable conflicts
arose, then Smith confidently counseled the believer not to retreat
into the private sanctuary of faith but resolutely to demonstrate the
incompatibility of the opponent's position with sound reason.[31]

In another bow to his German teachers Smith next argued that the
centerpoint of Christianity was located in the person of Jesus Christ.
Christianity, Smith stated in language reminiscent of Neander, was
"an organic, diffusive, plastic, and triumphant force in human history,
and in this history . . . the centre around which all revolves is the
person of Jesus Christ." This view provided the focus in Smith's theological enterprise for the rest of his life, yet before he finished speaking
Smith drew one final practical conclusion for his listeners: these
Christological doctrines are "the soul of our Puritan theology," and it

was high time to stop bickering between ourselves and to recognize that errors, not persons, should be the object of our admonitions. Smith was calling for a truce to the internecine theological battles in New England, much as the proponents of church union had done in Germany. Beyond that he was announcing that not all German theology led to infidelity but that, in fact, German theologians could provide some of the resources that Americans needed so badly in their present controversies.[32]

Further elucidation of Smith's position came in his inaugural lectures at Union Theological Seminary of New York, first as professor of church history in 1851 then as professor of systematic theology in 1855. As others before and after him have done, Smith complained that Americans had little true regard for history. Too often, he stated, history is regarded as "a collection of bare names, arid facts, and lifeless dates. It is learned by rote and kept by mnemonic helps. . . . [It is] investigated for aid in present polemics, not to know the past but to conquer in an emergency."[33]

Smith dismissed this approach and instead called for a true appreciation of church history as science. Taking pains to explicate this concept of science, Smith noted three characteristics. First, historical study must subsume its facts within a broader set of generalizations, or laws. If history was too often approached as the mastery of atomistic units of information, then the fault lay in an inability or unwillingness to link these units properly into a broader picture. Second, the correct schema for church history was a developmental one, one that encompassed both the causes that produced these facts and the ends to which they were directed. In this emphasis on cause and purpose Smith demonstrated once again his indebtedness to those broadly nineteenth-century Romantic and specifically German influences, which placed such a premium on developmental schemas as the proper framework for explanation. Finally, Smith insisted that a proper methodology must have checks and tests to verify the facts and validate the generalizations. In filling out this third requirement Smith placed the Scriptures within the broad interpretive framework of his theology of mediation as the appropriate testing ground. Here was all the verification one could require, Smith argued, for, in his mediational principle of reconciliation between God and mankind in Jesus Christ, Smith claimed to identify a dynamic principle that could encompass all the diversity, rank all the developmental stages, and clarify all the meanings of church history.[34]

In combining his interest in historical scholarship with his commitment to Christian theology Henry Boynton Smith charted a new approach to the teaching of church history at Union Theological Seminary. His historiographical vision was a grand one; drawing on his German mentors, he portrayed each historical period as reflecting its own needs and developing its own theological controversies yet still contributing finally to the unfolding of essential scriptural truth beneath these outward forms of church history. Furthermore, as a theologian, he appropriated much of the current Christological work in Germany and presented it in a comprehensible form for his American audience. Though always suspect in some circles for his Teutonic interests, Smith made an important contribution to the attempt to reconcile science and religion through the category of historical understanding.

The breadth and significance of this developmental vision could be seen not only in the analysis of Christianity but also in the evaluation of non-Christian religions by Smith and other of the American mediational theologians. Potentially, historical research into world religions could be every bit as challenging as geological findings to the previously privileged status of Christianity. Was Christianity just one religion among all others, or was it special or even perhaps a unique case? What was the relation of Christianity to the other religions of the world? Were their messages all the same, or did they reflect specific contexts, environments, or circumstances? Attention to non-Christian religions by Christian commentators and other observers had a long previous history in European culture, and the question was to assume an even greater urgency during the late nineteenth and early twentieth centuries.

Although a body of scholarly literature on non-Christian religions was emerging in Europe, American discussions up through the 1800s largely ignored it. Instead, American depictions of world religions tended to go in one of two ways. First, there was the presentation of the rationalist, or Enlightened skeptic, who drew parallels between alleged pagan superstitions and more familiar Christian practices and beliefs so as to be able to rid all such supernatural religions of their superficialities and reduce them to a common core of reasonable beliefs. Second, there was the portrayal by the corps of present and past foreign missionaries, whose journal reports, Bible society announcements, and lecture circuits provided them with ample opportunity to reiterate that non-Christian religions were simply exercises in error and not deserving of the name religion. Within the context of these two perspectives the interest by the antebellum New England Transcendentalists—such as Ralph Waldo Emerson, Henry David Thoreau, Theodore Parker, and Bronson Alcott—in Asian culture and religion was striking. Though their knowledge did not always run deep and their enthusiasm often overstepped their comprehension, these Transcendentalists shared an abiding fascination with world religions and provided a context for their recognition and study in antebellum America.[35]

The Congregational clergyman Horace Bushnell clearly recognized the challenges posed by historical research. This "historical criticism," Bushnell stated, had been applied to the religions of Egypt, Greece, and the Mediterranean basin with the result that their beliefs had been reduced to fanciful tales of supernatural gods "charioteering in the sun, presiding in the mountain tops, rising out of the foam of the sea." Would Christianity suffer the same fate under the glare of historical investigation and comparison? Would it too be reduced to another set of fables and legends? Bushnell acknowledged that preliminary historical comparisons between Christianity and other religions had produced intriguing results. He cited the claim for a broad-based religious sentiment and the acknowledgment of the importance—indeed, the divine inspiration—of men such as Zoroaster, Confucius, and Mohammed as acceptable findings. Yet the signal failure of this historical approach, according to Bushnell, was its "bondage under the method of science," a method construed exclusively in rationalistic and materialistic terms. Consequently, Bushnell insisted on the existence of a symbolic as well as a literal dimension, an emotional as well as an intellectual sphere, in human affairs. Rationalism was fine in its own area, but the higher truths of religion were verified by faith and the heart, not cognition and the head. In the end Bushnell's analysis of world religions was incomplete and partial. He recognized their existence but always subordinated them unequivocally to Christianity.[36]

Henry Boynton Smith's consideration of non-Christian religions was further developed than Bushnell's. For Smith *religion*, as a generic term, implied "a sense of dependence on a higher power, and of obligation to its behest." Smith drew this definition from Friedrich Schleiermacher and his claim that a feeling of absolute dependence lies at the very heart of all religion. Equally familiar in nineteenth-century German Protestant theology was Smith's next move—the distinction between natural and revealed religion and the claim that revealed religion incorporated and elevated the attributes of natural religion into a new and higher stage of development. Finally, then, Smith concluded that all the other religions of the world found their culmination in the revelation of Christianity, for "the yearnings of paganism . . . are but immature and anticipatory efforts to realize that idea of Mediation through an Incarnation which came to its perfect embodiment in the person of Christ." Smith's Christological doctrine provided him with an explicit means of both linking together the religions of the world and still fulfilling his apologetic desire to see Christianity as the fulfillment of their development.[37]

James Warley Miles paralleled the theological conclusions of Henry Boynton Smith but contextualized his analysis in a more far-reaching manner than did Smith and thereby pointed out explicitly several important implications in the developmental presentation. Miles spoke of a scale of moral development upon which all the nations and religions of the world had their place. Every unit of the scale had its meaning and mission, for Miles's emphasis was not so much on the relative position of each unit as on the total development of the whole as a manifestation of divine Providence. Zoroaster and Buddha were reforming prophets analogous to Moses and Abraham, while Hinduism, Buddhism, the religions of Greece, and Judaism all contained important moral dimensions and insights. Like Smith, however, Miles considered Christianity the completion of this development, with Jesus as the ultimate and final prophet.[38]

Miles recognized two possible implications in his position and accepted their consequences. For he argued, first, that it was necessary for the non-Christian religions to precede Christianity in order to prepare the way for the revelation of Jesus. On Miles's account human history was one great providential plan, and without the religions of Greece, Asia, and Palestine, Jesus' message would have been unintelligible. Miles's developmental schema, then, was rigidly and hierarchically ranked. Where the conceptions of another developmentalist, Johann Herder, could conclude in pluralistic ends derived from different and equivalent causes, Miles's unitary framework was less elastic. He recognized the contributions of other religions to the development of moral law, yet he subordinated those religions to the final authority of Christianity. In so doing Miles recognized a second implication of his position: his developmental schema consigned all religious believers before Jesus and all who had not yet heard of Jesus to spiritual thralldom with no hope of achieving a higher moral life.

Such an inescapable situation seemed incompatible with the highest law of moral development manifested through Christianity. In response Miles suggested that, in their context, these past believers' own religions, however limited, were the ones best suited to their needs and level of development. And, as for the present day, Miles, as a former missionary himself, supported the efforts in his contemporary society to evangelize in foreign and domestic missions and hoped that these efforts would succeed.[39]

In 1846 Philip Schaff, professor in the German Reformed seminary at Mercersburg, Pennsylvania, also explored the significance of world religions within a developmental context. Schaff's discussion had much in common with that of Smith and Miles, though it was not identical to theirs. Schaff, for example, insisted that the true root of religion was not a feeling of dependence but, rather, a quest for reconciliation between the divine and the human. All religions aim at this reconciliation between God and mankind, but, Schaff argued, all non-Christian religions either fail outright or else achieve at best an imperfect anticipation of this goal. Like Smith and Miles, Schaff, too, found Christianity to be the final stage in the long historical development of world religions. Moreover, Schaff argued that both nations and religions played a part in a larger developmental scheme. The purpose of this development, he continued, was the progress of humanity and the exhibition of God's glory. Here Schaff drew conclusions every bit as stern and deterministic as Miles. For it was the "historical" nations, races, and religions, those that "have made themselves felt in a living way upon the actual development, inward and outward, of the world's life as a whole," which played a role in this development. Other non-historical groups, identified by Schaff as "the Hottentots, Caffrarians, Negroes, and New Zealanders," had played no role in this historical saga. Beyond that Schaff insisted that the development among historical groups was not simply a quantitative advance but a qualitative leap. Where Miles and Smith depicted development in essentially fluid and continuous terms, Schaff propounded a dialectical view in which the synthesis not only grew out of its predecessors but abolished them as well. Illustrating his point with the example of Christianity and Judaism, Schaff stated that Christianity "is not to be viewed as an advance simply upon the Jewish system, exalting it to a higher state. It must be regarded rather as a new creation, by which a new principle, a divine life is communicated to humanity itself."[40]

Here again world religions were recognized, but once again the radical challenge of comparative historical studies was turned away by a theological rejoinder and a Euroamerican cultural bias. Comparative studies contained a powerful dissolvant, one that could strip away the outward facade and melt the foundation of many a privileged idea. During the antebellum era in America, however, this corrosive agent remained bottled up, and an uneasy equilibrium between the demands of faith and history remained intact to await a later generation's renewed interest and efforts.

The Organic Vision of Philip Schaff

It was characteristic of Philip Schaff to discuss issues in historical terms. Coming to America from Europe in 1844, he taught church history first at Mercersburg then later at Union Theological Seminary in New York City. At the time of his death in 1893 Schaff had published voluminously and was recognized as one of the foremost church historians in America. Schaff was born on 1 January 1819 in Chur, Switzerland. As a youngster, Schaff received his primary education in Stuttgart and was heavily influenced by the pietism then prevalent in Württemberg. An energetic student, Schaff succeeded in his university studies and began to pursue an academic career, a decision encouraged "by my beloved professors, Drs. Schmid in Tübingen, Tholuck and Müller in Halle, Neander, Twesten and Hengstenberg in Berlin." Schaff's list of mentors was impressive, but he acknowledged that it was August Neander "who interested and helped me the most." For in Neander Schaff found a sweeping interpretation of church history, one grounded in a thorough, firsthand knowledge of primary materials and combined together with a life of piety and devotion to Christianity. These qualities impressed the young Schaff, and he sought to duplicate them throughout his own professional career. Yet Schaff's historical analysis was no simple recapitulation of Neander's ideas. For, above all else, Schaff saw his own mission as that of a mediator between German and Anglo-American theology, as an interpreter of the meaning of Christianity from its ancient past to its turbulent present. In the accomplishment of this task Schaff eminently qualifies as one who strove in antebellum America to reconcile science and religion through the medium of historical understanding.[41]

Schaff combined an encyclopedic knowledge of church history with an explicit concern for the nature and method of historical investigation. In a bow to his university instructors, the historians F. C. Baur and Neander, Schaff listed "a thorough use of original sources, clear apprehensions, organic development, lively and interesting delineations, strong but liberal and universal church feelings, and fruitfulness in the way of practical edification" as the basic prerequisites for the successful writing of church history. Schaff's list testified to his appropriation of Romantic categories of interpretation, particularly the characteristic emphasis on organic development (versus mechanical enumeration or simply chronicling of unrelated facts), and the desire to evoke the meaning of past experience in all of its vitality for the further enhancement of the present generation.[42]

Moreover, in this undertaking the historian labors on behalf of all humanity, not simply for an isolated cause. The modern historian, Schaff remarked, "has too exalted an idea of truth, to think of confining it to the narrow horizon of an individual or party." Parochial or apologetic historical study was obsolete, Schaff went on, for all the actors on the stage of human history had a part to play in this drama. Thus, the historian sought both to evoke the spirit and texture and to delineate the moral and historical significance of the past, by bringing the actors of the past forward into the present as flesh-and-blood human beings with recognizable motivations, aspirations, and failings.[43]

As Henry Bowden has pointed out, Philip Schaff viewed church history as ultimately a theological discipline. For Schaff historical scholarship was grounded in two important assumptions. First, Schaff believed in a providential interpretation of human history, one that found the ultimate explanation for all events in the divine plan of God for the human race. Historians could debate the proximate causes of events in world history, but they needed to recognize in that very history "the hand of an over-ruling, allwise Providence who is here breaking new paths . . . and opening new and boundless prospects for the further development of humanity and the kingdom of God." Schaff's providential interpretation always contained this dynamic and developmental element in which new possibilities were continuously emerging as older forms withered and disappeared. So too Schaff's interpretation always retained a sense of mystery, in that the meaning of the divine plan, though warranted by revelation, was not always clear and, indeed, might not be known until the end of time. Providential interpretations of history were characteristic of Christian communities all the way back to Augustine; with his characteristic emphasis on organic development, however, Philip Schaff placed a nineteenth-century stamp on his proposal.[44]

The second assumption of Schaff's scholarship asserted the importance of church history not only for the life of the Christian church but also for a proper understanding of world history. Indeed, Schaff simply stated that, without a proper knowledge of its history, the church denied itself its surest guide to success in its present activities. Schaff was well aware, as he put it, that, "as a general thing, we are too much taken up with the present, to trouble ourselves much about the past." Even the mere introduction of a fundamentally historical and developmental principle could lead to misunderstanding, as it had in Schaff's own case when he was tried for heresy in 1845. Yet, just as he had been vindicated in that trial, so Schaff felt confident that the practical usefulness of historical understanding would be borne out.[45]

More portentous, if not problematic, than the practicality of church history was Schaff's contention that ecclesiastical history encompassed the meaning of world history. On one level the Christian church had been at the center of world history for eighteen hundred years, Schaff maintained. Little or nothing had transpired on the stage of world history which did not bear some connection to the church and which did not "acquire its true historical significance precisely from this relation." That such a claim confined world history to a European and Mediterranean locale was clear, yet it also illustrated Schaff's view that "only that can be called historical, strictly speaking, which has exercised a determining influence upon the progress of humanity." Progress and Christianity were identical, and only those features that contributed to their development were to be considered historically important in Schaff's analysis.[46]

If Schaff's conception of history was a presumptuous one, then it was a conceit based not simply or exclusively in racial or ethnic identity (as was often the case in this era), so much as in theology. For in unequivocal terms Schaff saw the direction of ancient history leading to Jesus' life and all subsequent experience illumined and measured by that event. Here, then, in an appropriation of the mediating theology of Karl Ullmann and August Neander, Schaff portrayed Jesus as the union of human and divine natures, Christian theology as the reconciliation of scientific reason and divine revelation, and the Christian church as the mediation of the principles and institutions of sacred and secular history. In Philip Schaff's panoramic presentation human history found its measure in Christian revelation, and Christian theology found its method in the careful display of the organic development of church history as the bearer of world history.[47]

During the 1840s and 1850s, in an extended series of essays and books, Philip Schaff applied his theological reflections on the nature of church history to his adopted country of America. The centerpiece of these reflections was Schaff's *America*, a set of lectures delivered in Germany in 1854 on the political, social, and religious character of the new nation, observations that Perry Miller judged to be "one of the most searching analyses of the national character composed in his [Schaff's] century." There was much that impressed and much that depressed Philip Schaff about the American scene. Fundamentally, however, Schaff was hopeful, for even in 1848, as Europe convulsed with revolution and America confronted its own version of spread-eagle nationalism, he saw portents of America's destiny. "We find ourselves in a process of transition," Schaff wrote, "whose end result is concealed to human eyes. The present is quite chaotic, however at the same time full of fresh life, youthful energy, the bold spirit of enter-prise and joyful hopes. . . . America is in an eminent sense the land of the future and appears more and more destined to become the chief scene of world and church history."[48]

Schaff often underscored the importance of America, highlighting its discovery by Columbus and equating that discovery with the inven-tion of the printing press and the beginning of the Reformation in significance. Continuing this assessment, Schaff startled his German audience with the prediction that "the ultimate fate of the Reforma-tion will be decided in America; that it will there be proven, whether the work was of God or of man." That the Protestant Schaff might doubt the ultimate sanctity of the Reformation was bad enough; how-ever, that the test might take place in America rather than in Europe, or especially Germany, was rank heresy for many of his listeners.[49]

Mention of American religious life during the late eighteenth and early nineteenth centuries brought to the minds of literate Europeans visions of convulsive conversions and rambunctious revivals. Beyond that rumors of the results of the separation of church and state upset European ideas of a territorial church and a state-supported clergy. Finally, American Protestant theology, with its characteristic empha-ses on hellfire and brimstone, the necessity and availability of immedi-ate conversion, and the importance of benevolent activities, lacked the grandeur, the depth, and the richness of its European counterpart.

Ironically, in view of these European misgivings there was a recognizable tradition in America which insisted that it was, indeed, in the New World that God's redemptive efforts were to take place. The Puritans of New England, with their vision of "a city upon a hill," articulated an early version of America's role as a chosen nation. In the 1740s Jonathan Edwards continued the tradition, suggesting that America, and perhaps even New England itself, would be the location of such providential efforts. By the time of Schaff's address racial and nativist elements had entered into the rhetoric, and removals of American Indian peoples, incursions by military forces, and national expansion from sea to shining sea had all taken place in the name of manifest destiny and Christian religion.[50]

Thus, Schaff was not alone in his prediction of momentous things for America. Schaff's message was distinctive, however, in its explicit use of the Hegelian dialectic of history—that is, the view that conflict between opposite parties was necessary and that out of this conflict came a new solution, which canceled the old antagonism. In the context of America such conflict for Schaff meant neither violent confrontations, such as the burning of the Ursuline convent in Charlestown, Massachusetts, in 1834, nor the incessant bickering between various Protestant sectarians, an indulgent bigotry, which Schaff derided as "rabies theologorum."[51]

Instead, Schaff looked to America to be the "Phenix grave" of European nationalities and European Christianity. Schaff hailed the legal separation of church and state, for example, with its assumptions of voluntary support for religious bodies as proof that no transplanted European Christian group nor native-born religious organization would ever be capable of becoming the established church in America. Each would vie for support, some would prosper, others might die off, but "out of the mutual conflict of all something wholly new will gradually arise."[52]

Out of this conflict, "not in Europe . . . but on the banks of the Hudson, the Susquehannah, the Mississippi, and the Sacramento," would come what Schaff called "evangelical Catholicism." Such a development would vindicate the Protestant Reformation while still showing the Reformation's deep roots in medieval Christianity. Such a development would demonstrate the final organic unity of Christianity, despite the fragmentation and splintering introduced by the Protestant Reformation and made so evident in the sectarian rivalries in America. Such a development would combine the special contributions of Germanic thought, spirit, and piety together with the Anglo-American genius for organization and practical enterprises. Finally, such a development would reconcile science and religion, reason and revelation, through a true mediation, one for which there would be no opposition or contradiction.[53]

Philip Schaff thus saw the reconciliation of science and religion as a task of mediation. To an even greater degree than W. G. T. Shedd, James Warley Miles, or Henry Boynton Smith, Schaff placed ecclesiastical history within a broader theological agenda. Yet for all four men history was replete with the moral meanings of human life, it was a witness to divine activity, and it was the context for proffering a concept of development as a method for the reconciliation of science and religion in American culture.

Chapter Three

Biblicism Reaffirmed

Charles Hodge and the Science of Theology

In 1840 Charles Hodge assumed the chair of professor of systematic theology at Princeton Seminary. During his tenure at Princeton, which began in 1820 and lasted until his death in 1878, Hodge taught nearly three thousand students, edited an internationally recognized journal of theological commentary, published scores of articles and several biblical commentaries as well as his three-volume *Systematic Theology*. In these ways and more he helped shape both Reformed theology and religious culture in nineteenth-century America. His was a theology that reaffirmed the authority of the Bible and drew on the contemporary philosophy of Common Sense and utilized these resources to construct a theological program that prominently featured the claim that science and religion were reconcilable.

While commentators on Hodge have consistently noted his theological indebtedness to the Protestant Scholastics, such as Francis Turretin, it is clear that Hodge's argument for the reconciliation of science and religion was not merely a repristination of seventeenth-century dogmatics. Rather, drawing on the heritage of Scottish Common Sense, with a limited though important exposure to German mediational theology, Hodge argued that theology was a science and that induction was its proper method.

The circumstances that produced Hodge's direct encounter with German theology were serendipitous. In 1816 he had enrolled in Princeton Seminary. After three years of study under the institution's two professors, Archibald Alexander and Samuel Miller, he graduated. Although Hodge at this point anticipated leaving the seminary and taking up the life of a country parson, his expectations were transformed by the offer from his mentor, Alexander, of an appointment as an instructor in Hebrew at the seminary.[1]

Hodge threw himself into his new position; it is clear, however, that he felt ill prepared. In a widely publicized lecture on the importance of biblical literature, delivered and published in 1822, Hodge took up the issues of the composition of the biblical text and the interpretation of its meaning. He traced the efforts to overcome textual discrepancies and called for application of the grammaticohistorical approach to biblical interpretation. In this presentation Hodge acknowledged both the work of Moses Stuart and the "most distinguished" advances in the area of biblical studies taking place in Germany. Hodge considered his own training in biblical exegesis "very defective," and his concerns about the inadequacy of his scholarly background accounts for his decision in 1826 to leave his family temporarily and depart for Europe for further studies.[2]

But where to go? For a Presbyterian such as himself Scotland might be attractive. Paris had a well-known faculty, and, of course, in Germany there was Göttingen, Halle, and the new university at Berlin from which to choose. At first Hodge did settle in Paris to work on his language skills but then set off for Germany. In this plan Hodge followed the advice of Edward Robinson, who had himself spent a winter in Paris before moving on to Germany for further study. In a wide-ranging letter in response to an inquiry by Hodge, Robinson surveyed the advantages and disadvantages for Hodge's purposes of the various German universities. Robinson noted that he had been himself initially inclined to go to Göttingen; others had convinced him, however, that Halle was a better choice. "In Halle there are about 1200 students, of which 800 were theological," Robinson wrote, "the library is richer than that of Göttingen. As I have already said, Gesenius and Tholuck [both professors at Halle] are preeminent in Germany as to Biblical Literature." Wrapping up his recommendation, Robinson concluded, "If your object is theology in general, or Oriental and biblical literature in particular, you will find Halle much better adapted to your purpose." In making his suggestions Robinson's remarks also underscored the changing identities and differing reputations of the universities at Halle and Göttingen. With Johann Michaelis and Johann Eichhorn previously on its faculty Göttingen was famous for its higher criticism of the Bible. In Halle, by contrast, under the leadership of Wilhelm Gesenius, Emil Rödiger, and later August Tholuck, textual studies and linguistic criticism predominated. Beyond that Göttingen had kept its reputation for rationalism among its theological faculty, while Halle was returning to its pietist beginnings, particularly under the influence of Tholuck.[3]

In a different vein Robinson also reported to Hodge that he was one of only a handful of American theologians studying in Germany. "At Göttingen," he continued, "you will find Americans from Boston, pleasing and amiable young men, but their pursuits have no connexion with theology. I think of nothing further to add, unless it be that the best character for us is that of *learners,*—education with us is so far behind Germany, that if we come as learned, we only expose ourselves and our country to ridicule." As Robinson's comments demonstrate, it was not unheard of for young Americans to complete their studies in Europe. Natural scientists, such as Joseph Henry, Alexander Bache, and Asa Gray, went to Europe in the 1830s, and their experience is instructive. Like Hodge and Robinson, these men realized the deficiencies in their American education and the greater resources available in Europe. Fundamentally, the attraction for these Americans as well as those who were to follow them for several decades was the model of scholarship which European universities offered. This was particularly true for Hodge and Robinson, as both of them discovered during their German sojourns a new depth of commitment to scholarship as a profession. Beyond that both Hodge and Robinson (as did others of the American mediational theologians) developed friendships with individual German theologians which continued throughout their lives and both widened the Americans' perspectives and enhanced their professional reputations. Finally, while Hodge and Robinson went to Germany to absorb its advantages, their direct encounter with a wide spectrum of German religious life gave them both respect for its accomplishments and freedom from an uncritical subordination to its every whim.[4]

Thus, the journey of these Americans to distant universities was a rich and ultimately beneficial one. The numbers involved, however, were never large. As Robinson alluded above and subsequent historians have gone on to celebrate, George Ticknor and Edward Everett came to Göttingen in 1815 and were soon joined by Joseph Cogswell and George Bancroft. Göttingen had connections both to America and England; it was Halle, however, that drew American theology students, especially in the decades from the late 1820s through the 1850s. Thus, from 1810 to 1859 eleven out of seventy-six Americans who registered at Göttingen entered the theology faculty, while twenty-one of the twenty-two Americans who went to Halle did so for theological study.[5]

Charles Hodge arrived in Halle in February 1827 and was not to return to Princeton until September 1828. During this time he traveled throughout Germany and came in contact with the elite of the German theological world. He heard the lectures of Schleiermacher and Hegel, for exmaple, attended August Neander's course on church history and Ernst Hengstenberg's on the Old Testament, and became acquainted with scores of prominent German theologians. Beyond that Hodge became friends with the Gerlach brothers and through that connection met members of the Prussian royal court at evening parties and church conferences.[6]

Much that Hodge encountered in Germany was new and challenging to him. Hodge's Princeton mentor, Archibald Alexander, had recognized this possibility and, even though he had sanctioned the trip, had still explicitly cautioned his young protégé against being swept away by the intellectual fashions of the day in Germany. Writing to Hodge in 1827, Alexander warned: "The air which you breathe in Germany will either have a deleterious effect on your moral constitution, or else by the strength of faith required to resist its effects your spiritual health will be confirmed. I pray God to keep you from the poison of *Neology!* I wish you to come home enriched with biblical learning but abhorring German philosophy and theology."[7]

The German philosophy and theology upon which Alexander wished to impose his intellectual quarantine were hardly unified, nor were their purposes and backgrounds all the same. Yet for American Protestants such as Alexander the outlines and the implications of the developments in German thought during the late eighteenth and early nineteenth centuries were clear. Above all this approach was rationalistic, seeking not only to square faith and knowledge, but often to subordinate faith to the standards and findings of rationalist inquiry. Such an approach to the Scriptures, these Protestants emphasized, inevitably challenged the beliefs of the faithful, raising questions under the guise of learned scholarship rather than strengthening the doubting and confirming them in their faith. Challenges to the authenticity and integrity of the Scriptures were merely the best-known results of this higher criticism, and, thus, while Alexander accepted the legitimacy of linguistic study for his young colleague, he sincerely hoped that the latent corrosive of theological and biblical criticism would not erode his evangelical faith.

Schooled in Princeton orthodoxy and frequently admonished by Alexander's letters, Charles Hodge knew to be on his guard. Here the advice of Edward Robinson to go to Halle and his praise for August Tholuck proved to be decisive. For almost from the first day Hodge arrived in Halle, Tholuck filled the role of mentor and guide for the young American. Robinson had first described Tholuck to Hodge as "a man of most amiable character and of deep and fervent piety," and Hodge's sense of indebtedness to Tholuck for his friendship, for his introductions to others, but above all for his support of and sympathy with Hodge's religious faith and piety was nearly boundless.[8]

Hodge's letters and notes from this period show that he was exposed to much of the best of German erudition. They just as clearly indicate, however, that he sifted it all through the filter of his evangelical orthodoxy, testing it against Tholuck's valued counsel and finally appropriating bits and pieces and discarding much of the rest. At one level Hodge simply could not accept many of the philosophical assumptions upon which post-Enlightenment German philosophy and theology operated. As with all of Princeton and much of antebellum America, Hodge had been trained in the logic, presumptions, and perspectives of Common Sense philosophy. In the writings of men such as Thomas Reid and Dugald Stewart, later embellished and glossed by Princeton's own president, John Witherspoon, the reliability of sense perception was affirmed, and the certainty of moral intuitions of right and wrong was accepted. To Hodge the situation in Germany was quite different. Writing to Archibald Alexander, Hodge complained that in Germany "philosophy is utterly beyond the grasp of common english understanding, that *esse*, and, *non esse*, are identical, altho' rather a startling proposition, is here so evident that it forms the first sentence of Hegel's *Logic*."[9]

Hodge did accept one idea that his German professors presented: theology was a science. Hodge attended Tholuck's class on Theological Encyclopedia, and there would have been introduced to the standard topics of theological study. Ever since Friedrich Schleiermacher's *Brief Outline of the Study of Theology* (1811), not only the division of Christian theology into philosophical, historical, and practical theology but also the claim that theology was a science with a proper methodology, procedures, and goals had been emphasized. While Tholuck did not simply reiterate Schleiermacher's perspective, Hodge would have heard from Tholuck a strong defense of the scientific character of theology. Hodge would also have been given a survey of the competing philosophical systems in contemporary Germany, including Kant, Fichte, Schelling, and Hegel. Though these thinkers differed importantly in various matters, they would have agreed that science emphasized critical inquiry and a systematic presentation of the results of that inquiry. For his part Tholuck presented these broad conclusions and furthermore catechized his students that theology was the science concerning the knowledge of humanity and God and, as such, was the queen of all the sciences.[10]

The assumption that science was a critical principle of inquiry whose results were systematically presented was an important result of Hodge's German education. Among other things it obviously applied to the natural sciences such as geology and biology, but, equally important, it encompassed theology and the human sciences as well. Beyond that it underscored the legitimacy of systematic rather than simply biblical theology, which was a point upon which Hodge himself would often insist. Finally, it challenged the parochialism of contemporary theology and, as Hodge was well aware, those broad ranges of popular American Protestant theology with their suspicions of the findings of natural scientists, philologists, and historians alike.

These were important points, for, as Hodge confided in private correspondence, he felt disappointed with the results of his stay in Germany. "That I should gain but little is what you foretold and what I myself expected," Hodge wrote to Archibald Alexander in 1828, "but that it would be *so* little I *did not* expect." Mindful of Alexander's fears and doubts, perhaps Hodge tailored these remarks to fit his senior colleague's assumptions. He spoke somewhat more positively of the benefits of his European sojourn in a letter to his mother. Moreover, he remained in contact with Tholuck and several other of his German friends and acquaintances for many years and never lost his admiration for the quality of German higher education, even though he often lamented its specific theological results and consequences.[11]

In 1828 Charles Hodge returned to America and renewed his academic career at Princeton Theological Seminary. The American society and culture to which Hodge returned was growing fitfully and in spurts, expanding into western lands and increasingly asserting its independence from Europe, even as it distanced itself slowly from models of Federalist and Jeffersonian lineage and began to take up the rhetoric of Jacksonian democracy. It was an age of scientific accomplishment, technological advancement, and previously unmatched progress in communications and transportation. In these circumstances Charles Hodge made a significant contribution in the debate over science and religion by arguing for their methodological unity. As with many such attempts at mediation, his efforts were not always successful or even equally even-handed. Nevertheless, in his lectures for the next several decades Hodge reasserted the ultimate compatibility of science and religion through a repeated appeal to the scientific character of Christian theology. Though the occasions might change and the circumstances differ, Hodge's message remained the same: science, when properly performed, proceeds inductively; theology, when properly performed, likewise proceeds according to the procedures of induction.

In the handwritten notes for his lectures on "The Nature and Method of Theology," delivered variously between 1824 and 1849, Charles Hodge expanded on the meaning and significance of the inductive method for Christian theology. Railing against those who would use a "speculative," or deductive, approach, Hodge insisted that "theory is to be determined by facts, not facts by theory, or a priori assumptions." The parallel in theology was clear: one must examine the Bible and upon that basis construct one's theory, rather than assume a philosophical position and then "receive, reject, or modify the facts of Scripture according to its dictates."[12]

The very language of Hodge's proposal highlighted an important element in his theory of induction and an equally significant dimension in his strategy of mediation of science and religion. This element was his emphasis upon empiricism. Facts came first then theory for Hodge, not the other way around. In our present age, which has emphasized the sociological character of knowledge, the relevance of paradigms of inquiry, and even the preexistence of unconscious motives about which the individual is unaware, Hodge's faith in the existence of facts, untainted by theoretical filters, may seem naive. Nevertheless, it was a crucial point and, in a larger context, signaled again his allegiance to Common Sense philosophy in America.

Common Sense philosophy was in large measure a response to the Enlightenment and specifically the philosophy of David Hume. Hume had taken Lockean epistemology, with its claims that the mind is a blank slate upon which the environment strikes, impinges, and collides, and radicalized its conclusions. For Hume all the realities of everyday life—cause and effect, personal identity, even the existence of the external world—were epistemologically suspect because they were only verifiable in individualistic terms—that is, they were only a bundle of perceptions succeeding each other with extraordinary rapidity. And on Hume's accounting, if cognition devolved into these terms, then morality was nothing better than the individual acting on the perception of momentary self-interest.

These Humean conclusions were unnerving to the reflective portion of the religious population, and it was against this radical skepticism that the Common Sense philosophers directed their energies. In short they countered that there were minimal intuitional categories in human consciousness, categories without which human experience would be unintelligible. These categories, such as personal identity, cause and effect, or the existence of moral principles, were known intuitively, or through "common sense," to anyone who took the time to examine properly their own self-consciousness. And a "proper" examination for these Common Sense philosophers was an inductive examination, one that began with the "facts" of self-consciousness and from that basis built up an account of the world and humanity's place in it.

Common Sense philosophy was the dominant perspective in early and mid-nineteenth-century America. It was optimistic in outlook, practical and down-to-earth in its methods, and democratic in its ethos. Beyond that its emphasis on the perspicuity of nature paralleled the Protestant doctrine of the perspicuity of Scriptures, and this, together with its broad appeal to empirical facts, further underscored the reconciliation of science and religion in the antebellum era.[13]

Hodge's devotion to empiricism was thoroughgoing. At a more anecdotal level one biographer notes that Hodge's first wife, Sarah, was the granddaughter of that noted American empiricist Benjamin Franklin. Though the two never met, Hodge would have approved of the experimental approach of Franklin, whether he was tinkering with electricity or investigating political systems. Hodge's personal papers contain evidence of his own amateur interest in the physical sciences, especially meteorology. While disabled by a hip ailment for many years, Hodge kept a daily journal, which recorded weather temperatures, wind direction and velocity, and various other calculations.[14]

A second important element of Hodge's inductive methodology was its probabilistic conclusions. Rather than try to establish the absolute deductive validity of his conclusions, Hodge claimed that, like any good and proper scientist, he began "by collecting well established facts and from them infer the general law which determines their occurrence." Here again was a context in which Hodge chastised the speculative philosophy of Germany. For Hodge easily enough agreed that philosophical perspectives and assumptions informed theological enterprises. Not philosophy as such, then, or even German philosophy in general, but speculative, a priori, and deductive philosophy was the real object of Hodge's scorn.[15]

Hodge's empiricism and inferential conclusions dovetailed nicely with a third dimension of his methodology, the frequent use of analogical reasoning. With a commitment to the availability and retrievability of facts as his foundation, Hodge marshaled analogical observations and broader sets of generalizations in defense of the reconciliation of science and religion. In this way Hodge developed a theological methodology that resonated with the attitudes, challenges, and spirit of his times. It was designed to tether science and religion together through a common approach. With its insistence on consideration of *all* the relevant facts it sought to include information from the Bible and the common sense of humanity within the universe of scientific discourse and analysis. Such a strategy might ward off challenges hostile to religion by arguing that they had been selective or misguided in their use of inductive method. Such a strategy could, furthermore, declare that true religion was not inimical to scientific inquiry, thereby putting to rest earlier images of forced recantations by scientists or suppression of scientific research by clerical authorities. For Hodge, then, no radical disjunction existed between the scientist and the theologian. Rather, a unity of method joined them, and discrepancies or objectionable conclusions were due to improper procedures, hasty generalizations, or misapplied principles.

Both scientist and theologian, then, looked to empirical facts and sought to arrange and organize them into meaningful patterns. Whereas the scientist turned to the natural world for his data, the theologian, Hodge argued, looked to the Bible for his materials, "for all the facts of Christian theology are to be found in the Sacred Scriptures." While the parallel was neat, Hodge's statement raised the troubling issue of the infallible status of this scriptural storehouse of biblical facts. In other words, what did it mean to investigate biblical facts if it was already assumed that the facts as given were beyond question and incapable of error? Hodge believed in the plenary inspiration of the Bible; thus, he insisted that in their capacity as teachers of doctrine the biblical authors were incapable of error. Such a view, as it had with Moses Stuart, allowed that, insofar as the biblical authors taught and believed other things—for example, that the sun revolved around the Earth or that the Earth was a flat plane—this was simply a reflection of the current knowledge of the day.[16]

So much, but only so much, would Hodge concede to historicity. Hodge repeated time and again that, if scientists found evidence that disputed the biblical account, those scientists ought to check their facts again, for the Scriptures were true from beginning to end. Years later Hodge expanded this insistence on the inspired veracity of the Christian Scriptures, stating that "inspiration extends to all the contents of these several books. It is not confined to moral and religious

truths, but extends to the statements of fact, whether scientific, historical, or geographical. . . . It extends to everything which any sacred
writer asserts to be true . . . even that great stumbling block, that
Jonah was three days in the whale's belly."[17]

Beyond this reaffirmation of the doctrine of biblical inspiration
Hodge was making a broader point about the place of scientific investigation in the modern world. For, while Hodge felt obliged to review
the findings of scientific research for factual errors, he contended that
too often science overlooked, misunderstood, and disregarded much
of the reality of human existence. Though natural science and theology were one in method, Hodge still maintained that they differed
significantly in orientation and content. Hodge ceaselessly spoke of
"great religious truths"; he tirelessly invoked "fundamental religious
insights." What was at stake, finally, in such perorations was the conviction that the essence of human experience was ultimately not reduc-
ible into assays, crucibles, compounds, and experimental equations.

However well suited it may have been for its own era, Hodge's
approach was weakened by several flaws. Though Hodge extolled
empiricism, for example, his acceptance of the epistemological and
moral intuitionalism of Common Sense philosophy placed clear limits
on his empiricism. Moreover, while he championed analogical reasoning, Hodge was not adverse to using other types of argumentation, as
in his defense of both the ontological and cosmological arguments for
the existence of God. Finally, though he posed as the humble student
of the Bible, investigating its facts as the student of nature might
investigate the Earth's biological life, Hodge's commitment to the
veracity of the biblical account made practically impossible the falsi-
fication of any scriptural claim. Indeed, though he spoke of inferences
and criticized deductive approaches, Hodge began his own investigations with the assumption of the infallibility of the scriptural authors
and in this way distanced himself from an actual engagement with the
very inductive method that he prescribed.

James Henley Thornwell and the Holy Alliance of Science and Religion

Nevertheless, if logicians could point out that, in his appeal to a
common inductive method, Charles Hodge had not really proved the
compatibility of science and theology, historians could respond that

this argument for methodological unity and for a reaffirmation of biblical truths was still popular with large portions of American Protestantism. One example of a particularly striking resonance with Hodge's approach can be found in the work of the South Carolinian James Henley Thornwell. A leader among Southern Presbyterians and later a strong voice defending Confederate secession and the formation of independent Southern churches, Thornwell was also one who defended the reconciliation of science and religion. Much like Charles Hodge, whom he respected though also occasionally fought with over matters of Presbyterian polity, Thornwell fashioned an argument for the holy alliance between science and religion based on a shared method of inductive investigation.[18]

Thornwell was born in South Carolina in 1812 and in 1829, with the financial assistance of two patrons, entered South Carolina College. A fellow classmate once described Thornwell as "perhaps the most unpromising specimen of humanity that ever entered such an institution. Very short in stature, shorter by a head than he became in later life, very lean in flesh, with a skin the color of old parchment, his hands and face as thickly studded with black freckles as the Milky Way with stars, and an eye rendered dull in repose by a drooping lid." His physical deficiencies seemed at first to be matched by other problems as well, for Thornwell wavered between a career in law and one in the ministry and even flunked his first try at the admission test for the college. Yet the young man matured during his college years, achieving a reputation for intellectual ability and graduating at the head of his class in 1831.[19]

Unlike Charles Hodge and Edward Robinson, Thornwell never traveled to Europe for postgraduate studies. Closely identified with South Carolina throughout his whole life, Thornwell attended Columbia Theological Seminary. His first pastorate was in Lancasterville, South Carolina, but in 1837, after only three years there, he accepted a position at South Carolina College. For much of the rest of his life Thornwell devoted his energies to education. He served on the faculty then later as president of South Carolina College and in 1856 joined the faculty of Columbia Theological Seminary. Only twice during his lifetime, first in 1841 and then again in 1860, did Thornwell venture to Europe. By then his intellectual temperament was fully formed, and there is no indication of any real engagement by Thornwell with the intellectual currents on the Continent. Instead, traveling as a tourist, visiting churches and seeing the sights, Thornwell found much of Scotland to his liking but regarded the general religious condition of Europe to be vastly inferior to America's.[20]

In his 1857 inaugural lecture as professor of Didactic and Polemic Theology at Columbia Theological Seminary James Henley Thornwell proclaimed that theology was the queen of the sciences. Theology derived its scientific standing in that, as with other modes of inquiry, it arranged its materials and conclusions into a logical, systematic, and connected presentation. Moreover, Thornwell insisted that theology both animated investigation in the other sciences and integrated the findings of these other inquiries into one general system. The real key to the scientific aspirations of theology, however, was its use of the inductive method. Here Thornwell pointed to the career of Francis Bacon as representing a major turning point in modern philosophy and science. For all great discoveries in science, Thornwell stated, "have been made in consequence of the adoption and spread of just views of the true object and method of all sound philosophical investigation." Prior to Bacon, Thornwell argued, deductive assumptions independent of firsthand observation ruled scientific method and philosophy. Under the Baconian influence, induction became "the infallible touchstone of truth," and its application "produced an amazing reaction in all the departments of knowledge."[21]

Thornwell gained his first exposure to Baconianism as well as to its more influential successor, the Scottish Common Sense philosophy, during his first years at college. The works of Dugald Stewart, Thomas Reid, and William Hamilton provided the philosophic texts for Thornwell's most respected teacher, Robert Henry, and Thornwell continued to prize their work throughout his life. While historians have debated the manner in which other influences, such as Calvinism, tended to subdue or modify the allegiance of adherents like Thornwell to the Baconian ideal, they have agreed that Baconianism played a significant role in antebellum American religious thought. For clergymen, such as Thornwell, found in the emphasis on inductive observation of the natural world a clear reaffirmation of the importance and legitimacy of natural theology. Confidence in inductive method reinforced confidence in natural theology. And, as natural theology was believed to conform to revealed theology, the link from investigation of the natural world to interpretation of that investigation and its reconciliation with biblical revelation appeared unbroken. Here was the basis upon which the capacities and discoveries of reason and the revelations of divine activity in the world were joined together in a meaningful unity. Beyond that here was the line of thinking which forged the holy alliance between science and religion and which led many to anticipate in the findings of the scientist praise for the work of God.[22]

James Henley Thornwell endorsed this affirmation of natural theology. Religion had nothing to fear from science, he maintained, for the results of proper science and true religion would fit together as the Book of Nature complemented the Book of Revelation. "Let the earth be explored, let its physical history be traced," Thornwell wrote in reference to the current controversy over the age of the earth, "Geology and the Bible must kiss and embrace each other, and this youngest daughter of Science will be found, bringing her votive offerings to the cradle of the Prince of peace. The earth can never turn traitor to its God, and its stones have already begun to cry out against those who attempted to extract from them a lesson of infidelity or Atheism."[23]

Yet, though science and religion were reconcilable, Thornwell believed that clergymen should still monitor scientific findings to ensure that proper inductive methods were being used. Here was Thornwell's answer to the recurring examples of disagreement between scientific findings and religious traditions: scientists were reverting to deductive, a priori systems of investigation rather than induction. Prominent examples of this preconceived approach to inquiry in Thornwell's view could be found in Europe and especially in Germany. "The preposterous stuff which is deluging Germany under the name of Transcendentalism, France under that of Eclecticism and is creeping into the United States under the lying title of Psychology is not metaphysics," Thornwell wrote, "it is a monster which never should have seen the light. . . . Kant, Fichte, Schelling are only the miserable tools in the hands of the fiend of darkness for consummating his black designs of malice and of hate upon our wretched race." Nor was Thornwell's expletive exhausted on the Germans; he also found culprits closer to home. In 1834 Thornwell had gone to Andover Seminary to study and there got his first taste of "New England theology." Thornwell had originally intended to study with Edward Robinson; when Robinson became incapacitated, however, Thornwell transferred to Harvard. Thornwell enjoyed Unitarian Harvard little better than he had the more evangelical atmosphere of Andover. In fact, within a few short months Thornwell returned to South Carolina, citing as his reasons Robinson's absence, his exasperation with Unitarianism, and a physician's warning that a harsh New England winter might kill him. As for New England theology, Thornwell deplored what he considered its deductive approach, noting that it "resembles more the dry and crusty jargon of the Schools than the sober discussion of Christian men and protestant Divines. The consequence, is that their literature is almost as frozen as their climate."[24]

Just as James Henley Thornwell shared with Charles Hodge a common methodological argument for the reconciliation of science and religion, so too did the South Carolinian share one of the principal disabilities that weakened Hodge's approach. For Thornwell held to the verbal dictation of the Scriptures and the subsequent infallibility of its message. Just as with Hodge, this assumption of the prescriptive authority of the Scriptures preempted their rigorous empirical investigation. Any contradictory evidence was dismissed as the result of faulty method and misguided practitioners. For Hodge and Thornwell, at least, this seemed to be the price to keep the holy alliance between science and religion intact.

Edward Robinson and the Archaeology of Piety

Edward Robinson is best known for his work in biblical archaeology and as professor of biblical literature for many years at Union Theological Seminary in New York City. Robinson was born in 1794 and educated at Hamilton College. In 1822 he went to Andover Seminary and there quickly became the protégé of Moses Stuart and a firm disciple of Stuart's grammaticohistorical approach to biblical interpretation. In fact, Robinson's progress in linguistic study was so rapid that Stuart had him hired as an instructor in Hebrew at the seminary in 1823.[25]

Soon thereafter in 1826, however, Robinson determined that he needed to go to Germany for advanced scholarly training. In writing a letter of introduction for Robinson to August Tholuck, Timothy Dwight praised his countryman's accomplishments in language study but admitted that the paucity of scholarly resources in America severely inhibited first-rate biblical study. The four years that Robinson spent in Germany marked a personal and intellectual turning point in his life. For personally he would make lifelong friends in Germany, establishing a network of international colleagues as well as marrying Therese Jacob, the daughter of Ludwig Heinrich von Jacob, professor of philosophy and political science at Halle. Beyond that Robinson's intellectual life would be transformed as he became deeply immersed in German scholarship. In fact, it was to be Robinson's continuing project to absorb the findings of German biblical studies and transmit them to a broad American audience. In so doing Robinson infused German evangelicalism into American evangelicalism, thereby serving as an effective agent of mediation between the two religious cultures.[26]

As his advice to Charles Hodge indicated, Robinson found Halle vastly preferable to Göttingen for biblical study. Wilhelm Gesenius was still on the Halle faculty and was renowned for his work in linguistics. Yet Robinson's preference for Halle over Göttingen reflected once again the influence of August Tholuck. For Robinson, too, had befriended Tholuck upon his arrival in Halle, the "dear" and "kind" Tholuck, and, as would happen with Hodge, Robinson fell deeply under Tholuck's paternal and pastoral spell. Robinson's letters to Tholuck overflow with thanks for the German's solicitous care and suggest in their own way the depth of Robinson's misgivings about himself and especially the competency of his scholarly training. By all accounts during this period, ill at ease in social circles and painfully aware of shortcomings in himself, Robinson found Tholuck's pastoral concern reassuring and nourishing.[27]

Tholuck's influence on Robinson was matched, at another level, by that of the church historian August Neander and the professor of geography Carl Ritter. Both Neander and Ritter taught at Berlin and were in their prime when Robinson was there pursuing his own studies. Though the Berlin faculty at this time contained some of the best-known names in the history of modern philosophy and theology (Hegel and Schleiermacher to name but two), Robinson shied away from their lectures. He did not consider himself a metaphysician, and, as he reported to Tholuck, "I am no philosopher, at least no German philosopher; what little sense I have is too mere *common sense* to enable me to dive into the depths of the Berliner speculations; and I am quite willing that Brother Hodge should do for the philosophical representation of my country, since his mind seems to have a native bent to that species of inquiry."[28]

Robinson's remarks are intriguing because, if he was immune to German metaphysics, he did not completely escape exposure to and incorporation of important elements of German romanticism. This Romantic influence can be seen, for example, in the results of Robinson's archaeological investigations, in which one finds an avowal of the organic connection between the physical and spiritual, the material and the cultural, as well as a delicate statement of the inexplicable mystery of life. Beyond these aspects one also finds the conjunction of the analytical methods of the scientist and the believer's faith in the veracity of the Bible. In all of these dimensions the influences of Neander and Ritter can be discerned. Tholuck, Ritter, and Neander, then, are the main purveyors of this Romantic influence on Robinson, as attested in his private letters, public acknowledgments, and published works. Despite differences in scholarly expertise, all three of these German professors combined an evangelical piety with a commitment to critical methods in the study of religion. Moreover, all three were suffused with that Romantic awareness of the mystery of life, the interpenetration of the micro- and macrospheres, and the centrality of the organic metaphor as the proper symbolic representation of life processes. Thus, the German influence on Edward Robinson matched that of Moses Stuart and is extremely important in any accounting of Robinson's intellectual background.[29]

Whereas Charles Hodge argued for the unity of the sciences through inductive methods and, on theological grounds, contended for the infallibility of the Bible, Robinson's life work took up Hodge's theological contention and sought to prove it on an empirical basis. Confident of the Bible's truthfulness, Robinson invited exhaustive and comprehensive investigation of the biblical account. "We are not of the number of those, who fear the consequences of the closest scrutiny, or the most profound researches into either the nature, or history, or interpretation of the records of our religion," Robinson declared, "we believe the truths which these records reveal will shine with purer lustre, when the veil of ignorance by which they are yet in a measure shrouded, shall have been still farther removed." Between his return to America in 1830 and his retirement due to cataracts in his eyes in 1862, Robinson sought to put this scholarly evangelical faith into practice. He made two archaeological trips to Palestine, one in 1838 and again in 1856, and the results of these trips can be found in his famous studies, the three-volume *Biblical Researches in Palestine, Mount Sinai, and Arabia Petraea*, published in 1841, and the subsequent study, *Later Biblical Researches in Palestine and the Adjacent Regions*.[30]

Beyond its importance for his own life Robinson's explorations fit into a larger context within nineteenth-century American culture. For Robinson exemplified many features of what William Goetzmann has called "the Second Great Age of Discovery." In this age scientific activity focused on the mapping of the Earth's surfaces, the plotting of geological strata, and the classifying of animal species. The hero in these efforts and the dominant symbol of this age of discovery was the explorer and scholar Alexander von Humboldt, the Romantic scientist whose organic approach to geography emphasized the interconnection of everything in nature. If Europe had its Humboldt or Carl Ritter, America had Lewis and Clark, Fremont and Wilkes, Pike and Powell. Beyond that, if, as Goetzmann further argues, the development of the map into a chart of organic and systematic connections enabled geography to become the key science during this Second Age of Discovery, then this development was more than matched by the desire of explorer-scientists to get out into nature, to observe it first-hand, and to measure, weigh, and possibly even depict it through realistic drawings and paintings.[31]

Edward Robinson fit into the model of the Romantic explorer-scientist. Whereas Hodge and Thornwell extolled induction as the proper method for scientific study, Robinson called for a hermeneutics of empathetic understanding. In setting out the task of the student of biblical literature, for example, Robinson stated, "if we would comprehend the Scriptures fully, we must place ourselves in the situations of the Jews, hear as they heard, and understand the language as they understood it." The prescription reflected the influence of Moses Stuart and his defense of the grammaticohistorical interpretation of the Bible. For, like his Andover mentor, Robinson insisted that in order to understand a document we must place ourselves in the situation of the audience to whom the piece was first addressed. As Robinson expounded on this theme, he identified the various skills necessary for the would-be student of biblical literature: command of Hebrew, Greek, Arabic, and Aramaic; familiarity with the national histories and literatures of Egypt, Ethiopia, Persia, Assyria, Babylonia, and Phoenicia, as well as with Mediterranean basin history through the first century. So, too, thorough knowledge of the history of the Hebrews in their ecclesiastical, political, and daily experience would help, as Robinson put it, to place the student "in the position of the Jews themselves, enabl[ing] him to think as they thought, feel as they felt, judge as they judged, and understand as they understood."[32]

As significant as was his literary work, Robinson's true legacy resides in the area of biblical archaeology. During the early nineteenth century American experience and knowledge of the Middle East was confined to scattered reports by military officers, merchants, and missionaries. Moreover, the state of archaeological knowledge about Palestine prior to Robinson's efforts was sad, indeed. As Robinson's chief competitor, the Swiss geographer Titus Tobler, concluded, the archaeological discoveries of Robinson "surpass the total of all previous contributions to Palestinian geography from the time of Eusebius and Jerome to the early nineteenth century." Robinson himself observed that Palestine had been the goal and object of interest for centuries of pilgrims, yet none had ever gone there out of scientific interest or equipped with the necessary linguistic, geographical, or scientific tools. For his part Robinson confessed his own feelings of awe in the presence of many biblical sites, yet he joined this deeply felt sensibility to the scientific discipline to which he also felt an allegiance.[33]

Two procedural decisions that Robinson made early on in his archaeological researches exemplified his commitment to empathetic understanding and measurably improved his results. First, upon discovering that many of the names of sites were preserved in vernacular Arabic, he canvassed local tribal members wherever he went about names and the corresponding sites he sought. Second, Robinson quickly came to distrust common ecclesiastical traditions as well as local tourist guides regarding the location of sites and insisted on making his own fresh examination. Thus, through these procedures Robinson developed methods that successfully identified over one hundred sites. Robinson was also not adverse to rolling up his sleeves and trousers and unpacking his compass and measuring tape in order to take the dimensions of a site or, as in the case of the Fountain of Siloam, crawling through a partially filled water conduit on his hands and knees to make accurate measurements. Beyond these efforts to develop what Albrecht Alt called a "scientific Palestinology," it is clear that Robinson demonstrated the applicability of the historical-critical methods that he had learned from Stuart and Neander. Similarly, through the often rhapsodic prose that he used to describe the Palestinian geography and its influence on that region's people and culture, Robinson also illustrated the influence of Carl Ritter and his view of the study of geography as part of a broader cultural approach seeking to understand the human experience.[34]

Disavowing what he called "monkish tradition" and attending instead to verifiable vernacular place names, Robinson and his assistant, Eli Smith, traversed Palestine from March to July 1838. Shortly after his return to America, the publication of his *Biblical Researches* took place, and with it Robinson's international reputation was secured. Yet, despite the impressive array of facts amassed in Robinson's imposing three-volume work, the final conclusions never strayed far from his conservative theological presuppositions. For, in the end, all his research proved one point—that the Bible was "the best, and only accurate guidebook in the Holy Land." Here then, as with Charles Hodge and James Henley Thornwell, science was the handmaid of religion.[35]

If this troika of Hodge, Thornwell, and Robinson were joined together in their positive appraisal of an empirical approach to the reconciliation of science and religion, their orientations in Scottish Common Sense philosophy and romanticism respectively could well pull them in differing directions. Indeed, in the context of the preceding chapter's appeal to history with its deep imprint of romanticism as well as in the following chapter's discussion of language and the symbolic meaning that it contained, again so decisively shaped by the energies and impulses of romanticism, Hodge's and Thornwell's advocacy of a Common Sense approach might seem out of place. Yet it should not be overlooked that Hodge and Thornwell were every bit as committed to the reconciliation of science and religion as were their more romantically influenced colleagues. Moreover, Scottish Common Sense had a very wide appeal within antebellum American intellectual circles. Thus, the fact that the distinctive approaches of Scottish Common Sense and romanticism could be utilized in the mutual effort to reconcile science and religion merely underscores the broad-based desire within antebellum American culture to see that end achieved.

Chapter Four

Language Reinterpreted

In 1829 James Marsh, president of the University of Vermont and a writer with an interest in European letters and thought, brought out the first American edition of Samuel Taylor Coleridge's *Aids to Reflection*. As he stated in his introduction, in republishing the volume Marsh hoped to further the cause of "sound philosophy and true religion" and to make a contribution to "the science of words," particularly as the study of words was associated with the study of morals and religion. Marsh was well aware that the piece would cause disputes. Indeed, New England was rife with philosophical debates, and controversies over language—its nature, its provenance, and its meaning—occupied a major part of the deliberations over science and religion in antebellum America.[1]

"A Critical Understanding of Words"

Some of the fiercest conflicts in the history of American religion in the nineteenth century concerned battles over words and the effort to sort out the transient from the permanent, to balance the letter and spirit of the text, and to discern the true kernel amid the worthless husks of pulpit rhetoric. As American culture passed out of the first third of the nineteenth century and struggled to squirm out of the cocoon of Enlightenment patterns of thought, Marsh was one of those who wished to break up stalemated disputes, to explore new resources, and to chart new paths through perennial and still significant issues.

Marsh was born in Hartford, Vermont, in 1794 and received his education at Dartmouth College and Andover Theological Seminary. After working on a farm and holding a position at Hampden-Sydney College in Virginia, Marsh was appointed president of the University of Vermont in 1826. He remained at Vermont, first as president then, after 1833, as professor of moral and intellectual philosophy, until his death in 1842.[2]

By 1829 and his publication of *Aids* Marsh had already made two important contributions to literary criticism and the study of language. In 1822 he wrote a piece on "Ancient and Modern Poetry" for the prestigious *North American Review*. This journal specialized in articles on philology and historical literature and regularly reviewed

German, Italian, as well as English literature. In his essay Marsh distinguished classical from Romantic poetry, in a manner akin to the Schlegel brothers' famous typology and the spirit that characterized romanticism. Beyond that Marsh depicted the modern world as divided against itself, and he nostalgically posited an earlier golden age, when art, nature, and history, life, love, and imagination, were all fused together. Paradoxically, however, Marsh argued for the superiority of the modern age insofar as it turned its attention inward, elevating subjective experience over objective and minimizing materialistic values. Marsh ascribed this inward turn to the positive influence of Christianity and, thus, described an intimate, if complex, relation between religion and culture.[3]

In 1829, shortly before his edition of *Aids* appeared, Marsh also published a long review essay on *A Commentary on the Epistle to the Hebrews* by his former teacher at Andover, Moses Stuart. This article appeared in the *Christian Spectator*, edited by the Yale divinity professor Nathaniel Taylor, and established Marsh's theological independence from both the conservatives at Andover and the liberals at Yale. Marsh spoke out in defense of philology and its contributions to biblical criticism as well as to the nurturing of better literary tastes and habits. He recognized that, presently in the popular and literary lyceum circuits, prominent voices called for the promotion of useful, practical, and commercially remunerative works. Yet he regarded these summonses to concentrate on the simple and immediately understandable as naive and shortsighted. For, despite the prejudices against philological research, Marsh observed that there could be no adequate communication or acquisition of knowledge about things "without a critical understanding of words." As a means of cultivating the mental processes, forming powers of discriminating insight, and dispelling jargon, vagueness, and ambiguity, the science of philology was essential. Beyond that the language of a people was "the index of its intellectual and moral cultivation, the adequate representative of its substantial knowledge and improvement." Thus, for Marsh the demand for practical knowledge, for concentration on railroads and canals, for exclusive attention to tariffs and banking policy, was self-defeating without the associated efforts of philology, for "whether we study our vernacular, or a foreign, a living, or a dead language, the science of mathematics, or the objects of natural history, law, or theology, it makes little difference in this respect, we are everywhere met at the outset by *words*, and our business is everywhere the same, to *understand* them."[4]

In the remainder of his review Marsh repeatedly praised Stuart for his success in enabling his readers to understand the text before them. Marsh distinguished between grammatical and theological systems of interpretation and placed Stuart's work squarely within the first. As a former student, Marsh was well aware of the Andover professor's indebtedness to the work of Johann Ernesti as well as of Stuart's own familiarity with much of the new biblical scholarship coming out of Germany. Marsh was widely read in these German scholars, too, and he recognized the challenges to traditional interpretations of Christianity which many Americans saw in their work. For by the nineteenth century the science of philology could pose challenges every bit as severe as those of the science of geology to the authority of biblical texts and the religious faith that they grounded.

Marsh's rejoinder reaffirmed his support for European scholarship but also anticipated the direction of his later work. He readily conceded that much grammatically based biblical interpretation "has been abused in Germany for the purposes of infidelity." Yet he insisted that such were not the necessary results either in Germany or in America and that, in fact, in both countries errors and mistakes were being corrected. In a move that both characterized his edition of *Aids* and signaled the connection of philology and metaphysics in his own mind, Marsh stated, "we have more fear of injury to the cause of religion from the influence of superficial modes and systems of philosophizing, than from the principles of criticism."[5]

Inadequate metaphysics, or, more broadly put, inadequate philosophical grounds expressed by imprecise words and vague concepts— these were the real challenges, in Marsh's opinion, posed by the current religious situation. As he was to do at length in his edition of *Aids*, Marsh excoriated "the Paleian and the Caledonian school" and lauded the seventeenth-century theologians Archbishop Leighton, Isaac Barrow, William Bates, and Robert Riccaltoun. Whereas the former represented much that was wrong in contemporary religious discussion, Marsh believed that the latter group contained resources that the present generation could desperately use.[6]

In a letter to his fiancée, written in 1821, Marsh described in a more intimate and much less formal manner the challenge facing one who would take on "the ten thousand distracting questions, the harrowing doubts and maddening skepticism" and plunge into "the metaphysic depths of controversial theology." Each philosophical school had its own fierce defenders, while others claimed to have risen above the fray, embracing either reason in its purity or emotion in its passion. For his own part Marsh found difficulties in every theological system, yet he maintained the need to question both "on what grounds every received article of faith is rested by those who defend it" and the renewed faith that arose out of such interrogations.[7]

The 1829 edition of Coleridge's *Aids to Reflections* contained a long "Preliminary Essay" by Marsh. Marsh underscored the significance of the volume when he stated that it was "a philosophical statement and vindication of the distinctively spiritual and peculiar doctrines of the Christian systems." As he expounded on the meaning of his statement, Marsh again pointed out that attention to precise language analysis, rather than the popular usage of the words, showed that philosophical or rational meant reasonable or in accordance with reason. Marsh saw the demonstration of the reasonableness of Christianity as the whole point of Coleridge's book, for, as Marsh stated elsewhere in the essay, the genuine philosopher "has and can have rationally but one system, in which his philosophy becomes religious and his religion philosophical."[8]

Reiterating his point from the Stuart review on the superficiality of current philosophy, Marsh mounted a two-pronged assault on contemporary metaphysics. First, against those who decried metaphysics and claimed that they employed no philosophical system in their interpretation at all, Marsh retorted that metaphysical beliefs had formed a part of every age. Self-conscious and reflective philosophical work was the prerequisite for any true advance in the field of religion. Beyond that Marsh conceded that "every writer now-a-days on such [interpretive] subjects will assure us, that he has nothing to do with metaphysics but is guided only by common sense and the laws of interpretation. But I would like to know how a man comes by any common sense in relation to the movement and laws of his intellectual and moral being without metaphysics. What is the common sense of a Hottentot on subjects of this sort?" Marsh realized here that appeals to a common sense divorced from a proper metaphysics were vacuous. His statement was not intended as an admission of cultural relativism—that is, that common sense could signify radically different assumptions for a Hottentot versus an American. Rather, Marsh designed this as the opening salvo of his attack on "the prevailing system of metaphysics," the system of John Locke.[9]

Marsh's dissatisfaction with Locke—and here he essentially lumped the Common Sense philosophers Dugald Stewart, George Campbell, and Thomas Brown together with Locke—was twofold. On Marsh's account Locke's theory of the will denied human freedom by subjecting the whole universe (including humanity) to the laws of nature. Now Locke claimed that there was a sphere of free human activity, but Marsh found this to be a spurious concession. In Marsh's words Locke endeavored to "subject our whole being to the law of nature and then contend for the existence of something which is not nature."[10]

The fundamental problem, and here was Marsh's second disagreement, was that Locke and his followers had failed correctly to distinguish between Reason and Understanding. In so doing they had further failed adequately to distinguish the natural from the supernatural, or, as Marsh preferred to call it, the natural from the spiritual. The distinction between Understanding, "the faculty judging according to sense . . . of abstracting and generalizing, of contrivance and forecast," and Reason, "the power of ideal construction, the intuition of geometrical or other necessary and universal truths," was a hallmark of the Coleridgean system. The Lockean failure to differentiate these two faculties properly, Marsh contended, had fundamentally invalidated Lockean metaphysics. Coleridge's attention to the precise use of language had been the first step toward recognizing the problem. Unfortunately, the Lockean system presented its views as if they were self-evident and available simply on common sense. On Marsh's account this reaffirmed the need for clearer metaphysical thinking and, once this was begun, the replacement of the Lockean system with that of Coleridge.[11]

Marsh admired Coleridge for the Englishman's attempt to show that it was the philosophical grounds upon which Christianity was defended, rather than Christianity itself, which was the source of much popular and scholarly confusion over religious authority. For Marsh Coleridge's work began with close attention to language, progressed through rigorous philosophical examination, and arrived at the goal of "adequate and scientific self-knowledge." Marsh pointed out against certain of Coleridge's critics that the peculiarities of Coleridge's choice of language reflected either new or renewed uses of particular terms. And, as for those others who claimed that Coleridge's metaphysics were unintelligible, Marsh simply dismissed them as persons who prefer "to sleep after dinner" rather than to grapple with profound issues.[12]

For Marsh, then, philological controversies contained underlying metaphysical issues, and such basic metaphysical disagreements often revolved around vague or inadequate language. Accordingly, much of the clamor between the critics and defenders of religion was misplaced. Attention to metaphysics, expressed in a precise and felicitous language, as Marsh believed Coleridge did so well, could resolve the current strife troubling the religious community and the broader American culture.

After the publication of *Aids* Marsh maintained his interest in Coleridge, continued to deplore the hegemony of the Lockean system, and sought to keep abreast of Continental criticism. In 1830 he wrote to August Tholuck and explored the possibility of translating some of Tholuck's work. Marsh was struck with the parallels between Tholuck and Coleridge's work and, additionally, hoped to develop interest in Germany for Coleridge's philosophical approach. Indeed, he was sufficiently impressed with Tholuck's scholarship to suggest to one correspondent that Moses Stuart's work would be substantially improved if he would read Tholuck. Thus, while Marsh neither studied with nor met Tholuck, familiarity and engagement with German mediational theology also influenced James Marsh.[13]

W. G. T. Shedd and Romantic Discourse

In 1847, five years after Marsh's death, Noah Porter assessed Coleridge and his American disciples and praised Marsh for "opening new fields of inquiry" and displaying other "modes of viewing religious truth." Though he did not accept all of Marsh's proposed modifications, he concluded that Marsh's work "contended for a wakeful, thorough, and scientific theology, in which, let alarmists and incapables say what they will, rests the hope of the church." Yet, with Marsh's passing, it fell to others to explore the possibility of language as a means to reconcile science and religion. One of these was William G. T. Shedd, a former student of Marsh's and another prominent partisan of Coleridge. Shedd was well known for his reflections on history as a means for mediating science and religion. Nevertheless, his analysis of language also won him recognition. In his construal of language within organic terms, in his emphasis on the creative dimension of the writer (whether poet or historian), and, in his Romantic and specifically Coleridgean framing of epistemological and moral questions, Shedd established a clear connection between his deliberations on history and language.[14]

Shedd was born in Acton, Massachusetts, on 21 June 1820. He attended the University of Vermont and there fell under the influence of Marsh and, through Marsh, of Coleridge and romanticism. After graduating from college in 1839, Shedd taught school for a year in New York. From there he went back to New England and enrolled in Andover Theological Seminary, from which he graduated in 1843. Ordained the following year, he briefly served in a church before returning to the University of Vermont in 1845. The rest of Shedd's life was spent teaching, writing, and lecturing; he was successively professor of literature at Vermont (1845–52), professor of sacred rhetoric at Auburn Theological Seminary (1852–54), professor of church history at Andover (1854–62), and professor first of sacred rhetoric then systematic theology at Union Theological Seminary in New York City, until his resignation in 1893. Shedd died the following year.[15]

Shedd continued the project begun by his mentor, Marsh, in his production in 1853 of the first American edition of the complete works of Coleridge. Moreover, Shedd's writings reflect the influence of Marsh and, beyond that, of Coleridge and William Wordsworth. In a manner sympathetic to that of these two English Romantics Shedd contended that scientific investigation was not inimical to the growth and development of language and the arts. Wordsworth and Coleridge saw empirical knowledge offering a different kind of knowledge from that of poetry and, thus, ultimately complementing it. Shedd, characterizing theology as the "science of science" and the "science of the supernatural," contended that the profundity of the best of world literature was reinforced by, and indeed reflected, the contributions of theological knowledge and inquiry.[16]

Second, Shedd insisted in a lecture first given in 1848 that language developed organically, not mechanically, and that it was an expression of thought. The organic metaphor was, of course, one of the central symbols of the Romantic movement and clearly distinguished its aesthetic orientation from that of the neoclassicism of an earlier age. Beyond that Shedd argued that the specific origin of primitive language was an "instantaneous creation" from God available for Adam and necessary for the formal perfection of the universe. James Marsh had declined to go into the question of the origins of language, confining himself to the observation that thought preceded language and that, whatever the genesis of language, its evolution marked the progress of society. Shedd, on the other hand, pressed much further. Since God had initially made languages available for Adam's use in naming the creatures of the world, Shedd maintained that the development of language was plain to see and that, in expressing thought, it gave vent to an essential creative process.[17]

The view that language—in its various forms of poetry, prose, and speech—was an expression of some dynamic and natural genius within the individual, rather than the delineation or communication of a set of concepts through formal, uniform, and regulative laws, again marked Shedd's allegiance to Romantic rather than Neoclassic aesthetics. In the preface to the *Lyrical Ballads* of 1800 Wordsworth had called poetry "the spontaneous overflow of powerful feelings" and, in so doing, had declared his independence from the responsibility to imitate nature, reflectively like a mirror, or to edify his audience through calculated literary vehicles. For Shedd, too, the writer or rhetorician literally expelled, expressed, or ventilated his or her thoughts in an act of creation, one that provided form for the formless and analogically paralleled divine creation.[18]

Yet, whereas the creation of the world had been studied and self-conscious, Shedd insisted that literary creativity reflected a different style. Human literary creativity was free, pure, spontaneous, and unconscious. In yet another bow to the aesthetics of the Romantics Shedd described genuine creativity as an expression of individuality, rather than as conformity to uniform conventions. Genuine creativity showed that "plastic power" to shape and mold without effort or endeavor, which became the Romantic ideal and measure. Neither were such expressions exercises in artistic anarchy nor examples of self-indulgence, for Shedd, in true Coleridgean fashion, insisted that beauty and truth "in a work of Art, is conditioned upon the presence in it of some intelligible idea." Beneath or behind all the diversity of appearances and manifestations of individuality there existed transcendental principles or ideas. Truth, for Romantics like Shedd, was ultimately universal.[19]

The assertion of an inner unity beneath an outer diversity also gave Shedd a response to those who would deny the unity of the human race (and hence the biblical doctrine of a single creation of humanity) on the basis of the diversity of human language. Indeed, Shedd was not dismayed by such linguistic variety, for "all those different languages

are equally embodiments of thought, and of the same thought substantially . . . the vital principle—logical immutable truth in the form
of human thought—is here seen embodying itself in manifold forms,
with freedom and originality, and with an expressive suitableness in
every instance."[20]

Philology, Biblical Criticism, and James Warley Miles

Coleridge's influence was not confined exclusively to the precincts of
Vermont and its university. Down South, in the Palmetto state of
South Carolina, James Warley Miles drew on the thought of the sage
of Highgate as well as other European Romantics in his own philosophical explorations of language. Miles's eclectic career—Episco-
palian minister, missionary, litterateur, librarian, and college professor—suggests both the instability of his personal life as well as the
unsettled opportunities for a career in letters in the South. While his
penchant for scholarship often made him an object of solicitude for his
friends, Miles privately fluctuated between pride in his work and
despair over his lack of greater accomplishments. Yet his insights
regarding the nature of language as well as his previously noted reflections on history were important contributions to the debate over
science and religion in antebellum America.[21]

James Warley Miles was born on 24 November 1818 in St. Matthew's Parish, South Carolina. Even as a youngster, his attraction to
the study of language was evident. "His recitations have not been such
recently as pleased me," the headmaster of the school wrote to Miles's
father. "I fear he was too much absorbed in the study of German." In a
subsequent letter, however, the headmaster praised the young Miles's
diligence: "he is what he should be, modest, discreet, and studious. . . .
He is not backward in asking for books and it is a gratification to
supply him. I have witnessed his efforts at extemporaneous discussion
in the literary society, I think he stands decidedly first."[22]

While such a gift for eloquence would have directed many a South
Carolinian boy into a career in law or politics, Miles chose to study for
the ministry. He graduated from General Theological Seminary in
New York City in 1841. While at the seminary, he came under the
influence of the then contemporary Tractarian theology emanating
from England and the pens of John Henry Newman, John Keble,
Edward Pusey, and Hurrell Froude. By the time of his graduation

Miles had helped to draft a plan for a religious house of priests dedicated to spirituality and service, a plan later realized in the Nashotah House Seminary in Wisconsin. Yet, as events turned out, Miles never participated in the actual project but, instead, pledged himself to missionary work in Turkey. In fact, in his *Farewell Sermon* presented in 1843, just prior to his departure, he derided Tractarianism as "the mists of a new-fangled Theology from a distant Island" and re-embraced what he called "the sound views of the Reformers."[23]

Miles served as a missionary under Bishop Horatio Southgate and the Board of the Domestic and Foreign Missionary Society of the Episcopal Church in America. Working in Constantinople and Armenia, Miles continued his language study, adding Hebrew, Arabic, and Chaldean to his growing list of linguistic proficiencies. These years abroad were formative ones for Miles, particularly in his later thinking about the issue of slavery. Additionally, his own progress in language studies while a missionary pointed up the glaring lack of opportunities and facilities to continue such study in the South once he returned. To his knowledge, Miles complained in 1848, there existed in the South no "chair of literature, from which might proceed a guidance or direction to the literary researches of the student, furnishing a course of instruction which would give a systematic outline of literary history." This charge of the institutional backwardness and intellectual aridity of the South was echoed by friends and acquaintances of Miles, men such as William Gilmore Simms, James Louis Petigru, Alfred Huger, and Paul Hamilton Hayne. Others, such as Edmund Ruffin, Nathaniel Beverly Tucker, and James Henry Hammond, felt the same and sought platforms for their views in public service and lengthy personal correspondence. Separated by intellect, sensibility, and choice from the mainstream of Southern society, these spiritual exiles shared Miles's mixture of chagrin with the South of the present and hope for its future.[24]

Between 1851 and 1853 Miles published a pair of essays, which together characterized his thinking on the problem of language and religion for the rest of his life. Taking up the familiar question of the origin of language, Miles scorned both the theory of independent human creation of language as well as that of a divine gift of specific rules of grammatical construction for the formal systems of logic. Instead, invoking the Coleridgean language of a "progressive development under the laws of Understanding and Reason," Miles argued that language had evolved as the "result of certain fixed laws of the intellect and organization of man." Recent philological research had given up the earlier fascination with the external similarities of vocabulary, Miles stated, and had moved on to the more fruitful investigation of "the structure, the internal connection, and . . . the psychological characteristics of different tongues." Acknowledgment of the structural unity of human language allowed Miles to defend the fundamental unity of the human creation. There was but one unified original creation, Miles insisted. Yet he added that the disparities between the various races of humans attested to the equally significant diversity of human experience, a disparity that "pseudo-philanthropy" tampered with only in failure and error. This emphasis upon historical development couched in terms of different races was significant, for it would form the basis for Miles's defense of Southern slavery, not on the basis of the Bible but, rather, on his reading of human history.[25]

Miles had high praise for what he called the new "scientific philology." Sensitive to the dynamic character of language, these philologists had a splendid opportunity to examine the relationship between national language and national identity. Much like Marsh or Shedd, Miles was convinced that the "genius" of a people, in that favorite construction of the Romantics, found particular expression in their language. Miles was especially impressed by the work of Wilhelm von Humboldt, Francis Lieber, and the historian of Rome Barthold Niebuhr and celebrated them as examples of "the real Germanic Scholar," who "shrinks from no labor, is deterred by no difficulty, is sustained by unselfish enthusiasm in the pursuit of knowledge . . . and makes all the civilized world debtors to his instruction."[26]

Such effusive praise may reflect Miles's own aspirations for himself, it may reflect Miles's extensive familiarity with German theological and critical work, or it may reflect Miles's attempt to dispel contemporary American ignorance of German scholarship compared with English or Scottish works. Whatever the case, it is clear that Miles held up high scholarly standards for the aspiring student of philology. Yet, just as the personal demands were great, so too were the regions to be encompassed vast. For the scientific philologist, on Miles's account, will be led directly "to the study of those problems in the Philosophy of Language to which Comparative Philology is tributary, and in another direction, he will be led to those Historical, Ethnological, and Literary investigations, in which the extant Literature of Nations is subjected to the application of the Laws of Hermeneutics, guided by refined and enlarged criticism." Here, then, Miles explicitly connected the study of words with the laws of hermeneutics, just as James Marsh had drawn basic metaphysical issues out of precise attention to linguistic analysis. For both men believed that broader principles of criticism could be pressed out of the scientific study of language, and, armed with these interpretive principles, many of the outstanding disputes regarding biblical authority and textual commentary could be resolved.

In a series of fascinating letters written to Mrs. T. J. Young between 1857 and 1864 Miles filled out the meaning of scientific philology's relationship both to hermeneutical strategy and to such specific textual questions as the age of the Earth. Early on in his reflections about biblical language Miles stated, "what is recorded in the Bible is to be judged by Moral Laws, and nothing is true merely because found in the Bible." "Any theory of 'inspiration' which makes God an accomplice with or conniver at, immorality and crime is a blasphemous theory," he continued, for "it makes no difference to me however much error and low-morality may be pretended, or may be proved, to be found in the books of the Bible. All that, cannot in the least affect the really divine thoughts and instructions scattered throughout those books, and which appeal to my Reason and Moral Nature—i.e., to the Law of God within me."[27]

These dual themes of the limitations to the meaning of inspiration and the Bible as a moral guide reappear throughout Miles's correspondence, and, in a later comment over the perennial attempt to reconcile Genesis with the growing body of contradictory material from the physical sciences, Miles simply stated, "it is impossible to make a scientific record out of Genesis." For Miles it was enough that the biblical authors were inspired about religious and moral truths, for, about other subjects, "as chronology, sciences, etc., they were no wiser than their age."[28]

Miles often called for the application of "the principles of scientific criticism" to the Bible, and an illustrative, if fragmentary, example of his employment of these principles appears in a discussion of the book of Genesis. Miles began by noting the presence of at least two literary traditions in the text. In line with much contemporary Continental biblical criticism Miles identified an Elohistic and a Jehovistic tradition on the basis of breaks in the text. From here Miles suggested that two systems of interpretation were available: the first operated "according to the analogy of Universal History, and according to the laws of psychology," while the second method "interpreted by the narrow, literal methods of rabbinism." Furthermore, where the rabbinic mode of interpretation clung to the words of the text, the historicopsychological mode compared this account with other accounts from primitive societies and observed the regular occurrence of hero stories clothed in the forms of legends, epics, and fables. When interpreted from the historicopsychological perspective, Miles contended, the reader has a view of the growth of Israelite society and, more importantly, the development of the religious consciousness of Abraham. If interpreted through rabbinic literalism, however, the Genesis traditions were reduced to the level of stories,

> which makes them horrible, as representing God necessitating incest by the creation of only a single pair; puerile, as introducing a talking snake . . . impossible, as representing without object or reason individual men living centuries in spite of all physiological laws; untrue as representing the Noahic Flood as universal which geology and tradition and chronology contradict; fabulous and impossible, as representing the ark, and the preservation in it of all the species.[29]

In a manner paralleling James Marsh, then, Miles was aware of defective biblical criticism, yet he stoutly insisted that the "Bible's true majesty and divinity" could only be brought out by criticism. Miles went beyond Marsh, however, in explicitly recognizing the figurative, analogical, and mythical dimensions of language. To put the point in other words Miles saw language operating on both the literal and symbolic levels, he was sensitive to the multiplicity of meanings contained within a text as rich as the biblical one, and he hoped that many of the conflicts surrounding the authority of the Bible could be resolved by a proper appreciation of the means through which language functioned.

Recognition of the symbolic dimension of language is the leitmotif running from Marsh through Miles to Horace Bushnell. Miles, however, had two further points to make. First, in a bow to the implications of his developmental emphasis Miles conceded that language and its meaning changed over time. He believed that the spirit and message of Christianity—"the filial relation of man to God, the life of the soul in God"—remained the same. In this volatile situation words and formulas too often took the place of truths and moral insights; dogmas won out over beauty. Moreover, new scientific information, instead of being incorporated rightfully into religious life and thought, was suppressed by church authorities. The resulting alternatives for knowledgeable modern men and women were either to smother their intellectual powers and discard their knowledge or to accept banishment from their churches as heretics.[30]

Miles's second point expanded on this dolorous tendency of the Christian church, Protestant and Catholic alike, to indulge itself in "bibliolatry." By *bibliolatry* Miles meant regarding the Bible as an idol. While he considered the doctrine of plenary inspiration as untenable and discredited among scholars, Miles realized that it continued to hold a popular appeal. Miles found it ironic that bibliolators viewed themselves as exalting the authority of the Bible, when, in fact, their disregard for the circumstances, history, and form of the text degraded it. In defending the inspired veracity of every aspect of the text, Miles pointed out, bibliolatry provides every word with "a superstitious and equal value, and a fragment of a text becomes a valued whole as the basis of the most unjustifiable and unreasonable deductions." "It thus consults the Bible as it might a set of heathen oracles," Miles concluded, "and any and every utterance of the idol, clothed with the fantastic interpretation of the exegetist, is invested with the sanction of the Word of God."[31]

Miles's disgust with the obtuseness of literalism and the pettiness of bibliolatry was matched only by his indignation at the religious teachers and seminary professors of his day. Miles found them, as a group, scared of scholarship and tethered to the past. Not surprisingly, he chided their lack of philological training, chastised their deficiencies in modern biblical criticism, and castigated their ignorance of contemporary theological trends. The only antidote to this situation would be to send them all off to Germany and "put them through the severest course of the ablest anti-revelation and infidel lecturers and writers, for until our teachers know what is thought and argued, they never can be competent to prepare others to be teachers."[32]

It is interesting to note in this context that, although James Marsh and James Warley Miles were drawn to Romantic philosophy and literature and both called for a variety of pedagogical and intellectual reforms, neither of them felt much comradeship with the Transcendentalist coterie of Concord and Boston. Furthermore, while Ralph Waldo Emerson, as one scholar put it, developed a theory of language which articulated "the resurgent capacity for symbolic experience, based on a peculiar sense of the inherent power of language," neither Marsh nor Miles expressed any sympathy for him. Marsh, for example, turned down an invitation to contribute to George Ripley's *Specimens of Standard Foreign Literature* and in 1838 derided Emerson's lectures as "Epicurean Atheism." Finally, in 1841, in his strongest criticism, Marsh characterized Ripley's Brook Farm experiment as misguided and "the whole of Boston transcendentalism" as "rather a superficial affair. . . . They have many of the prettinesses of the German writers, but without their manly logic and strong systematizing tendency. They pretend to no system or unity, but each utters, it seems, the inspiration of the moment, assuming that it all comes from the universal heart, while ten to one, it comes only from the stomach of the individual."[33]

Miles's relationship to transcendentalism was both less personal and less acerbic than Marsh's. He was familiar with and drew on the same wealth of Platonic, English, and Continental thought which played such a formative role in the development of the New Englanders. He was indebted to Coleridge, and the Englishman's influence, along with that of men such as Thomas Arnold, Friedrich Schleiermacher, August Neander, and August Tholuck, helped to frame Miles's understanding of the compatibility of reason and faith and the reconcilability of science and religion. Yet, despite these intellectual affinities, Miles had no personal contact with the Transcendental cognoscenti, and in his only recorded use of the word he describes himself as "ungifted with the seven-league boots of Transcendentalism" and, thus, unable to leap to their conclusions.[34]

In 1874, one year before his death, Miles delivered an address that both drew together many of the central themes of his thinking and demonstrated the continuity of his intellectual peregrinations. For, once again, he acknowledged Coleridge's distinction between Understanding and Reason, reminding his listeners that Christianity "presents herself in her vital power, as a voice from God, directly to the Reason or intuitive consciousness of man." In so doing, Miles continued, Christianity accorded with both biblical testimony and human conscience in illustrating its validity. For the heart of Christianity was the awakened religious consciousness, and, in a plea that reached back to the very core of the Romantics' protest against the Enlightenment, Miles insisted that the Bible was a repository of spiritual truths and that no amount of historical evidences or factual errors could elevate or diminish its value. Empirical evidence neither added to nor distracted from the Bible's authority, for such allegations were superfluous to the fundamental truths available to the spiritually alive individual. In the end Miles reaffirmed the possible reconciliation of science and religion, for religion needed philologically sound texts, freed from historical excrescences and supernumerary literary traditions, while science needed to demonstrate the applicability of its methods. And the result, Miles confidently predicted, would be that, "after every concession is made, which true science can exact or demand, the spiritual truths of that Book still shine."[35]

"Language Two Stories High"

In 1832 an anonymous reviewer responded to charges of obscurity in current philosophy and literary criticism with the remark, "what great science, we would ask, is not obscure before its nomenclature is understood and its definitions studied?" This, of course, had been the retort of James Marsh to critics of Coleridge, and the observation likewise readily summarized the challenge that Horace Bushnell took up when he made his own contribution toward the clarification of the science of words. Moreover, this sense that something of value existed just outside one's grasp and would be available with diligent work also pertained to Bushnell's own introduction to Coleridge. Bushnell recounted spending six long months working through *Aids to Reflection*. Though he continually found the book fascinating, he was never sure that he understood its full consequences. "I was quite sure that I saw a star glimmer," Bushnell recalled, "but I could not quite see the stars." This image of glimmering semblances of meaning, vaguely discerned lineaments of importance, and dimly perceived yet still strongly sensed constellations of significance could well serve as a model for Bushnell's mature considerations of the nature of language and its own capacity for hidden meanings.[36]

Significantly, as he later stated, Bushnell's assiduous study of Coleridge paid off, opening new vistas on the nature of current religious issues for him and providing insights that fueled his own further thinking. Yet Bushnell never became as self-conscious a disciple of Samuel Taylor Coleridge as had Marsh, Shedd, or even James Warley Miles. Invocations of the Coleridgean distinction between Reason and Understanding do not pepper his writings, and, while Coleridgean influences can be discerned, there are few intellectual pledges of allegiance.

Bushnell's professional career was a controversial one, and the total corpus of his writings touched on both the classic issues of Christian doctrine and the ephemeral reports of the national press. And, if it was his fate to spend his entire ministry at one church, it was likewise his destiny to arrive at his calling through a most circuitous route. Born in Bantam, Connecticut, in 1802, Bushnell spent his youth on the family farm. Bushnell described himself, as a youngster, as "a church-going, thoughtful man" who sought "to dig out a religion by my head." If a collegiate reminiscence is to be believed, this rationalist tendency was strengthened by Bushnell's teenage membership in an "infidel club" whose head was a devotee of Tom Paine.[37]

Reluctant to leave the familiarity of this rural environment and the comfort of his family, Bushnell finally agreed to go to Yale College in 1823. After graduation he taught school in Connecticut, only to leave to accept a job as a newspaper reporter and editor in New York City. In 1829 Bushnell returned to Yale, this time to study law, with the hopes of eventually moving to the West. He remained at Yale, studying law and serving as a tutor in the college until 1831. This was to be a memorable year in Bushnell's life, for, during a religious revival that took place on the campus during that winter, Bushnell decided to become a minister. Transferring to the Divinity School, where he studied under Nathaniel W. Taylor, Bushnell finally graduated and accepted a call to North Congregational Church in Hartford, Connecticut, in 1833. Bushnell remained at this church until 1859 and ultimately died at Hartford in 1876.[38]

Like the other mediating theologians in this study, Horace Bushnell believed that science and religion were compatible with one another. In an essay he wrote while still a student at Yale Divinity School Bushnell characterized science as an analysis based upon the systemization and classification of empirical data. In his own sphere, Bushnell continued, the scientist was justified in his efforts to catalog, explain, and even predict natural phenomena. Bushnell protested, however, against the extension of these efforts into the human sphere. For natural laws, he argued, did not control human affairs, and any such efforts were doomed as attempts "to systematize in science where there is not system in fact." For Bushnell it was not only that human affairs contained a multiplicity of motives, which had defied previous attempts to reduce them to common first principles, but also, as Bushnell adopted from his reading in Coleridge, that the moral and spiritual realms were fundamentally distinct from the physical and natural ones.[39]

As late as the 1850s, Bushnell was reiterating this basic position. Christianity had no conflict with the facts of science, he stated, and, correctly presented, science and religion constituted complementary systems of knowledge. Remonstrating once again, however, against the arrogance of scientism, that bondage, which asserted that "nothing could be true, save as it is proved by the scientific method," Bushnell insisted that the truths of religion were of a higher and different nature, verified by the heart and not by the head.[40]

Why was it important to distinguish the physical realm from the spiritual, the natural sphere from the moral? What implications could be drawn out from such a distinction, and what new insights did it produce? For Bushnell the answers to these questions came out in his theory of language. As early as 1832, Bushnell sketched out in a student essay the contours of his later conception of language. Language had its origin, he announced, "purely in the phenomena of sense, and it is thus shown to be a series of arbitrary sounds agreed upon to represent visible phenomena which phenomena are symbols naturally significant." Rising to his point, the young divinity student concluded that "the whole sensible world is a significant language and that the language is possible only as it is a recombination of terms found in the language of nature."[41]

In later years Bushnell expanded his contention that sense experience was the basis of all language and its corollary, that the physical world comprised a symbolic system, into a full discussion of human language. At this point in his life he confronted other problems. When he first entered college Bushnell admitted that he "had no language and if I chanced to have an idea, nothing came to give it expression. The problem was, in fact, from that point onward, how to get a language and where." Seeking a vocabulary and grammar of expression adequate to his thought, Bushnell first turned to Paley then to Coleridge. Initially, he struggled with Coleridge's style, but by about 1831 he had had a crucial insight. "I discovered how language built on physical images is itself two stories high," he wrote, "and is, in fact, an outfit for a double range of uses. In one it is literal, naming roots or so many facts of form, in the other it is figure, figure on figure, clean beyond the dictionaries, for whatever it can properly signify." Although Bushnell only indirectly credited Coleridge with the impetus for this insight into language, it is clear that Coleridge had an important influence on the young Connecticut theologian. Indeed, many years later Bushnell confessed that "he was more indebted to Coleridge than to any extra-Scriptural author."[42]

Bushnell's mature thought presented a linguistic theory that both was consistent with the work of Marsh, Shedd, and Miles and also went beyond them. For Bushnell's analysis of language explicitly centered on the symbolic nature of human communication and, in so doing, captured the distinctive nature of the reinterpretation of language as a method of mediation. In addition to purportedly ameliorating the claims of the scientific and religious communities, Bushnell held out the hope that the proper understanding of the nature, capabilities, and meaning of language could also adjudicate the warring factions within Christianity. That many of these disputants were located in his own backyard in New England was not lost on Bushnell, nor was the recognition of what his subsequent reputation in American religious history would be, if he could successfully accomplish his goal. Unfortunately for Bushnell, his contemporaries were disdainful and sometimes hostile toward his suggestions, while more recent commentators have criticized his views for other reasons. Nevertheless, for his own and the succeeding generation of liberal Protestant thinkers, Bushnell remained a formidable presence.[43]

Bushnell's treatise "Preliminary Dissertation on the Nature of Language," first published in 1849, was dedicated to illuminating the significance of language and revealing the "power and capacity of words taken as vehicles of thought and of spiritual truth." To accomplish this end Bushnell began by differentiating language into two large classes: physical language and the language of intelligence. For it was in their "mode of origin," Bushnell stated, that their real power was revealed. The first of these categories referred to material things, and Bushnell claimed that even animals could be taught this class of language. The other—and, for Bushnell, ultimately more significant—class was composed of rational, emotional, spiritual, and moral meanings articulated through some outward form of expression. In a manner reminiscent of his student essay Bushnell further maintained that all the words of the language of intelligence were originally based on physical realities and appearances. Bushnell's hypothesis was an ambitious one, and, as one scholar has pointed out, nothing less than an inventory of all known human language could prove or disconfirm Bushnell's contention.[44]

Beyond its significance as an account of the origin of human language Bushnell's discussion is important in two other ways. First, Bushnell probably adopted the concept of the physical basis of language from his Yale teacher Josiah Gibbs, Sr. Gibbs was a well-known and highly respected nineteenth-century philologist, who taught that "intellectual and moral ideas, as expressed in language, are derived from physical," from the world of natural phenomena. Though he was not one to acknowledge his intellectual debts extensively, Bushnell did praise the works of Gibbs, the Englishman Horne Tooke, and the German Wilhelm von Humboldt and cited their influence on his thinking. If nothing else, such acknowledgments and the use Bushnell made of these authors demonstrated his familiarity with contemporary philological discussions.[45]

Second, Bushnell asserted that external and physical objects served as typological references or images for internal and spiritual states. Typological thinking had, of course, played a prominent role in colonial American culture, and Bushnell was familiar with the tradition. In this earlier orientation an aspect of the Old Testament was interpreted as foreshadowing a later occurrence in the New Testament, while even national experiences (e.g., that of ancient Israel) were seen as modeling later experiences (e.g., that of America). In Bushnell's presentation the physical world was a "vast dictionary and grammar of thought," one that contained symbolic meanings that awaited proper interpretation and expression in language. Here was the true importance of Bushnell's claim regarding the interrelationship of the physical and intellectual realms. For the physical world was no longer simply a collection of recalcitrant facts but, instead, a vast reservoir of latent meanings, no longer a catalog of potential ambushes or embarrassments for the religious believer but, rather, a system of symbols available for interpretation, exegesis, and understanding.[46]

From an analysis of the classes of language Bushnell next turned to a discussion of how language functioned. Building on his earlier exposition, Bushnell described two levels of language—a literal and a figurative. The literal level drew on physical language, while the figurative drew on the language of intelligence. Both levels coexisted within all human language, and it was the great error of classic and contemporary thinking not to differentiate these levels when analyzing language. Indeed, it was the utility of this distinction which excited Bushnell, for he believed that its recognition promised a way out of theological wrangling as well as a means to defend the integrity of religion's most important claims.[47]

For, on Bushnell's reckoning, theologians had too often failed to realize the limits of language as vehicles for spiritual truths. Bushnell likened words to earthen vessels and contended that the truths and meanings contained therein were always greater than and separable from their containers. These great treasures of meanings, exhibited at best only approximately in their lumbering linguistic transports, posed challenges to correct interpretation. The recognition that life, and all its linguistic expressions, were better understood in organic rather than in mechanical terms, Bushnell contended, was an important first step. Likewise, Bushnell hoped that the physical sciences could contribute by "setting outward things in their true proportions, opening up their true contents, revealing their genesis and final causes . . . and weaving all into the unity of a real universe." This expansion of knowledge of the natural universe and the concomitant expansion of physical language might then provide a basis, Bushnell hoped, for more exact usages of the language of intelligence. Finally, Bushnell suggested that understanding, especially of religious language, would be enhanced if scriptural texts were approached "not as a magazine of propositions and mere dialectic entities, but as inspirations and poetic forms of life."[48]

The path of future progress lay in a "more cultivated and nicer apprehension of symbol," Bushnell proclaimed to his readers. Proper awareness of the limitations of language as well as sensitivity to its multiple layers of meaning would help settle the disputes of fractious theological sectarians as well as those between stubborn scientists and their equally bullheaded religious opponents. Beyond that flexibility in grasping the changing forms in which meaning presented itself, a tolerance for ambiguity and a respect for the difficulty of finding suitable outward expressions of inward determinations—these were all the supplementary mechanisms that Bushnell's irenic appeal to language proffered. Nor, in Bushnell's opinion, was this admission of the poetic dimension of language a capitulation to subjectivity or egoistic self-absorption. For his analysis of the nature of language, he believed, was rigorous and accurate; it illuminated the true essence of language and charted an escape out of the shoals of old controversies.[49]

From James Marsh's investigation of the metaphysical foundations of language through James Warley Miles's call for scientific criticism to Horace Bushnell's pronouncement of the literal and figurative levels of language, the reinterpretation of language and the emphasis upon its symbolic nature provided a rich resource for the reconciliation of science and religion in nineteenth-century America.

"Das Gelehrte Berlin" (The Savants of Berlin), by Julius Schoppe. *Front row:*
Wilhelm von Humboldt; *middle row:* Christoph Hufeland, Carl Ritter, Alexander von
Humboldt; *back row:* August Neander, Georg Friedrich Hegel, Friedrich
Schleiermacher. Photograph by Hans-Joachim Bartsch, Berlin; courtesy of Berlin
Museum, Berlin, Germany.

August Tholuck. Courtesy of Staatsbibliothek zu Berlin, Preussischer Kulturbesitz.

Henry Boynton Smith. Library of Congress, Brady-Handy Collection; reproduced from the *Dictionary of American Portraits*, Dover Publications, 1967.

Philip Schaff. Engraving by J. J. Cade; reproduced from the *Dictionary of American Portraits*, Dover Publications, 1967.

Charles Hodge. Courtesy of Speer Library, Princeton Theological Seminary.

James Henley Thornwell. Courtesy of South Caroliniana Library, University of South Carolina.

Edward Robinson. Reproduced from the *Dictionary of American Portraits*, Dover Publications, 1967.

W. G. T. Shedd. Library of Congress, Brady-Handy Collection; reproduced from the *Dictionary of American Portraits*, Dover Publications, 1967.

James Marsh. University of Vermont; reproduced from the *Dictionary of American Portraits*, Dover Publications, 1967.

Horace Bushnell. Portrait by Jared B. Flagg; courtesy of Wadsworth Atheneum, Hartford, Connecticut; endowed by C. N. Flagg and Company; Wadsworth Atheneum.

Chapter Five

Religion and the Science of Society

Reflection and commentary upon contemporary society have been characteristic of American church leaders since the days of the Puritans, and the antebellum mediating theologians were no exception to this rule. Moralistic in tone and conservative in outlook, the social thought of these men was both an extrapolation from their interpretive principles for the reconciliation of science and religion and an application of the pastoral definition of their social role. Thus, examination of their views on society further displays the depth and significance of the mediating theologians' contributions to the American religious scene.

In eighteenth- and early nineteenth-century America the study of society had not yet developed into a scholarly profession. Instead of a specialized field of analysis, sociology (or "moral science," as it was often called) remained a broad-based inquiry, one that reflected normative assumptions and was not immune to, or often even distinct from, religious values and opinions. Beyond that, given their class position and the prominence of the roles they occupied, the clergy's opinions on current political and social events were sought out, listened to, and often heeded. Thus, it is not surprising that later, during the Progressive era, when sociology as an academic specialty in America finally emerged, the majority of its first generation of practitioners came from ministerial families and backgrounds.[1]

Scriptural Politics

By the conventional standards of nineteenth-century America Charles Hodge was a conservative. His often cited statement that he produced no original idea in theology displayed his respect for Princeton's theological heritage and his distrust of religious innovation. Politically, he had been raised on the principles of Hamiltonian federalism, and he identified with the Whig party. Not surprisingly, then, Hodge opposed the policies of Andrew Jackson on several counts. He favored, for example, continuation of the Second Bank of the United States.

When Jackson vetoed the bank's charter in July 1832 Hodge wrote to his brother deploring Jackson's action and concluding that "our institutions will not long survive his reelection." Likewise, as Jackson and his allies sought to extinguish the Indians' title to their lands and to remove them to the western territories, Hodge expressed fear that "our national character will be deeply strained by their disregard of solemn treaties."[2]

During his European trip of 1826–28 Hodge befriended many prominent German political and church officials, such as Leopold von Gerlach and Ernst von Hengstenberg. His journal and letters recount discussions with these advocates of monarchy and Hodge's own difficulties in defending democracy against their criticisms. Hodge was never entirely happy with American political practices or theory. Writing to his brother in 1837, Hodge stated: "If we could have a Republic with the right of suffrage restricted to householders, who can read and write, and have been at least ten years in the country, we could get along grandly. But a democracy with universal suffrage will soon be worse than an aristocracy with Queen Victoria at the head."[3]

Given the racial and gender restrictions on suffrage in antebellum America, Hodge's concerns about universal suffrage were clearly misplaced. Hodge's apprehensions about cultural degeneration in American society were reflected, however, in other issues besides suffrage. He predicted that the "paupers of Europe" and the "mob of foreigners" who were immigrating to America would overwhelm the native born. He insisted on an end to Sunday mail delivery, stating that America was a Christian country and that any dissenters should conform to the cultural and religious customs of the majority. He applauded the growth and achievements of the temperance movement, especially as it pertained to working-class and immigrant families. In all these ways Charles Hodge revealed not only his social conservatism but also his identification with an older conception of a natural aristocracy, one that by birth and upbringing was entitled to rule. At first represented in the early Republic by the Federalists and later taken over by the Whigs, this prescriptive politics had little sympathy with Jackson's appeal to the common man. It rested power in the hands of persons, as Hodge put it, of "intelligence and property" and had no patience with the relativism implied by a laissez-faire approach to economics or a utilitarian approach to morality.[4]

Hodge was also dissatisfied with the voluntaristic assumptions underlying the social contract view of politics. For this Princeton theologian regarded the state not as a voluntary association composed of consenting individuals but, rather, as a holy institution that acquired its authority from divine sanction. Neither the existence nor the legitimacy of the state derived fundamentally from the populace, nor especially from a simple majority of that populace, in Hodge's view. Eternal moral laws and time-honored biblical precepts instead of Enlightenment political theory and the capricious results of majority opinion—these were the foundations of politics in Hodge's reckoning. Moreover, authority, whether biblical or secular, must be firmly and securely anchored, Hodge insisted, and punishment must be swift. For just as religious authority was secured by divine wrath, so was civil authority backed by the threat of the use of force by the state. As Hodge once quipped to his brother, "whatever it may be for Quakers, gunpowder is a very necessary evil for all other sorts of Christians and I have no doubt that it is one of the best prescriptions for saving life and limb that could be made."[5]

Of all the issues that antebellum Americans faced none was greater than that of slavery and secession. Charles Hodge defended the legitimacy of slavery in America. In so doing he staked out a position for which he claimed biblical warrant and constitutional legitimacy. Central to Hodge's argument, however, was the assertion of the unity of humankind, as described in Genesis. Thus, Hodge dissented from the increasingly popular "American school" of anthropology, associated with Josiah Nott, Samuel Morton, and George Glidden, which posited separate origins for the various human races.

Monogenesis, the descent of all human species from a common source, was the prevailing ethnological assumption of Enlightenment philosophers and Christian theologians during the eighteenth century. By the middle of the nineteenth century, however, this concept faced stiff competition among many scientists in the United States. In essence advocates of polygenesis, such as Nott, Morton, and Glidden, claimed to find biological, historical, and statistical evidence that the "white, red, black, and yellow races" were probably created separately, that they remained distinctly different, and that they would forever be hierarchically ordered in terms of intelligence, ability, and talents.[6]

For Hodge there would be no appeal to scientific allegations of racial inferiority in his defense of slavery. Instead, he referred once again to the Bible and the indisputable fact that slavery occurred in the Bible, thus proving that it could not be unscriptural. Whereas abolitionists argued that the whole spirit of the Scriptures ran opposed to the enslavement of human beings, Hodge rejoined that the letter of the Bible revealed its legitimacy. Upon this basis, then, Hodge fashioned a definition of slavery after that of the eighteenth-century theologian William Paley, a definition that identified slavery as simply an obligation to labor for a master without contract or consent. Beyond this Hodge argued that slavery was only a local institution and, as such, subject only to municipal jurisdiction and law. The significance of this position became clearer in the debates during the 1850s over whether slavery was protected by the United States Constitution or only by municipal laws of property, especially when slaveholders took their slaves into free states or new territories and demanded federal protection.[7]

Charles Hodge regarded himself as a moderate on the slavery question, rejecting what he called the "vituperation" and "gross exaggerations" of the abolitionists but also stating that there should be limits to the expansion of slavery. Restrained or not, Hodge's position was criticized in both the North and South. Lewis Tappan, a leader in the Northern antislavery movement, wrote Hodge in 1849, expecting that he had surely changed his earlier views in support of slavery, while many Southerners, Hodge noted himself, lumped the Princeton theologian together with the Northern abolitionists. Yet, to all such critics, Hodge responded that his position had not changed, and, indeed, he considered it the only biblically warranted one.[8]

One Southerner who appreciated Hodge's biblical approach to the slavery question was James Henley Thornwell. Like Hodge, Thornwell insisted that blacks and whites shared a common origin from Adam, and, thus, there were no grounds for either allegations of separate creations or for charges of innate racial inferiority. Furthermore, Thornwell also insisted that the Bible clearly justified slavery. "Certain it is," he wrote, "that no direct condemnation of slavery can anywhere be found in the Sacred Volume. . . . The Scriptures not only fail to condemn slavery, they as distinctly sanction it as any other social condition of man." Whereas Hodge allowed that the Scriptures passively acquiesced in the existence of slavery, Thornwell pushed further, claiming a positive recognition and sanction for the institution. Thus, in the end Thornwell rejected the abolitionists' invocation of the spirit of the biblical text just as Hodge had done, and he likewise dismissed abolitionism as a political movement, calling it "a species of madness:" "It is hot, boiling, furious fanaticism." Not subjective and predetermined interpretations of the text, as the abolitionists allegedly produced, but straightforward examinations of the plain words and simple declarations of the Scriptures—this was what Thornwell wanted.[9]

Thornwell saw the slavery controversy within a global context, one in which "the world is the battleground, Christianity and Atheism the combatants, and the progress of humanity the stake." In this conflict the parties "are not merely Abolitionists and Slaveholders; they are Atheists, Socialists, Communists, Red Republicans, Jacobins on the one side, and friends of order and regulated freedom on the other." Thus, the fundamental issue in the controversy was "the relations of man to Society." In highlighting this dimension Thornwell could put his own gloss on many of the charges made by abolitionists. For example, he too cited William Paley's definition of slavery, with its emphasis on the master's right only to the labor of the slaves. Masters ought not to mistreat their slaves, Thornwell insisted, not only from the standpoint of economic investment but also because they had no claim to the person of the slave. Work and obedience by the slaves were to be expected, but sexual exploitation or physical abuse of the slave had no justification.[10]

Moreover, Thornwell also favored religious instruction for the slaves. Yet, as he expanded on the meaning of such instruction, it became clear that these were simply opportunities to preach submission to those in authority and the legitimacy of the South's peculiar institution. "Our design in giving them the Gospel," Thornwell stated, "is not to civilize them, not to exalt them into citizens or freemen, it is to save them." The fruits of such efforts were contentment in this life and future rewards in the next. Christian freedom, Thornwell explained, was spiritual and not political. Complete equality of person and rank was socialism, not Christianity. And the desire for universal happiness here on earth was a perfectionist notion contradicted by the doctrine of original sin and the everyday examples of its consequences. Finally, as to the role of the church, Thornwell was explicit: the church ought to confine its activities to preaching the Gospel, comforting the afflicted, and saving souls. It ought not to meddle or interfere in social and political systems, as continually called for by abolitionists such as William Lloyd Garrison or Theodore Weld. Instead, Thornwell reiterated that the church's duties were spiritual and not political; the church and state inhabited different realms. Society for Thornwell was an organic entity, deeply rooted in the distant past and dimly projected into an unknown future. Change must be very slow and would properly occur through the cumulative

efforts of individuals, never through the sudden cataclysms of revolution and upheaval. Thus, the church contributed to this progressive
development by raising up good Christians, who in their own individual ways would influence politics and society.[11]

Hodge and Thornwell joined, then, in a biblically based defense of
slavery. They both contrasted their own approaches to what they considered to be the politically motivated readings of the Scripture which
the abolitionists gave in the name of the spirit of the text. Finally, they
conceded that the slaves ought to receive religious instruction, adequate food and provisions, and protection from abuse. Both writers,
however, left these guarantees entirely to the master's discretion, and,
thus, their strictures scarcely touched the reality of the slave system. If
Hodge and Thornwell were generally in agreement in their discussion
of slavery, the issue of secession just as clearly separated them. At first
James Henley Thornwell supported the Union and gloried in its
achievement. In 1841, writing to his wife from London, Thornwell
declared that "America is immeasurably superior to England. . . . I
admire what is excellent in England, but I see so much of an opposite
character that I must still sigh for my native land." Ruefully, he concluded, "abolitionism is, if possible, more fanatical here than in America." In 1841 Thornwell could hardly have guessed at the significance
of his remarks. Yet, twenty years later, he believed that abolitionism
and "Black Republicanism" had made secession inevitable, and he fell
in line in support of the Confederate States, preferring the alternative
of war to that of submission.[12]

Thornwell identified the cause on behalf of which the South se-
ceded as "constitutional freedom," and he blamed the North for abro-
gating the Constitution through the actions of its congressmen in
limiting slavery's expansion into the territories. As Thornwell
developed his apologia, his resonance with sources as disparate as the
ancient Greeks and John Calvin, eighteenth-century American antifederalism and nineteenth-century Romantic nationalism, was apparent. For, together with the ancient Greeks and Calvin, Thornwell saw
the state as a divinely instituted association, a realm where freedom
was regulated and (for Aristotle at least) slavery was legitimate. Closer
to his own day, Thornwell spoke of the Confederate States as following their own genius, spirit, or divine spark—all terms widespread
among the Romantic proponents of early nineteenth-century Romantic nationalism.

Nevertheless, it is when Thornwell turned to a discussion of constitutional government that the loudest echoes, those of his Anti-federalist predecessors, can be discerned. In the Constitutional Convention at Philadelphia in 1787 the Antifederalists were an insightful coalition of opponents to the adoption of the federal Constitution. They articulated the fears of many Americans regarding a new central government and its influence over their lives. Thus, they sought to limit the authority and restrict the power of the national government. The Antifederalists saw the clash of economic and political interests as probably unavoidable and primarily sectional. On the whole they tended to be suspicious concerning the capacity of the people to act wisely and favored representative over democratic forms of government. In a like manner Thornwell argued that the states of the North and South diverged in their political interests as a result of different climate, production, and industry. The individual states, in this context, had ceded only limited and specific powers to the federal branches and had done so on the understanding that such federal power represented only a "treaty" or "alliance" between the states and that the federal Congress operated with indifference between the regions, the "organ of neither and the agent of both." Thus, for the federal Congress, at the behest of the North, to legislate against the interests of the South was wrong. In so doing, Thornwell insisted, the North was actually breaking the Constitution. Moreover, insofar as Congress claimed a democratic mandate for such actions, it had degenerated from a properly representative government to a despotic popular one. As far as Thornwell was concerned, to identify the majoritarian voice of the people with the divine voice of God was simply blasphemy and confusion.[13]

Thus, although initially committed to national unity, Thornwell ultimately endorsed secession and, moreover, wrote one of the major defenses of and played an important role in the establishment of the Presbyterian Church in the Confederate States. Behind his convoluted political odyssey lies Thornwell's unquestioned devotion to his home state of South Carolina and his often repeated pledge to support it in whatever course it finally took. Likewise, one does not have to read far in Thornwell's defense of Southern secession and Southern Presbyterianism to see his fundamental commitment to the preservation of slavery as the essential prerequisite to the continuance of Southern society.[14]

For his part Charles Hodge neatly reversed Thornwell's position. Whereas Thornwell defended the expansionist claims for slavery,

Hodge granted it only local sovereignty. Thornwell accepted secession; Hodge damned it as unjustified and immoral. Thornwell saw the
Federal Union trampling liberty; Hodge depicted the very same
Union as a bright hope for mankind. Finally, whereas Thornwell
called for the church to keep out of politics (at least so far as it intruded
on Southern prerogatives) and to deal exclusively with spiritual matters, Hodge countered that the church was chartered by Scripture to
bear witness against sin and in favor of truth and righteousness. In the
end, though neither Hodge nor Thornwell would admit it, the fires of
the Civil War had smelted the politics out of their biblicism. The
extract, respectively blue and gray, clearly showed how many extra-
biblical elements were to be found in this strain of antebellum
biblicism.[15]

A Rising Phoenix?

While Hodge and Thornwell referred their social positions to biblical
perspectives, Philip Schaff and James Warley Miles drew their so-
ciopolitical lessons from history. Both Schaff and Miles regarded human history as a depository of moral lessons and divine truths. Both
men fashioned theories of organic historical development and argued
that these categories provided serious religious thinkers with an intellectual context and a hermeneutical strategy for their engagement
with the recent findings of the scientific community. Finally, both
individuals constructed a set of conservative political views out of their
organic categories and applied them to the issues of the day.

As Philip Schaff assessed the meaning of the American experience,
he was guarded but hopeful. America was the land of the future, in
Schaff's opinion, yet the country was troubled by

> the filibuster spirit which scorns all international laws and rights
> . . . the piratical schemes of our manifest-destinarians, who
> would swallow in one meal, Cuba, all Central America, Mexico
> and Canada into the bargain, [and] . . . the unbridled passion for
> the almighty dollar, which fosters a mean and heartless utilitar-
> ianism and tends to extinguish all the nobler aspirations of the
> human mind.[16]

These challenges clouded the immediate scene, yet a trio of other
problems—immigration, slavery, and the Civil War—emerged as
deeper issues in Schaff's thinking. As a close observer of the swelling

waves of newly arrived Europeans to America and as an immigrant himself, Schaff made an important contribution to the discussion of the significance of the immigrant for American life. Schaff liked to say that he was a Swiss by birth, a German by education, and an American by adoption, and this remark signaled the cosmopolitan nature of his analysis of the issue. For Schaff believed that America was the "Phenix grave" of all European nationalities and that the republic could give rise to a new nationality, one that would preserve the superior elements while eliminating the worst characteristics of each national group.[17]

As a product of the best of German education, Schaff highly respected Central European culture and its role in world history. Yet, on the American stage, Schaff always envisioned Anglo-American practicality moderating the Teutonic speculative imagination and leading the way. Other groups might enter into view—the Chinese, for example, with "their quiet disposition and mechanical culture, their industry, avarice, and filthy habits," or the Irish, "on the whole, the roughest class of the American population." It remained for the new Anglo-German hybrid, however, to carry forward the work of progress in America.[18]

The cultural assumptions of such statements were clear: the Anglo-Saxon race was superior to the Celtic race, and the Occident was superior to the Orient. Yet Philip Schaff's views on race were not unique or unusual in the America of his day. They formed part of that complex of ideas called Romantic nationalism, which played such an important role in American culture during the second third of the nineteenth century. Derived from the larger European traditions of romanticism, this perspective on nationhood had two mutually reinforcing forms. In its more general form Romantic nationalism broke with the eighteenth-century Enlightenment's emphasis on the universal features of mankind and, instead, focused on the particular, the different, the special characteristics of human experience. Romantic nationalists in America, such as James Polk, took pride in the American spirit, the genius of the American people, and the special qualities of the nation's institutions. It was this emphasis on the *genius* of a people, those ineffable and unique national characteristics, which permeated the writings of these Romantic nationalists.

In its second form Romantic nationalism took on a racial hue, in that its proponents alleged that what infused the genius and institutions of a people was its racial heritage. Early nineteenth-century

American historians such as George Bancroft, John Motley, and Francis Parkman all identified the Anglo-Saxon birthright of America as the true source of its distinctive character and free institutions. Moreover, Romantic nationalism, in either form, often contained a strong rationale for territorial expansion in the name of extending the benefits of its special spirit and institutions to other more "primitive" peoples. Although he recoiled at jingoism and saber rattling, Philip Schaff's belief in the Anglo-Saxon leadership of a future American society clearly places him into the broad context of Romantic racial nationalism.[19]

Schaff also believed that all immigrants must learn the English language if they were to survive and prosper in America. In nineteenth-century America, when newspapers and hymnals, dramatic productions and orders of worship, still appeared by the scores in European languages, Schaff's point was a telling one. It set him off, for example, from a variety of ethnic leaders who strove to maintain the tongue as well as the traditions of the Old Country. Yet Schaff argued that the cultural links between America and the English-speaking world were too strong and to struggle against them "must be just as idle as to swim against the sea." Characteristically, Schaff blended Continental and New World resources together into his vision of the future. He refused to accord any single element undue influence, for his own view of human existence was too deeply penetrated by a dialectical perspective to allow one movement, one race, or one institution either to exist unchallenged by its necessary antithesis or to represent the culmination of human history.[20]

Schaff's use of the dialectic reflected the influence of Hegel on his thought and, more broadly, his commitment to a principle of historical development. A concept of historical development undergirded all of Schaff's social as well as theological concerns. Three features characterized this principle. First, human history was teleological—that is, it was a process organic in nature and directed to a goal. In language that drew on his roots in European romanticism Schaff depicted human history as a "living organism" and as "the struggle of centuries to actualize in full the deep meanings of life." The end of this process of human history was everywhere the same, "the exhibition of God's glory," though not, Schaff lamented, everywhere as simply seen.[21]

Schaff's invocation of the organic metaphor testified to the influence of romanticism on his thinking. Indeed, the use of the organic rather than mechanical image was one of the telltale signs of nineteenth-century romanticism and marked its break with the Enlightenment. Models of the universe as a growing, maturing entity replaced those of an efficient machine finished, complete, and set in motion for all eternity. Beyond that Romantics claimed that life was an ineffable mystery and understanding its deeper meanings required an intuitive insight, not simply a rational calculation. Schaff's intellectual background was a complex one; nevertheless, romanticism played a significant role in shaping his thinking.[22]

The second feature of Schaff's principle of historical development emphasized the dynamic nature of human history. History revealed the struggle and challenges presented to individuals and societies; it witnessed the victories achieved and the reverses suffered. It is important to note Schaff's basic confidence and optimism regarding the progressive outcome of human history. Nevertheless, in the short run, or in any specific instances, setbacks, failures, and regression were always possible. Moreover, he was never so theologically passive or self-assured as to suggest that human activity had no role in the outcome of human history. Regarding the newly arrived immigrants, Schaff stated, "make the foreigners good Christians, and we are sure to make them good citizens." Such a statement not only emphasized the utility of religion in the Republic; it also underscored the importance of human activity in the accomplishment of human destiny.[23]

Finally, Schaff's principle of historical development recognized a hierarchical ordering of societies and groups, one that not only distinguished differences but also normatively ranked them. Though some organicist thinkers, such as Johann Herder, portrayed human development as a multiplicity of equally legitimate possibilities, Schaff's conception of teleology posited one comprehensive line of development to which all human development served and by which it was to be judged. Because human history was dynamic, no single group in the present should assume that it was the crown of creation. The accomplishments of all groups were relative when placed under divine judgment, Schaff insisted. Yet it was clear that, in Schaff's social thinking, not all groups were equal; the more developed were superior to the less developed, and the first would not become the last nor the last become the first, at least in this terrestrial sphere.

Schaff's social thinking was also rooted in a set of paternalist assumptions, which was typical among individuals of his educational, professional, and cultural background. The essence of social and political paternalism in the nineteenth century was a set of general values and clearly defined social relationships. Paternalist values assumed the superiority of European civilization over Asian, discerned divine activity in the cultural and economic development of the West, believed Christianity to be the only true religion, and expected to be rewarded for its efforts in this life and the next. Beyond that paternalist relationships did not depend so much on actual acquaintanceship as on mutually understood expectations. It was a world in which one naturally paid respect to one's "betters" and, in return, received charity, goodwill, and counsel as a matter of reciprocal expectation. Schaff articulated this point of view when in 1851 he justified the existence of poverty as enabling the poor to grow "in humility, in contentment, in thankfulness, in freedom from envy," while providing the rich with "a constant opportunity for the exercise of love and benevolence."[24]

Schaff drew on this developmental framework in discussing an even more significant issue—the "riddle," as he called it, of black slavery. Writing in 1854, Schaff characterized slavery as the "tendo-Achilles" of the American Republic. Slavery was clearly incompatible with the principles of freedom contained in the Declaration of Independence and at least partially achieved in America's history. Yet, Schaff continued, free blacks in the North suffered various discriminations and often were more badly treated than slaves in the South. In giving an empirical description, Schaff overlooked the many achievements of Northern free blacks and underestimated the significance of the lack of legal freedom for the slaves. Still, Schaff's broader point was to distribute responsibility for slavery equally between all Americans, rather than to assign it simply to Southerners.[25]

Schaff scorned the work of abolitionists such as William Lloyd Garrison or Theodore Parker, dismissing their efforts as "unsound, fanatical, and extremely radical in all political and social questions, and infidel in religion." Instead, Schaff favored the work of the American Colonization Society to manumit slaves and assist any willing blacks to return to Africa to live. Schaff noted two reasons for approving this colonization plan. First, as he was pessimistic about the chances for blacks to achieve social equality in America, such a plan appeared to him as a realistic alternative to either continued bondage or a precipitous freedom. Second, once in Africa repatriated American blacks could carry out the work of "a general Christian civilization for the wild negro tribes around." The two themes of civilization and Christianization were standard ones in the rhetoric of American

Christian missionaries, and Schaff was simply grafting them to his own developmental schema, as he envisioned the "dreadful curse of America slavery" finding its resolution and becoming "an incalculable blessing to the pagan savages of Africa."[26]

In 1861, as discussion of black emancipation floated about Washington, D.C., and the North, Schaff again discussed slavery. His essay *Slavery and the Bible* expressed his pessimism about race relations in America and his skepticism about political solutions in the case of such intractable problems. For Schaff insisted that Christianity made no direct challenge to the legal and social basis of slavery; it gave no warrant for John Brown's raid and no comfort to abolitionism. Not proclamation of political liberty for a captive people but, instead, promises of spiritual transformation for established institutions—this was Christianity's legacy, Schaff maintained. Thus, while Schaff envisioned the eventual extinction of slavery by an all-wise Providence, he echoed, with his Calvinist colleagues Hodge and Thornwell, the theme of the need for religious instruction of the slaves.[27]

Schaff recognized a further dilemma beyond slavery, for "the negro question lies far deeper than the slavery question. Emancipation here is no solution. . . . American slavery in spite of all its incidental evils and abuses has already accomplished much good. It has been thus far a wholesome training school for the negro from the lowest states of heathenism and barbarism to some degree of Christian civilization." For Schaff, as for other white Americans north of slavery, adjudication of the slavery issue only opened up the more fundamental question of race relations in American society. Operating within his hierarchical assumptions, with its paternalistic inclinations, Schaff recognized what he considered to be Southern accomplishments in educating and Christianizing black slaves, and here again he muted his dissatisfaction with slavery by placing that institution within a developmental framework. Schaff's paternalistic conservatism matched his Romantic organicism in respecting existing institutions. The result was a puzzled but hopeful assessment of the riddle that slavery and race represented for America.[28]

Schaff's concern with the future destiny of America is nowhere more clearly expressed than in his analysis of the meaning of the Civil War. Already in 1854 Schaff recognized that slavery might divide the Union and produce civil strife. Though he often balanced his criticisms of the Southern slaveholders with admonishments of abolitionists, Schaff was a fervent believer in the Union and saw in its persistence a symbol of freedom for the world. Thus, Schaff stood with Charles Hodge and many other Northern Protestants in viewing the Union as an agency of divine activity and its reestablishment as legitimate grounds for justifying the war's bloody prosecution.[29]

In 1865, in a series of lectures first given to audiences in Germany and published the following year, Schaff expanded on the meaning of the now completed conflict in America. Unequivocally, he held the South responsible for the breakup of the Union and pictured the Civil War as "a struggle of freedom against slavery, of Christian humility and civilization against an antiquated institution of oppression and barbarism." Unlike other groups in the North, however, who demanded a victor's revenge upon the vanquished, Schaff insisted that, since the North and South were both implicated in the existence of antebellum slavery, so did both regions share ultimate responsibility for the war. The lessons to be drawn from the war, he insisted, concerned less the assignment of guilt for the war and more the question of America's postwar fate. Would the republic rise phoenixlike from the ashes and trials of war to achieve that reconciliation of peoples which Schaff had earlier foreseen as its role in human history? Would there be a new regenerated nation emerging from this baptism of blood, or would America forfeit its destiny and miss its historical opportunity? The questions remained open and unanswered for Schaff. His theological interpretation of providential activity gave him hope for its eventual accomplishment, and his developmental view of history gave him a conceptual framework within which to discuss its possibility, as this ecumenical and erudite Swiss-American sought to proclaim that vision of mediation which was so uniquely his own.[30]

Geographical location and intellectual background played as decisive a role in the social thought of James Warley Miles as they did with Philip Schaff. A born and bred South Carolinian, James Warley Miles was a firm supporter of the Confederacy and a defender of black slavery. Unlike many Southern clergymen, such as James Henley Thornwell or Robert Dabney Lewis, Miles, however, did not defend the Southern institution of slavery on a biblical basis. Miles conceded that such a biblical justification could be made, but he regarded it as fundamentally flawed. For in Miles's opinion the Bible justified the institution of slavery as such, but it did not specifically justify the institution of black servitude. "The sacred writers mention only Semitic and Caucasian races," Miles wrote; "the notion that the negro has been mentioned in the Bible has arisen from theoretical views, and not from scientific examination of the sacred text. Abraham's slaves were white; the slave sent back to his master by St. Paul was white. The relation of the negro to the white Southerner was not known or contemplated any more than was the voyage of Columbus, or the discoveries of Newton."[31]

Thus, Miles argued that interpretations that saw allusions to blacks in biblical references were based on mistranslations and misunderstandings of the text. For Miles these biblical arguments could as easily defend white slavery as they could black slavery. And, as a former missionary to the Middle East, where he had witnessed the enslavement of whites, and as one interested solely in the perpetuation of the South's peculiar institution, Miles believed Southerners would do better to look to other sources than the Bible for their justifications of chattel slavery.[32]

Miles's analysis of slavery was a clear expression of his broader social and philosophical positions, for in discussing slavery he returned to his characteristic developmental view of history. Again he argued that human history was dynamic and unfolding, an evolutionary development that was ultimately the progressive embodiment of the divine plan for mankind. Reflection upon the record of human experience clearly revealed a division between successful and unsuccessful groups, or historical and nonhistorical races, as Miles preferred to call them. Why certain nations or races were advanced and successful versus backward and primitive was a secret known only to God, Miles admitted. Nevertheless, the difference was clear in Miles's view, and he identified the predominance of European stock over Middle Eastern, Asian, and Pacific races. Within Europe itself "the Teutonic races are the only natural soil of real Liberty," Miles wrote, for, with regard to the exercise of true liberty, "it is foolish to attempt to give to Irish, or French, or Hungarian, or Turk, or mongrel modern Greek or Italian what they cannot receive."[33]

Miles applied this distinction between historical and nonhistorical races to the relation of blacks and whites in the South in an extended essay he published in 1861. Simply entitled *The Relation between the Races of the South*, this pamphlet proposed an allegedly scientific justification for the institution of black slavery. Appealing to ethnological evidence, Miles defined slavery as the subjection through conquest or force of one race by an equally endowed opponent and pointed to captives from Israelite, Greek, and Roman military victories as examples of such slavery. On this account, however, Miles insisted that the "negro in the South is not properly a slave. He is really in his highest and most favorable position as a human creature."[34]

The meaning for Miles of this curious statement was that blacks had flourished in their subjugation in the South, especially in comparison with free blacks in the North and those blacks remaining in Africa. "Other races, inferior to the white race, such as the North American Indian, the inhabitants of the Pacific Ocean, etc. gradually perish away before the white race," Miles wrote, "but the black race alone, [is] thriving, becoming elevated, from the degrading slavery of savage heathenism to the participation in civilization and Christianity." Moreover, Miles maintained that, as a historical race, whites in the South fulfilled their duty by protecting and directing their bondsmen, while the blacks fulfilled their divinely appointed mission by cultivating the crops of cotton, rice, and sugar and by obeying their white masters.[35]

Significantly, although Miles dissented from the scriptural defense of Southern slavery, he did accept the traditional biblical account of one origin for all mankind and the universalism of the Christian offer of salvation for all, even blacks. Thus, like Hodge, Thornwell and Schaff, James Warley Miles acknowledged the master's responsibility for protection and spiritual instruction of his slaves. Yet, in a bow to the changing modes of thought in his day, Miles still insisted that the relation "of the white and black races is a matter of science, of induction, of historical observation." In thus focusing on the utility of scientific findings, Miles underscored his own belief in the compatibility of science and religion. Beyond that, while his justification for slavery was different from the polygenetic apologia of Josiah Nott, the biblical account of James Henley Thornwell, and the politico-economic defense of many Southern politicians, Miles's use of ethnological materials, his claims for a positive christianizing influence in black slavery, and his derogatory comparison of free blacks in the North with black slaves in the South made him an ally to all these other champions of Southern slavery.[36]

Since Southern blacks were really in their highest stage of development as bondsmen to white Southerners, Miles further maintained that any proposals for altering their conditions would be unwise. Not surprisingly, Miles strongly opposed the suggestion of Jefferson Davis in 1865 to arm the slaves and reward their participation in the defense of the Confederacy with emancipation. For the abolition of slavery in the South, Miles wrote, "would deprive us of the great conservative element in our institution, and we would rapidly run into that worst of all political conditions—an utter democracy—the very thing we are fighting against."[37]

Properly understood, the Confederate States were not intended as simply an experiment in states' rights and surely not as an example of popular democracy. Rather, in a college commencement speech, Miles contended that the true mission of the Confederacy was to embody "the foundations of a political organization, in which the freedom of every member is the result of law, is preserved by justice, is harmonized by the true relations of labor and capital, and is sanctified by the divine spirit of Christianity." At this level, then, Confederate conservatism stood opposed to the despotism of popular democracy and demagoguery, the exploitation of supposedly free labor, and the excesses of antinomian religion characteristic of the North. At another level, however, and here Miles had recourse to familiar themes from his other writings, the cause of the Confederacy represented the working out of "a great thought of God—namely the Higher Development of Humanity in its capacity for Constitutional Liberty. 'Humanity' is a conception of the Divine Mind and must be realized in its full import, in the progress of History and towards that realization our struggle is contributing."[38]

In short, for Miles the Confederate States had taken up that glorious and divine mission of presenting true, well-ordered liberty to the world, a task that had been originally entrusted to the American Republic but which it had failed to carry out successfully. Beyond that historical level the Confederacy represented a theological conception, one that attested to the nature and direction of God's presence in history. By casting his analysis of the Confederacy in terms of historical development and sacred duty, Miles not only located his defense squarely and consistently within the structures of his own overall philosophy; he also chimed in with those many other interpreters who saw divine purpose behind the Confederacy's existence.[39]

Ironically, then, conceptions of divine purpose and national mission understood within a framework of historical development had been the basis for both Philip Schaff's and James Warley Miles's respective understanding of the significance of the Civil War. Whereas Schaff saw the development and vindication of a union of diverse peoples arising out of the turmoil and bloodshed of the conflict, Miles saw the Confederacy emerging from the struggle, ennobled by its suffering, and providing a tempered example of the constitutional liberty, which was its own special calling. Both Schaff and Miles regarded their own conclusions as valid expressions of their philosophies of historical development, and both were influenced by several of the same distant European philosophical, literary, and theological resources.

Yet, to paraphrase Abraham Lincoln, though both of these historical theologians prayed to the same God and invoked his assistance for their cause, it was the Southern defeat that forced the Southerner, Miles, to review the meaning of Confederate reverses and their implications for his view of historical development. As late as January 1865, for example, Miles hoped for Confederate victory. Still, even if the Confederate forces were defeated, another nation in another time and place would be given the "mission of showing that man is capable of Constitutional Liberty." For, in spite of any provisional setbacks, "it is the ultimate triumph of this [i.e., the development of Constitutional Liberty] which I think it is treason to doubt."[40]

After Lee's surrender at Appomattox Miles joined many other Southern clergy and laity in blaming Southern losses ultimately on the failure of the Southern people to live righteous lives equal to the challenges presented to them. Such an interpretation was a piece of that broader pattern of Southern jeremiad, which explained the defeat in battle by reference to the failures and moral corruptions of the people. What distinguished Miles from many other postwar Southern religious leaders, however, was his retention of an ultimately optimistic view of historical development. For Southern religious thought, shaped by the individualism of the camp meeting, spiritualized by the pervasive dynamics of slavery, and now chastened by the loss of the war, assumed during the Reconstruction decades an even more pronounced premillennial cast, one that was pessimistic about earthly life and focused more and more earnestly on the rewards in the hereafter.[41]

For his part James Warley Miles continued to speak of historical development, yet, whereas previously he had represented this development exclusively in terms of progressive evolutionary growth, now he included setbacks and reversals in history. This new portrayal depicted history as "a cycloidal curve of successive ascents and descents, forming continued parallelisms, but each point of descent and ascent being in advance of the previous one." Change over time was still central to Miles's perspective, yet now he explicitly acknowledged the problem of evil and the reality of defeat within his metaphysics of historical development.[42]

Miles never lost that organic and optimistic view of human potential grounded in a theory of historical development. As late as 1874, one year before his death, Miles still envisioned the "perfect or complete development of the Idea of Humanity," that fulfillment of human possibility which originated with divine creation and which was always located in but never bound by the parameters of human history. Together, then, with Philip Schaff, James Warley Miles provided the "moral science" of antebellum America with one of its most comprehensive historical theoretical foundations.[43]

Podiums, Pulpits, and the Future of the Republic

By contrast with Hodge and Thornwell or Schaff and Miles, the social commentary of James Marsh was limited. Marsh died in 1842, and, thus, while he faced many political and religious conflicts, he was spared the anguish of the secession crisis and the Civil War. Marsh's most forceful social observations appear in his reflections on the nature and goals of education in the young American Republic. For education—its purposes, meaning, and content—was a lifelong avocational interest of Marsh as well as an object of explicit professional concern during his sixteen-year association with the University of Vermont.

In a characteristic statement Marsh once declared that the aim of education was not "to shape and fit the powers of the mind to this or that outward condition in the mechanism of civil society, but by means corresponding to their inherent nature, to excite, to encourage, affectionately to aid the free and perfect development of those powers themselves." Marsh's emphasis was on the highest development of the full range of potentialities that the individual possessed. Spiritual, intellectual, and aesthetic capacities were each developed and harmonized with the other. Yet such a process concluded not simply in the solipsistic exaltation of the individual but, rather, finally in the liberation of the human spirit. For Marsh insisted that the full development of the individual inevitably produced the cultivation of the community and the emancipation of humanity.[44]

Marsh's views of education were probably influenced again by Samuel Taylor Coleridge and the Englishman's conception of the capacities of Reason and Understanding, now pressed in their organic complementarity into the service of a pedagogy of the individual and society. Interestingly, Marsh's opinions about education paralleled those of his Continental contemporary Wilhelm von Humboldt and of that German tradition of *Bildung*, of which von Humboldt was such a conspicuous example. For the life of this Prussian nobleman and educator stressed conscious striving for self-cultivation, by which was meant the highest possible development of the self into a well-proportioned whole. Service to others, as such, was not emphasized but was expected naturally to develop and to find appropriate expression.[45]

Much of Marsh's educational philosophy was prefigured in his own educational experience. He entered Dartmouth College in 1813 and graduated four years later. These were precisely the years of institutional upheaval which resulted in the famous Dartmouth College Case. In this conflict the Federalist trustees of Dartmouth College squared off against the newly elected Democratic legislature of Vermont. After the trustees fired the president of the college the legislature impounded the buildings, revenues, and seal of the college. In the end, after Daniel Webster's celebrated plea on behalf of the trustees, Chief Justice John Marshall ruled in the trustees' favor. Thus, for some time James Marsh, along with his classmates, attended a college that did not formally exist. In these circumstances the students gathered with their professors for improvised lectures, met with each other for discussion, and often studied alone. Here out of the exigencies at Dartmouth came a pattern of education which allowed self-cultivation, individual preparation, and informal group meetings for reading and discussion. It was a model of instruction which Marsh was to use often in his life and one that he found well suited to that development of the powers of the human spirit, which was his goal for education.[46]

After further study at Andover Theological Seminary and a tutorship at Hampden-Sydney College in Virginia, Marsh was appointed to the presidency of the University of Vermont in 1826. Marsh served as president for seven years before resigning to become professor of moral and intellectual philosophy on the Vermont faculty. Marsh's tenure as president was marked by his initiation of a series of curricular reforms, all of which aimed at his goal of individual development and many of which had been tried previously during his Dartmouth days.

Moreover, the times seemed ripe for reform in higher education, for, as one historian has written, American higher education "required adaptation to the needs of a developing republican society." Reform proposals ran from simple course modifications to the whole-scale establishment of institutions. The work of European educators, such as Johann Pestalozzi and Friedrich Froebel, with their concern for the nurturing influence of primary education, or the news of Wilhelm von Humboldt's reorganization of the Prussian education including the establishment of the University of Berlin, provided important examples for American educational reformers. Closer to home, George Ticknor's reshaping of the curriculum into departments at Harvard, Eliphalet Nott's emphasis at Union College on parallel study of modern languages and natural science, and Thomas Jefferson's role in the founding of the University of Virginia also contributed to the reform spirit in higher education.[47]

New England collegiate education was also undergoing a social transformation, one that gave pedagogical reform an extra impetus. The model of education at the early American colleges, such as Harvard and Yale, was built on the expectation that a class of young men, all of whom had roughly the same preparation and knowledge of required texts, would attend classes and live together in a residential college under faculty supervision until their graduation more or less as a cohort four years later. Yet, by the end of the eighteenth century, this pattern of collegiate education was dissolving, particularly in the newer education institutions outside of Cambridge and New Haven. Changes were underway in schools such as Brown, Williams, Bowdoin, Amherst, and Vermont, schools with less direct connection to traditional European models of college education and greater proximity to that exodus during the post-Revolutionary era of young persons moving off the farm and into new social settings. The upshot was that New England colleges, such as the University of Vermont, faced a social transformation of their student body, as persons diversely prepared, too poor to afford room and board costs, and older than the typical pre-Revolution student shattered the preconditions of the former pedagogical paradigm.[48]

Marsh's reforms as president reflected both the general desire for change and the contemporary developments concerning his own institution. Marsh wanted, for example, to classify students not by their class year but, rather, by their attainments within the curriculum. In this perspective students would move at the pace of their own development and complete their degrees in accordance with their talents and application. Additionally, Marsh called for admitting part-time students and others who wished to pursue a nondegree program of study.

Though such proposals were anathema to the well-ordered march of four-year cohort graduation, they obviously reflected the change in circumstances and the partial demise of those earlier educational expectations. Finally, Marsh advocated a greater degree of choice among subjects by students and, very importantly, shifted the focus of discipline from faculty-inflicted penalties to faculty-led attempts at moral persuasion and simple expulsion from the institution for those too obdurate.[49]

In his inaugural address in 1826, as president of the university, Marsh expressed the broader social view that provided the foundation for these specific educational reforms. Pervading his address was an emphasis on education as an active process, one designed to excite, encourage, and nurture the development of the student's mental abilities. This process recognized, in good Coleridgean fashion, the differing capacities of Reason and Understanding and proceeded to shape instruction with the differing nature of the two in mind. Curriculum was not molded exclusively by present issues and conflicts, nor did it seek to conform to or mimic ancient pedagogical models. Rather, sensitive to the free play of imagination and the development of individual insight, proper education infused the student with the spirit of well-ordered liberty.[50]

Marsh had high praise for the American system of free public education. Indeed, he contrasted the "spirit of society among a free people" with that "among a passive and humbled peasantry" and furthermore criticized the examples of Athens and Rome for the narrow slave-based foundations upon which their greatness was based. This nationalist gesture on Marsh's part not only expressed his pride in America's educational accomplishments in comparison to Europe and the ancient world; it also signaled the break by the Romantics from that mode of literary classicism and New World parochialism which always measured America against these standards and usually found it wanting. Here again pride in America's accomplishments and optimism in its future underscored the variety of pedagogical reforms ranging from Noah Webster's American speller to Horace Mann's design for free public education.[51]

Finally, Marsh applauded education as an agent of rejuvenation for American society. In theory, at least, free public education helped to equalize all classes and individuals and to substitute for hereditary privilege "the free and fair competition of talents in the general struggle for advancement" as the only arena for conflict. Beyond that Marsh supported the nascent, and by 1826 now nearly complete, legal separation of church and state. Like that other Federalist, the Connecticut patriarch Lyman Beecher, Marsh had happily come to find the role of religion growing within American society, undergirded by voluntary support and expanding steadily in the profusion of voluntary benevolent associations. That many of these associations interpreted education and culture in a sectarian spirit and that American education did not truly erase distinctions of class, race, and gender should not obscure the purpose of Marsh's statements. For education in his view was a tool for the reform rather than the static preservation of society, and its scope encompassed the laborer as much as the literati.[52]

Although James Marsh's social commentary was focused on the concept of education as self-development and cultivation, it is still possible to press out the broader implications of his views for a wider set of issues. Marsh criticized slavery, for example, but not for its barbarity nor for its disjunction with the Gospel. Instead, in occasional letters he condemned it for its inhibition or prevention of the full development of the human capacity in the individual. In making a historical observation, Marsh had insisted that ancient Athens and Rome could never really prosper, could never really achieve full development, so long as they maintained slavery. So too, on the basis of his personal experience as a tutor at Hampden-Sydney in Virginia, Marsh explained that all plans for moral or intellectual improvement in the South were mocked, if not destroyed outright, by the heavy incubus of slavery. Thus, he hoped to write an antislavery tract to contribute his part "to wipe away the dark stain of slavery," thereby enabling America as a whole to strive truly to become "the soberest, wisest, and most Christian people of these latter days."[53]

The prospects for American Christianity in "these latter days" was likewise a topic of anxious debate in the first third of the nineteenth century. Camp meetings in Kentucky, collegiate conversions supervised by Timothy Dwight and Nathaniel W. Taylor at Yale, and urban revivalism under the direction of Charles Grandison Finney were the best-known expressions of religious activity during the Second Great Awakening. Yet, just as Jonathan Edwards had his James Davenport, so too did leaders such as Finney have their even less restrained and even more extravagant imitators. At least that was Marsh's opinion when, in the winter of 1835, an itinerant evangelist by the name of Jedidiah Burchard roared into Burlington.

In 1815, at the age of twenty-one, Marsh had his own conversion experience. It had been a model of slow and painful soul-searching, an examination for signs of grace more akin to the spiritual excavations of the Puritans than the "worked-up" means of Finney. Six years later, in a revealing letter to his fiancée, Marsh confessed to continuing doubts about his faith. Though he was not "wholly indifferent to experimental piety," his chosen path of scholarly study and investigation precluded the unquestioning confidence of the "simple unlearned Christian, who knows only his Bible." Such a person sees nothing of "the ten thousand distracting questions, the harrowing doubts and maddening skepticism" that habitually afflict the scholar. Moreover, most who engage in scholarship never even raise fundamental questions but, instead, coast "the shores of this mighty deep in the cockboat of their own opinionated self-confidence." And those few who do persevere will be counseled to dance to "some German metaphysical bagpipe," to listen exclusively to their emotions, or just as readily to let Reason alone guide them. In all of this Marsh was again displaying his emphasis on education as a process of development, be that the development of the spiritual or the intellectual capacities of the individual.[54]

As Marsh stood by and watched, the revivalist Burchard remained in Burlington for several days. His efforts typically caused much controversy, and he found support among many who were impressed with the results of his work and accepted his justification for the revival in terms of the numbers converted. While Marsh did not deny that some of these conversions might be genuine, it was clear that he regarded Burchard's efforts as superficial. For Marsh the religious life was a struggle of energetic, almost titanic proportions and always more than the simple emotional indulgence and pragmatic justification that he saw so prominently featured in the message of contemporary revivalism. True spirituality, Marsh insisted, included Reason and Understanding, heart and head, in a reconciliation that was deep, genuine, and authentic.

If Marsh sought mediation in religious experience, he sought moderation in politics. He expressed characteristic reservations about political action during the nearby Canadian Rebellion of 1837. In this complicated conflict, which took place in both Upper and Lower Canada, specific constitutional, ethnic, and religious claims were pressed in the context of a general call for political reform. Many New Englanders watched from the sidelines. Others joined the fight when rebel leaders slipped across the border into the United States and organized filibustering expeditions some dozen years before William Walker and others made the term even better known in Central America. Finally, in 1838 the United States government took action to halt further American participation, and the revolt soon ended.[55]

In correspondence with his son-in-law, David Read, Marsh disapproved of the rebellion and denounced the Americans who joined it. His basic premise was that government in general ought to be supported unless truly tyrannical acts had been committed. For Marsh the British colonial government had perpetrated no such deed and, in fact, was training Canadians for their own future self-government. Significantly, Marsh suggested that the Democratic administrations of Andrew Jackson and Martin Van Buren, and not some foreign power, were the real examples of high-handed demagoguery and had brought America to "the very brink of anarchy and revolution." In line with many former New England Federalists and present-day Whigs, Marsh saw little good or wise coming out of the politics of Jackson and his appeal to the common man.[56]

A final slant on Marsh's social views can be gained by examining his relationship with New England transcendentalism. As noted previously, Marsh had a low estimate of the philosophical profundity of the Concord group. Beyond that Marsh considered George Ripley's communal experiment at Brook Farm to be woefully misguided. "They aspire," Marsh observed, "to redeem the world by a sort of dilettanti process, to purge off grossness, to make a poetical paradise in which hard work shall become easy, dirty things clean, the selfish liberal, and the churl a churl no longer." However noble such dreams, they were fundamentally at variance, in Marsh's view, with the basic fact of human selfishness.[57]

Ultimately, neither political revolution nor social reconstruction were the correct paths for reform in Marsh's view. Instead, education—construed as spiritual liberation, as freedom from the bondage to natural selfishness, as that reconciliation between self and society such that each shall do that which is the best good for all—provided true and lasting reform. Marsh believed that such emancipation represented the most genuine fruits of Christianity, and it was an enterprise to which he gave his best energies as a scholar, an educator, and a Christian.

In 1856, during a visit to the West Coast, Horace Bushnell was offered the presidency of the University of California. Bushnell declined the position in order to remain as pastor of North Church in

Hartford, Connecticut. Whereas James Marsh saw in education his agent for true social change, Horace Bushnell preferred the power of the pulpit as the means for shaping society.

Bushnell was a successful and influential preacher, and one prominent theme in his public addresses concerned the moral basis of society and the conditions for true American nationhood. In expounding upon this issue, Bushnell drew on a framework of Romantic nationalism similar in many respects to that of Schaff, Miles, and Marsh. Though the circumstances might vary during the second third of the nineteenth century, when many of these occasional essays were written, a recurring set of ideas and images shaped Bushnell's discourse, giving consistency to his social thought and gaining him a wide audience in antebellum America.

Writing in 1843 on the moral character of the age, Bushnell described the progressive development of human society from the satisfaction of exclusively physical needs to the fulfillment of moral requirements. This symbolic growth from the primitive to the civilized state was slow and often uneven; Bushnell, however, had no doubts that the direction of human society was toward improvement. Such optimistic commentary was often found in early nineteenth-century America, particularly among the many supporters of the benevolent empire, that legacy of the Second Great Awakening which had spawned so many evangelical reform associations for the improvement of human society.

Yet, like the majority of these other supporters, Bushnell was careful to insist that, while he was optimistic about the future social direction, he harbored no notions of Christian or humanist perfectionism. Charles Grandison Finney or John Humphrey Noyes might speak in those terms, but Horace Bushnell was a reasonable son of New England and was made of sterner stuff. Moreover, Bushnell insisted that the forces of evil were still strong and ever present, and, thus, watchfulness and courage were the orders of the day. In the end, however, the dominion of evil will give way, and Bushnell indulged his audience in a vision of the future when "beauty, reason, science, personal worth, and religion will come into their rightful supremacy, and moral forces will preside over physical and mind over body."[58]

Bushnell played out this confident depiction of social development in a number of ways. He emphasized, for example, that society was a developmental and organic entity, not a mechanical aggregation nor a voluntaristic agreement built on a social contract. Too much of contemporary politics, weaned on Jefferson and Jackson's rhetoric of democratic sensibilities, refused to recognize the value of this alternative approach. The result, Bushnell suggested, was an electorate "morally drunk at the polls," one so intoxicated by the appeal of the moment as to be oblivious to such obligations as decades-old treaties with the Indians and so enamored with present opportunities as to ignore any warnings of long-term dangers. Indulging in a favorite complaint of the Whigs against Andrew Jackson and his followers, Bushnell castigated the introduction of party discipline and the spoils system, remarking that this "party spirit" had become so prevalent as to nearly snuff out any signs of conscience or independent thinking. While such criticisms contained no small measure of Whig rhetoric within them, they did underscore the location of Bushnell's social conservatism within early nineteenth-century American politics, and they highlighted his prescriptive view of society, in that favorite image of the Romantics, as an organic body, maturing in shape and content through time.[59]

If deep roots and slow growth were the signs of a healthy organic society, then the counterimage was a society confused, stunted, and cut off from its vital sources. While party politics agitated Bushnell, a deeper menace to the moral sources of society, a more radical evil threatening organic society, emanated from what he called the "bowie-knife style of civilization." This was the challenge of America's expansion into western lands, territories, and states, and its implications terrified Bushnell. Instead of naturally paced development, Bushnell saw the artificial growth of the hothouse, and the result too often, in his opinion, was social barbarism. Here, on the frontier, only temporarily acknowledged concerns rather than deep and vital traditions united people. Here religious views were narrow and animosities always bitter. Here the knife and the gun, vigilantism and hastily passed legislation, sought to provide law and order. Here flourished a type of individual, "prompt to resent an injury, slack to discharge a debt; educated to ease, and readier, of course, when the means of living fail, to find them at the gambling table or the race grounds than in any work of industry." Here was a world, in short, which was totally at odds with the urbane, middle-class environment that Bushnell experienced, valued, and projected into his writings.[60]

While for many Americans Romantic nationalism justified territorial expansion in the name of the civilization of so-called savage or inferior cultures, it caused Bushnell to ponder the capacity of the

American nation to incorporate even more territory and peoples. The Mexican War particularly provoked Bushnell into further reflection, and he concluded that the war originated in ignoble causes. Consequently, its successful prosecution would only further advance the forces of barbarism within the American body politic. For, especially in his antebellum writings, there was a consistent identification by Bushnell of American destiny with white, Anglo-Saxon Protestants. In 1837, for example, he rhapsodized over America as "the theater wherein better principles might have room and free development. Out of all the inhabitants of the world, too, a select stock, the Saxon, and out of this the British family, the noblest of the stock, was chosen to people our country." America's destiny was ill served by territorial aggrandizement, which thwarted the possibility of truly achieving that destiny by incorporating large tracts of sparsely inhabited lands and alien peoples.[61]

The racial dimension in Bushnell's thinking came out most prominently in his discussion of black slavery. Bushnell's writings on slavery fit into his other writings, for again the twin themes of confrontation with evil in the achievement of America's destiny as well as a racial casting to his Romantic nationalism are evident. Bushnell believed that slavery was an evil that ought to be opposed by Christians and all persons of goodwill and conscience. He stated that Southern slavery's treatment of slaves denied the institutions of marriage and family, offered little or no protection to the individual, and repudiated blacks as fellow creatures of God along with whites. Despite these criticisms, Bushnell also opposed the techniques of the abolitionists and called on Northerners to extend "sympathy and gentleness" to the slaveholders of the South.[62]

Instead of abolitionist direct action, Bushnell looked to patient individual counsel with slaveholders to convince them to give up their slaves. Beyond that he believed that slavery would eventually die away on its own if it were not allowed to exist in the new territories. Indeed, in 1857, upon hearing of the successes of antislavery forces in Kansas, Bushnell exclaimed, "human slavery is now doomed in the United States, doomed not by any philanthropic scheme of abolition, but doomed to feel a pressure on its border . . . so as to give way, lose confidence, crumble in fatal demoralization, and finally to cease and be a fact forgot."[63]

And yet there was a double edge to Bushnell's argument. For, if demographic pressure and territorial confinement spelled the doom of slavery, he believed the situation of postemancipation America spelled extinction for blacks. Though some Americans looked forward to a time of racial harmony and beneficence, Bushnell saw competition and conflict between whites and blacks in this new future era. Citing the decimation of the Native American population (but neglecting to indicate the diseases, liquor, and land frauds introduced and initiated by whites, which were its real causes), Bushnell predicted a similar fate for blacks by concluding: "there is no example in history, where an uncultivated and barbarous stock has been elevated in the midst of a cultivated and civilized stock. . . . my expectation is that the African race, in this country would soon begin to dwindle towards extinction in the same way."[64]

Like Schaff and Miles, then, Horace Bushnell saw the genius of the American nation through the lens of a Romantic racial nationalism, one that for him placed leadership and responsibility squarely in the hands of white, Anglo-Saxon Protestants. Other groups played symbolic roles in the pageant of the world, though for Bushnell they were often only antagonists to the Anglo-Saxons—for example, the Irish, who Bushnell dismissed as the inhabitants of "alms-houses, and prisons, and potter's fields," or else figurative predecessors such as the Greeks and Romans. Conflict with evil, or at least confrontations with obstacles to improvement, likewise characterized Schaff's, Miles's, and Bushnell's views, though here again Bushnell often portrayed these conflicts in terms heavily symbolic rather than precisely historical. Finally, Schaff, Miles, and Bushnell all shared a fundamental optimism about the "moral tendencies and results of human history," as Bushnell once put it. They shared a providential interpretation of human history which placed America (or at least the South for Miles) in the role of a new Israel, a nation chosen, protected, and ultimately redeemed by God.[65]

The full meaning of Bushnell's confidence in America's destiny and the nation's place in human history can only be appreciated with reference to his analysis of the meaning of the Civil War. In 1864, for example, in a Thanksgiving Day address, Bushnell assigned himself the task of taking the measure and exploring the meaning of this agonizing national test. Once again he reminded his audience that the government, whatever its form, had its origin in eternal laws of right and divine principles of morality. Too many had believed that governments were formed out of human consent, and the upshot of this incorrect view had been the blasphemous doctrines of states' rights and secession. Consequently, for Bushnell the war was being fought to reunite the Union, to vindicate America's destiny as a people, and to reestablish the loyalty of the American nation to the true principles of morality and religion.[66]

Bushnell next sketched out the progress of America's political development. As with his earlier pronouncements, this process was blocked by obstacles, and the stages were heavily weighted with symbolic meaning rather than literal significance. As with many other Romantic nationalists, Bushnell located the true origins of nationhood in a remote and dim past—in the case of America in the distant days of Anglo-Saxon England. From these providential beginnings the American colonists first declared their independence, thereby signaling their own appearance on the stage of world events. Next came the formation of the Constitution at Philadelphia, at which time a consciousness of Americans as a distinct people, a distinct nation with its own special genius, was forming and thereby displacing an earlier regional or state allegiance. Both the Declaration of Independence and the Constitution were for Bushnell symbolic moments when national unity and identity overcame a wide array of challenges and achieved a deeper and more sustained existence.

The present crisis, Bushnell declared, represented the third stage in America's development. The conflict had been costly, but the cause was important. True liberty would be realized as the "pestilent heresy" of states' rights was exterminated. Black slavery might be ended, though emancipation of the slaves was not in Bushnell's opinion the primary goal of the Union forces. Yet who could doubt, Bushnell added, that God marched with the Federal armies, for "every drumbeat is a hymn, the cannon thunder God, the electric silence, darting victory along the wires, is the inaudible greeting of God's favoring word and purpose." The scales of righteousness assayed the Union's cause, and Bushnell hoped that the people of the North would not be found wanting in their willingness to sacrifice even to the last measure on behalf of the war effort.[67]

In July 1865, shortly after the cessation of formal hostilities, Bushnell offered another set of reflections on the meaning of the war. Entitled "Our Obligations to the Dead," he reasserted that the war had been a crusade to vindicate national unity and that the dead had fallen for a worthy cause. Indeed, in describing the soldiers' sacrifices, Bushnell accorded them the martyr's homage, for through their baptism of blood a new union had been consecrated and sanctified. As he

developed his meditation, Bushnell expanded on the new opportunities and the renewed responsibilities that were placed before
America. Out of the trials of the war had come a deepened understanding of America's destiny, for this had been a people's war and not simply
campaigns by a military elite. Out of these challenges had emerged a
self-confident American nation, inspired by its history and ready now
to take its place among the nations. Finally, though the Southern states
must expect some fair measure of further chastisement for their sins,
the true challenge for American society, having successfully passed
through this Armageddon, was "to champion, by land and sea, the
right of this whole continent to be an American world, and to have its
own American laws and liberties, and institutions." Now no longer
doubtful of America's ability to incorporate other lands and peoples
and flushed with a confidence that perceived divine purpose in military victory and divine sanction in soldiers' graves, Horace Bushnell
saw the symbolic consummation of America's past and its legacy for
the future in the outcome of the war.[68]

Thus, through biblical exegesis, historical theory, and symbolic interpretation, the mediational theologians made a substantial contribution to the moral science of mid-nineteenth-century American
culture. Like much of their thought generally, this contribution drew
on European intellectual resources and adapted those resources to the
American scene. Finding applications for their various hermeneutical
strategies for the reconciliation of science and religion in the pressing
social issues of the day, these mediational theologians interwove divine
purpose and human history, they invoked scientific authority for their
moral pronouncements, and they drew conservative conclusions from
their social experience.

Yet, as the Gilded Age of American history began, this intertwining
between science and religion which they had worked so hard to craft
was already coming apart. Perceptive observers noted that strong challenges continued to assail the union of science and religion. These
observers were agreed, however, that an even more powerful challenge
had emerged, a challenge they summarized in just one word: *Darwin*.

Epilogue

The publication of the *Origin of Species* in 1859 and the ensuing debates over its meaning and significance are usually taken as marking the beginning of a new chapter in the history of biological sciences. Whatever its impact in the sciences, Darwin's book certainly accelerated the controversy between science and religion in America, as it posed new challenges to the reigning cultural consensus regarding the reconciliation of science and religion.

Indeed, even a cursory reading of Darwin's volume displayed its variance with the inherited tradition of interpretation. Whereas American Protestants had perceived the world in categories of moral freedom and the exercise of personal responsibility, Darwin described an unremitting biological determinism. Whereas American Protestants had viewed nature as a vast illustration of that purposeful revelation that formed the basis of natural theology, Darwin pictured the natural processes as often violent and always random. All biological life was the result of chance variation, rather than of superintending and providential beneficence. Finally, whereas American Protestants had regarded the human species as the crown of creation and the image of divinity, Darwin insisted on the continuity and uniform applicability of the laws of nature and vehemently denied any possibility of special creation or other unique divine actions within biological history.

Embedded in the elaboration of the implications of these post-Darwinian considerations was what one historian has called a gradual epistemic shift from a supernaturalist to a positivist point of view. In the biological and physical sciences, for example, such a positivist perspective assumed the uniformity of natural laws and causes rather than the possibility of special divine interruptions into the natural sphere, it rejected teleological explanations for ones grounded in scientific examination and verification, and, finally, it understood the goal of scientific inquiry to be explanation of phenomenon and, by extension, the accumulation and refinement of these explanatory generalizations into laws of science. Here again such laws reflected observable regularities in behavior and action, rather than a priori conclusions regarding divine will. In this way patterns of emotional and intellectual authority and structures of legitimation and validation shifted slowly from religious to scientific frames of reference.[1]

The exemplary power of the developments in the biological and physical sciences could be seen in the adoption of this positivist epistemology in the humanities as well. In American literature the fiction of Hamlin Garland, Stephen Crane, Frank Norris, Jack London, and later Theodore Dreiser all strived to reflect the new scientific spirit of the age in their naturalistic, realistic depictions of life. Parallel developments could be seen in the rise of scientific history, with its willingness to dispense with references to the Holy Spirit as a causal explanation in human history. Instead, transferring the empiricism, objectivity, and naturalism of the laboratory into their own historical seminars and studies, historians such as Herbert Baxter Adams, Justin Winsor, Ephraim Emerton, Williston Walker, and Arthur C. McGiffert sought to purify the historical discipline of both pietistic perceptions of providential interventions and categories of organic purposefulness. The chasm between this understanding of historical inquiry and the earlier Romantic developmentalism of Philip Schaff, W. G. T. Shedd, and James Warley Miles was nearly insurmountable.[2]

Further implications of this shift in standpoint could be seen in the emergence of the scientific study of the Bible and the development of historical-critical methods of textual exegesis. To be sure, the earlier philological investigations of James Warley Miles had challenged the logic and cogency of the popular bibliolatry within American Protestantism, and Horace Bushnell's emphasis on the symbolic nature of much biblical language could likewise dislodge a literal reading of texts. Moreover, the introduction of German biblical criticism by many of the mediational theologians may have helped to gain recognition for these approaches in the last decades of the nineteenth century. Here again, however, the adoption of a positivist approach construed in terms of an exclusively historical and genetic attitude toward those texts was quite different from that of Bushnell or Marsh or Miles, whose real question concerned the appropriation of these symbolically complicated but always available texts by a modern reader.[3]

Thus, by last quarter of the nineteenth century ways of thinking in American society, and especially in the scientific community, were changing. Reverential invocations of Baconianism seemed anachronistic, and familiar assumptions that the scientist should simply gather facts rather than test explanatory hypotheses seemed equally out of place. Moreover, conceptions of explanation which saw purpose in nature were now often dismissed as speculative holdovers from Romantic philosophy. Philosophy, as such, might still have something to say, but the chances were good that the books cited now were those by Herbert Spencer or John Fiske. And, if dynamic teleology had given way to statistical regularity as the basis for promulgating scientific laws, so too had the understanding of science as a broad-based critical inquiry into the world of nature been eclipsed by the conviction that science had become a realm for specialized inquiry.

Along with these conceptual revisions there were social transformations that were also significant. For, coincident with the post-Darwinian debates, there occurred in American science a change in the profile of the scientist. Previously, the ranks of American science contained and often commended amateur investigators, individuals without formal scientific training but with an avid interest in the natural world and an eagerness to explain its significance. During the second and especially the last third of the nineteenth century American science became more professional, and its practitioners received more formal training in their fields. Graduate education became the norm, and the image of the university-trained and -employed scientist replaced that of the autodidactic amateur. Along with this upgrading in the training of individuals came a specialization in the areas of competence. The study of natural history, for example, gave way to the emergence of scientific botany and zoology, and, as the field of expertise shrank, so did the willingness of the scientific community and increasing sectors of the American public at large to recognize pronouncements by individuals outside their area of qualification.[4]

The professionalization of American science challenged the authority of the Protestant ministry. Lacking the credentials that verified their competence to speak on scientific issues, Protestant ministers often found their remarks dismissed in discussions and evaluations of the findings of science. This diminution of ministerial authority helps to explain the limelight that men such as Louis Agassiz and Asa Gray enjoyed. Both were trained scientists, members of the faculty at Harvard University, and, although Agassiz was a critic of Darwin while Gray was a supporter, the attention that they received in the popular press and religious circles reflected their roles as accredited scientific referees in a controversy that increasingly recognized the authority of properly credentialed experts.[5]

The waning of ministerial influence in the face of these conceptual and social changes was not ignored. Henry Ward Beecher, for example, called on his clerical colleagues to confront the new challenges posed by recent scientific findings and to infuse their ministries with a fresh spirit of investigation and openness. "You cannot wrap yourselves in professional mystery," Beecher warned, and failure to engage the issues of the day would quickly relegate ministers to intellectual obsolescence. "If ministers do not make their theological systems conform to facts as they are, if they do not recognize what men are studying," then, Beecher predicted, "the time will not be so far distant when the pulpit will be like the voice crying in the wilderness. And it will not be 'Prepare the way of the Lord,' either."[6]

Beecher often serves as the emblem of the successful Gilded Age Protestant preacher. Willing to accept the conclusions of recent scientific results, albeit in simplified and popularized form, Beecher became one of the great Gilded Age princes of the pulpit, along with Phillips Brooks and Russell Conwell. For, as Beecher, Brooks, and Conwell demonstrated, even if preachers lacked scientific expertise, they could still exert leadership and influence through the pulpit. Earlier in the century Edwards Amasa Park had sought this goal and identified the need for homiletic eloquence as the best way to achieve the result. Park insisted that doctrinal integrity should not be sacrificed; he underscored the need, however, for graceful presentation together with intellectual rigor and evangelical fervor in reaching the men and women of the day. In individuals such as Beecher and Brooks it was not simply doctrinal purity or even rhetorical brilliance but also the personality of the preacher which became the cement holding congregations together. And, whereas the preacher united the congregation in worship, assembling the parishioners for social and devotional purposes in a newly added church parlor brought them together during the course of the week. Innovations in style and setting, then, played a role in the reconfiguration of American Protestantism in the decades after the Civil War.[7]

Beyond these homiletic and sociological strategies to exert continuing influence on the lives of their parishioners, new directions in theology also became apparent. In general the shift amounted to a move in Christian theology away from metaphysics, away from proofs for divine existence based on analogies in nature, away from attempts to ape scientific standards of experimental verification, and toward an appraisal of that deep wellspring of the religious experience of God. Here the focus was on the inner murmurs of the heart, the conscience of the individual, or, writ large, the historical moral sense of humanity.

William Newton Clarke's *An Outline of Christian Theology* (1901) not only signaled his theological indebtedness to Schleiermacher and Bushnell but also the dogmatic reorientation of theology, when he made religious experience the foundation of Christian theology. Here was a realm outside the purview of the scientists, a sphere of self-authenticating sensibilities whose unique qualities defied the calculus of scientific explanation. By relocating theology in experience, in moral sentiment, and in individual conscience, these Protestant theologians implicitly recognized the now familiar distinction between knowledge and belief, verification and faith, at the same time that they also sought to safeguard the authority of the clergy in a realm beyond the grasp of science.[8]

Historians of religion in America have extensively mapped the landscape of the post-Darwinian controversies. In the center of this terrain stand the sturdy perennials of modernism and fundamentalism, each with identifiable limbs branching off a central trunk. On either side of these, overshadowed perhaps but still discernible, are the luxuriant flora of harmonial religion and the sparser sprigs of the religion of science. In this context the mediational theologians played an important, if sometimes unintended, role in providing nutritious resources for the development of the territory generally, and especially modernism and fundamentalism.

The mediational theologians were not sympathetic to Darwinism. Philip Schaff, James Warley Miles, and W. G. T. Shedd, for example, although they all championed a developmental view of history which would seem compatible with the whole thrust of evolution, ultimately differed profoundly with Darwin. Indeed, even though the word *evolution* can be found in their writings, Schaff, Miles, and Shedd depicted human history in teleological terms. Categories of providential purpose and assumptions of divine superintendence structured their theologies of historical development. Consequently, with their deep roots in European romanticism and the historical traditions of nineteenth-century German theology, with their emphasis on images of the organic development of inherent principles, the perspective of Schaff, Miles, and Shedd contrasted sharply with Darwin's insistence on random development in response to the demands of the external environment.

Here it should be noted that the debate over the purposefulness or randomness of evolution was also one of the principal objections to Darwin's theory within the scientific community. As historians of science have pointed out in some detail, although Darwin's theory ultimately found wide acceptance, its popularity during the nineteenth century seesawed between supporters and opponents. Thus, even among those scientists sympathetic to evolution disputes over the mechanism of evolution continued into the twentieth century.[9]

The reality of divisions within the scientific community became clear with the emergence during the last quarter of the nineteenth century of American neo-Lamarckism. In the work of Alpheus Hyatt, Edward Drinker Cope, and Alpheus Packard the assertion of purpose in evolutionary development found scientific backing. Hyatt and Packard had studied with Louis Agassiz, while Cope was clearly influenced by the Harvard scientist. With its emphasis on adaptive behavior, which was then passed on to later generations, with its insistence upon purposeful development rather than random variations, Lamarckism represented a scientific alternative to Darwinian natural selection which many religious believers found attractive.[10]

Writing in 1868, Horace Bushnell also took the measure of Darwin's writings and found them wanting. True to his antebellum precedents, Bushnell maintained that science and religion were reconcilable, for "God is in the book of science, quite as certainly as in the book of religion . . . being the same God in both, no truth can ever be discovered in one, that contradicts, or at all impinges on, the truth from the other." He further noted that many scientists seemed to take delight in raising issues critical of traditional religious doctrines, while some religious believers cringed at the announcement of every new scientific discovery. Seeking to reassure his readers, Bushnell suggested that most of the scientific controversies of the day could be resolved through proper scriptural interpretation and done so "without any sense of loss, or diminished respect for revelation."[11]

One class of controversies, however, contained more disturbing and far-reaching consequences. This was the Darwinian claim that species could change and transmute. The issue was straightforward for Bushnell: "what is science, anyhow, but the knowledge of species? And if species do not keep their places, but go a masking or really becoming one another, in strange transmutations, what is there to know, and where is the possibility of science?" Here again such criticism had its counterpart in the contemporary scientific community. For acceptance of the theory of the fixity of species was commonplace in scientific circles since the seventeenth century, and, if it was finally to give way to evolutionary theory, such a change was not yet complete during

Bushnell's lifetime. Thus, in his own mind Bushnell could consistently argue that true science and religion were indeed compatible, for Darwin's theory was not simply deceptive but flat-out wrong. True science, he insisted, would not give up on a stable and fixed natural order, and science and religion could remain united in their pursuit of truth.[12]

The nature of true science also concerned Charles Hodge, and in 1874 he weighed in within his extended essay *What is Darwinism?* In developing his analysis Hodge was careful to distinguish Darwin the scientist from Darwinism the theory. Hodge described Darwin as "simply a naturalist, a careful and laborious observer; skillful in his descriptions and singularly candid in dealing with the difficulties in the way of his peculiar doctrine." Moreover, Hodge noted that, "to account for the existence of matter and life, Mr. Darwin admits a Creator." Thus, unlike some popular critics of Darwin, Hodge and the mediational theologians engaged neither in ad hominem arguments nor slanderous innuendo to make their criticisms.[12]

Having distinguished the messenger from the message, Hodge unabashedly denounced Darwinism as atheism. In so doing Hodge pointed to three issues that clinched the case in his view. First, Darwinism was incompatible with biblical accounts of the nature and destiny of mankind. Hodge recognized, however, that the *Origin of Species* was not a work of biblical exegesis or theology and so left this criticism undeveloped. Second, Darwin's scientific methodology was not inductive, and therefore his theory was nothing more than a speculative hypothesis. Reflecting his lifelong commitment to Scottish Common Sense and his insistence that all true science must be inductive, Hodge dismissed Darwin's claims as unworthy of the stature of science. Darwin's own admission that the fossil record was often too sketchy to verify species transmutation again suggests that scientific controversies as well as religious commitments played a role in the responses to Darwin. Finally, Hodge came to the main point of his argument—namely, Darwin's exclusion of design. For Hodge insisted that to deny design or purpose in the natural world was tantamount to denying the existence and Providence of God. Here again the issue of design was crucial, particularly for the manner in which it reflected the anxieties of Gilded Age America and starkly posed for many the alternatives of Christian supernaturalism versus scientific materialism.[14]

Historical reality, however, was more complicated than a neat division between supernaturalism and materialism, and several different religious responses can be identified in the post-Darwinian era. One response included the aggregation of religious impulses, which has been called harmonial piety and includes Christian Science, New Thought, and the proponents of such medical remedies as homeopathy, hydropathy, and osteopathy. These movements traced their roots back into the early nineteenth century, and they or their descendants, as William James predicted with great foresight, have continued as a force in late twentieth-century American religion. Whatever their internal differences or historical divergences, these groups claimed to have discovered the correspondence between the physical and metaphysical realms. On this basis personal well-being could be achieved through conscientious application of their empirically derived principles. The invocation of empiricism, in the sense that the universe was studied and its laws were discovered, signaled the scientific aspirations of these champions of cosmic consonance. Yet, as William James noted in his own evaluation, these harmonial groups disparaged the increasingly popular identification of science with positivism and, instead, sought a reconciliation of science and religion on more flexible and elastic grounds.[15]

Another rather different position was that of the religion of science. Enamored with the results of scientific investigation, wedded to what one historian has aptly called "justification by verification," intellectuals such as G. Stanley Hall, Walter Lippmann, and John Dewey depicted scientific endeavor itself as a religious vocation. In this context Dewey could equate the inquisitive outlook of the scientist with the attitude of prayer, while Hall could identify the pursuit of scientific research with the voice of the Holy Ghost. In its claims for the seriousness and nobility of its undertaking, in its reaffirmation of the need to study nature, albeit no longer with the purposes of natural theology in mind, and in its praise for the ethical spirit of scientific inquiry, the religion of science represented a limited but distinctive alternative in the late nineteenth and early twentieth centuries. For its advocates the pursuit of knowledge became the equivalent of a religious mission, and, though the conception of science tended to be astringent and positivistic, the ethos of the enterprise represented its purposes in terms that esteemed the aspirations of both science and religion.[16]

While harmonial piety and the religion of science emerged in the late nineteenth century, modernism and fundamentalism figured more significantly in the configuration of religious responses to science. Modernists, or Protestant liberals more generally, were willing to make adjustments to interpretations of Christianity in light of the new findings of the age. Insisting that God was immanent in human history and revealed through especially the progress of that history, they often interpreted evolution as the presence of the divine in the forces of nature, revealing himself, as Washington Gladden once wrote, "not so convincingly by occasional interruptions of the order as by the order itself."[17]

Similar appraisals of evolutionary theory, often shorn of Darwin's mechanism of natural selection, facilitated Henry Ward Beecher, Lyman Abbott, and others in accepting a brand of theistic evolution and recommending it to their widespread audiences. Beecher, for example, wrote that scientists were not undermining religion but, rather, deciphering "God's thought as revealed in the structure of the world." Similarly, Abbott reassured his public that evolution was simply, "God's way of doing things."[18]

Such comfortable assessments of the meaning of evolution were augmented by forceful reassertions of purpose in biological life. Implicit within the apologia of Beecher and Abbott was the assumption that the structure and method of the operation of God's world reflected his superintending guidance. Other Protestant evolutionists consciously revitalized a concept of purpose in their explanation of evolutionary theory. The scientist and Christian layman Asa Gray argued that the variability that Darwin described was less random and more purposeful than the Englishman admitted. For Gray Darwin's theory did not supplant arguments of design in the world but, rather, specified another of the means by which it worked. The Congregational clergyman and Brown University professor Lewis Diman similarly perceived design in operation. For the combination and convergence of so many varied environmental factors, Diman intoned, was impossible to conceive as the result of simple chance. Again Protestant defenders of evolution saw order in the universe, and where there was order they insisted that there one would also find a source responsible for it. Thus, whether it was in attempts to resuscitate concepts of design or to excise natural selection from evolutionary theory in the hopes of fashioning a satisfying theistic evolution, Modernists sought to recast the relationship of science and religion so as to illustrate their continued compatibility in these post-Darwinian circumstances.[19]

Any assessment of the post-Darwinian controversies should take into account the legacy of Horace Bushnell for the Modernist movement. As one scholar of modernism has noted, Bushnell did "more than any other single person to create the possibility in America of a professedly Christian modernism." And, if this estimate applies to the movement generally, then it has equal relevance for its understanding of the relation of science and religion. Protestant liberals in general appreciated Bushnell for his positive evaluation of scientific inquiry, even while they acknowledged that Bushnell himself opposed Darwinism. Beyond that they found in Bushnell's emphasis on experience rather than dogma and his view of language as a fluid and multivalent medium with which to express doctrinal concerns a tonic for the ailments they faced. Washington Gladden, for example, acknowledged his indebtedness to Bushnell, calling his *God in Christ* "an emancipation proclamation which delivered me at once and forever from the bondage of an immoral theology." Bushnell, then, in his evaluation of the relationship of science and religion provided not so much a set of conclusions as an attitude, which the succeeding generation of Protestant liberals found decisive for their own reflections.[20]

Just as Horace Bushnell sowed seeds that the Modernists reaped, so did Charles Hodge bequeath a substantial legacy to conservative, and especially fundamentalist, Protestantism. Whereas liberal Christians were willing to entertain some adjustments of the faith in order to perpetuate it amid changing times, conservative Protestants were much more reluctant. Within such a context fundamentalism, despite the different theological emphases it contained, amounted to a militantly antimodernist form of American Protestantism.[21]

Although fundamentalism has been popularly caricatured as anti-intellectual and opposed to science, in fact it has articulated a conception of science whose roots lie in the Baconian and Scottish Common Sense movements of the eighteenth and nineteenth centuries. It is no surprise, then, that for such a tradition, as one historian has noted, Charles Hodge's response to Darwinian evolution represents the "classic formulation of the conservative position." Hodge's criticisms of Darwinism for its denial of design, incompatibility with the Bible, and improper scientific methodology were all taken up by conservatives and used to assail evolution. Beyond the theological and biblical aspect of the rejoinder here was a familiar description of scientific methodology, which insisted that the inductive collection, observation, and generalization of the facts was the only proper method for science. "An ounce of fact is worth a ton of theory," stated the fundamentalist leader A. C. Dixon, and William Jennings Bryan was thus merely exemplifying the same conclusions when he observed, "evolution is not truth; it is merely hypothesis—it is millions of guesses strung together." In contrasting facts and theory, evidence and guesses, truth and falsity, science and chicanery, Protestant fundamentalists in twentieth-century America were simply descanting on Hodge's earlier strictures concerning the methods and goals of true science.[22]

Further evidence of the influence of this Baconian and Scottish Common Sense perspective can be seen in the tradition of dispensationalism. Dispensationalism is usually considered an important part of modern American fundamentalism, and, though scholars debate the nature and degree of its relationship to the theology taught at Princeton Seminary, they all recognize the connection between Princeton and dispensationalism. For individuals such as Reuben Torrey, C. I. Scofield, and Arthur R. Pierson human history had been divided into seven eras or dispensations. The current age was drawing to a close, and the seventh dispensation, the millennial age, was about to dawn. This millennial age would include the return of Jesus to earth and his reign for a thousand years, after which there would be a new heaven and earth. Correct interpretation of the signs of the times necessitated thorough familiarity with and rigorous investigation of the prophecies, predictions, and promises of the Bible. Invoking Baconian method and the pedigree of science attached to it, dispensationalists claimed that their approach to the Bible was inductive, empirical, and thoroughly scientific. Thus, the appeal to the facts of the Bible and to the truths available to common sense and guaranteed by the inerrancy of the Scriptures were themes that again harked back to Charles Hodge's teachings and indicated the persistence of the Baconian model of science into the twentieth century.[23]

Writing in 1882, Noah Porter described the present era as one in which the reasons for faith were dissipating before the advance of science and culture, "as morning clouds melt before the morning light." Echoing Porter's remarks, historians ever since Arthur Schlesinger, Sr.'s, influential article in 1932, have depicted the last quarter of the nineteenth century as a critical period in American religion. Debates over science and religion, biblical criticism, the influx of immigrants and the study of the religions that they brought with them—all of these issues are taken to constitute a particular time of crisis for American Protestantism. While the scale and intensity of the discussion may have been greater, as this volume has demonstrated, examination of these issues began much earlier. Indeed, these controversies not only have their roots in the antebellum period; many of the specific issues received sustained investigation and discussion in this previous era.[24]

The attempts by the mediational theologians to respond to these and other issues and, thereby, to reconcile science and religion has been the focus of this volume. Examination of the efforts of the mediational theologians should remind scholars that there is no abstract single relationship between science and religion. Rather, differing contexts and oscillating encounters characterize the historical engagement of science and religion. Beyond that, certainly up through the early twentieth-century professionalization of science, the scientific and religious communities in America often shared overlapping organizational situations and conceptual understandings. Finally, both American science and American Protestantism were transformed during the nineteenth century. Neither were monolithic entities, but, in fact, were traditions undergoing volatile shifts. Both found that earlier self-understandings regarding their meanings and functions within American society were changing as that society itself changed over time.

Moreover, while scholars have emphasized the role of Scottish Common Sense and Baconianism in the American reflections on science and religion, this volume has shown that other intellectual resources in the form of German mediational theology and Coleridgean romanticism also played important roles. Acknowledgment of these broader contexts enriches our understanding of the background and significance of the era and its efforts.

Utilizing contemporary forms of European thought together with inherited traditions of Christian theology, the antebellum mediational theologians fashioned a coherent and sophisticated response to the controversies over science in their day. Prescient enough to recognize that fundamental issues of authority lay beneath the disputes over scientific discovery, they fashioned a series of interpretive strategies that sought to recognize scientific contributions at the same time that they bolstered familiar sorts of religious authority. Often overlooked for their impact on the controversy over science and religion in America, these mediational theologians made a significant contribution to nineteenth-century American Christianity.

Notes

Prologue

1. See Theodore Dwight Bozeman, *Protestants in an Age of Science: The Baconian Ideal and Antebellum American Religious Thought* (Chapel Hill: University of North Carolina Press, 1977); James R. Moore, *The Post-Darwinian Controversies* (Cambridge: Cambridge University Press, 1979); David C. Lindberg and Ronald L. Numbers, eds., *God and Nature* (Berkeley: University of California Press, 1986); and John Hedley Brooke, *Science and Religion* (Cambridge: Cambridge University Press, 1991).
2. See Bentley Glass et al., eds., *Forerunners of Darwin: 1745–1859* (Baltimore: Johns Hopkins Press, 1959); and Peter J. Bowler, *Evolution: The History of an Idea* (Berkeley: University of California Press, 1984).
3. See Thomas S. Kuhn, *The Structure of Scientific Revolutions*, 2d ed. (Chicago: University of Chicago Press, 1970); and David A. Hollinger, "T. S. Kuhn's Theory of Science and Its Implications for History," *American Historical Review* 78 (1973): 370–93.
4. George M. Marsden, *Fundamentalism and American Culture* (New York: Oxford University Press, 1980), 19.

Chapter One: The Crisis of Religious Authority

1. Edward Hitchcock, *The Religion of Geology and Its Connected Sciences*, new ed. (Boston: Phillips, Sampson, 1859), 2–5.
2. For biographical information on Hitchcock, see *The Dictionary of American Biography* (1932), 5: 70–71; Edward Hitchcock, *Reminiscences of Amherst College* (Northampton, Mass.: Bridgmen and Childs, 1863).
3. Hitchcock, *Reminiscences*, 291; *The Highest Use of Learning* (Amherst, Mass.: J. S. Adams, 1845), 21, 33–35.
4. See Herbert Butterfield, *The Origins of Modern Science, 1300–1800*, rev. ed. (New York: Free Press, 1965); Alexandre Koyré, *From the Closed World to the Infinite Universe* (Baltimore: Johns Hopkins Press, 1957).
5. See I. Bernard Cohen, *Revolution in Science* (Cambridge: Harvard University Press, 1985), 146–51.
6. See Brooke Hindle, *The Pursuit of Science in Revolutionary America, 1775–1789* (Chapel Hill: University of North Carolina Press, 1956); John C. Greene, *American Science in the Age of Jefferson* (Ames: Iowa State Univer-

sity Press, 1984); George H. Daniels, *Science in American Society: A Social History* (New York: Alfred A. Knopf, 1971), esp. chap. 7 ("The Democratic Age in American Science").

7. For a thoughtful analysis of the professionalization of nineteenth-century American science, see Nathan Reingold, "Definitions and Speculations: The Professionalization of Science in America in the Nineteenth Century," in *The Pursuit of Knowledge in the Early American Republic*, ed. Alexandra Oleson and Sanborn Brown (Baltimore: Johns Hopkins University Press, 1976), 33–69.

8. See Greene, *American Science in the Age of Jefferson*, 291–300, 312–38; George Daniels, *American Science in the Age of Jackson* (New York: Columbia University Press, 1968), 137.

9. See Greene, *American Science in the Age of Jefferson*, 135–56; Daniels, *American Science in the Age of Jackson*, 202–3, 210–12.

10. See Greene, *American Science in the Age of Jefferson*, 163–70, 176–82; Margaret Rossiter, *The Emergence of Agricultural Science* (New Haven, Conn.: Yale University Press, 1975), 91–124.

11. A. Hunter Dupree discusses federal support in *Science in the Federal Government*, rev. ed. (Baltimore: Johns Hopkins University Press, 1986), 43. For analysis of other contexts, see Donald M. Scott, "The Popular Lecture and the Creation of a Public in Mid-Nineteenth-Century America," *Journal of American History* 66 (March 1980): 791–809; Ronald Numbers and Todd Savitt, eds., *Science and Medicine in the Old South* (Baton Rouge: Louisiana State University Press, 1989); Daniels, *Science in American Society*, 160–61, 193–98.

12. Richard S. Westfall, *Science and Religion in Seventeenth-Century England* (Ann Arbor: University of Michigan Press, 1973), 3.

13. See Daniels, *Science in American Society*, 159.

14. George R. Noyes, "Causes of the Decline of Interest in Critical Theology," *Christian Examiner* 43 (November 1847): 325–44; Samuel Harris, "The Demands of Infidelity Satisfied by Christianity," *Bibliotheca Sacra* 13 (April 1856): 275; John C. Greene, *American Science in the Age of Jefferson*, 20.

15. "Life of Sir Isaac Newton," *Christian Examiner* 12 (July 1832): 287; "Academy of Natural Sciences of Philadelphia," *Scientific American* 7 (22 May 1852): 285.

16. "Natural History in Its Relation to Georgia," *DeBow's Review* 16 (April 1854): 361, 367–68; John Jay Dana, "The Claims of the Natural Sciences on the Christian Ministry," *Bibliotheca Sacra* 6 (August 1849): 462–63.

17. See Edward Grant, "Science and Theology in the Middle Ages," in *God and Nature*, ed. David C. Lindberg and Ronald L. Numbers (Berkeley: University of California Press, 1986), 50.

18. See Greene, *American Science in the Age of Jefferson*, 14–17; "The Logical

Relations of Religion and Natural Science," *Princeton Review* 32 (October 1860): 579.

19. See "Vestiges of Creation and Its Reviewers," *New Englander* 4 (January 1846): 119.

20. See "The Argument for Natural Religion," *Christian Examiner* 19 (November 1835): 145–46; and, for discussion of the influence of Paley in America, Wendell Glick, "Bishop Paley in America," *New England Quarterly* 27 (September 1954): 347–54.

21. Lewis Saum has noted that, "in popular thought of the pre-Civil War period, no theme was more pervasive or philosophically more fundamental than the providential view." See Lewis O. Saum, *The Popular Mood of Pre-Civil War America* (Westport, Conn.: Greenwood Press, 1980), 3.

22. A. B. Muzzey, "Family Worship," *Christian Examiner* 61 (September 1856): 193; *Scientific American* 2 (6 February 1847): 160.

23. "Revelations of the Microscope," *New Englander* 5 (April 1847): 237; Dana, "Claims of the Natural Sciences on the Christian Ministry," 462–66; "Moral Aesthetics or the Goodness of God in the Ornaments of the Universe," *Princeton Review* 24 (January 1852): 38.

24. John C. Greene, "Science and Religion," in *The Rise of Adventism*, ed. Edwin S. Gaustad (New York: Harper and Row, 1974), 50.

25. James Ussher, *The Annals of the World* (London: E. Tyler, 1685); for further discussion of Ussher and his significance, see H. R. Trevor-Roper, *Catholics, Anglicans, and Puritans* (Chicago: University of Chicago Press, 1988), 120–65; and Francis C. Haber, *The Age of the World* (Baltimore: Johns Hopkins Press, 1959).

26. See Arthur Lovejoy, *The Great Chain of Being* (New York: Harper and Row, 1960).

27. See John C. Greene, *The Death of Adam: Evolution and Its Impact on Western Thought* (Ames: Iowa State University Press, 1959), 15, 129.

28. James Hutton, *Theory of the Earth*, 2 vols. (Edinburgh: Cadell and Davies, 1795), 1:200. See A. Hallam, *Great Geological Controversies* (New York: Oxford University Press, 1983), 25; and Peter J. Bowler, *Evolution: The History of an Idea* (Berkeley: University of California Press, 1984), 30, for a discussion of fossil investigation.

29. See Stephen Jay Gould, "Eternal Metaphors of Palaeontology," in *Patterns of Evolution*, ed. A. Hallam (Amsterdam: Elsevier, 1977), 1–26; for a detailed historical discussion of the debates surrounding vulcanism, neptunism, catastrophism, and uniformitarianism, see Mott T. Greene, *Geology in the Nineteenth Century* (Ithaca: Cornell University Press, 1982).

30. See Richard H. Popkin, *Isaac La Peyrère* (Leiden: E. J. Brill, 1987).

31. For the emergence of polygenesis in the nineteenth century, see William Stanton, *The Leopard's Spots* (Chicago: University of Chicago Press, 1960); George M. Fredrickson, *The Black Image in the White Mind* (New York:

Harper and Row, 1973); Stephen J. Gould, *The Mismeasure of Man* (New York: W. W. Norton, 1981); Reginald Horsman, *Race and Manifest Destiny* (Cambridge: Harvard University Press, 1981).

32. Josiah Nott, *Two Lectures on the Connection between the Biblical and Physical History of Man* (New York: Bartlett and Welford, 1849), 22, 7; and "Ancient and Scripture Chronology," *Southern Quarterly Review* 18 (November 1850): 401. For discussion of Nott's career and thought, see Reginald Horsman, *Josiah Nott* (Baton Rouge: Louisiana State University Press, 1987).

33. See Richard H. Popkin, "Pre-Adamism in nineteenth-century American Thought," *Philosophia* 8 (1978–79): 205–39.

34. For a discussion of responses to polygenesis, see Thomas V. Peterson, *Ham and Japheth* (Metuchen, N.J.: Scarecrow Press, 1979); William G. McLoughlin and Walter H. Conser, Jr., "'The First Man was Red'— Cherokee Responses to the Debate over Indian Origins, 1760–1860," *American Quarterly* 41 (June 1989): 243–64.

35. See the discussion of Enlightenment rationalism in Henning Graf Reventlow, *The Authority of the Bible and the Rise of the Modern World* (Philadelphia: Fortress Press, 1985).

36. For a discussion of organicism, see Maurice Mandelbaum, *History, Man, and Reason* (Baltimore: Johns Hopkins University Press, 1974), 41–49; M. H. Abrams, *The Mirror and the Lamp* (New York: Oxford University Press, 1958), 202–5.

37. For a relevant discussion of biblical interpretation, see Hans Frei, *The Eclipse of Biblical Narrative* (New Haven, Conn.: Yale University Press, 1974); and Robert Morgan, *Biblical Interpretation* (New York: Oxford University Press, 1988). For specific discussion of the Old Testament, see John Rogerson, *Old Testament Criticism in the Nineteenth Century: England and Germany* (Philadelphia: Fortress Press, 1985); and for the New Testament, see Werner Kümmel, *The New Testament: The History of the Investigation of Its Problems* (Nashville: Abingdon Press, 1972); and Stephen Neill and Tom Wright, *The Interpretation of the New Testament*, rev. ed. (New York: Oxford University Press, 1988).

38. Eleazar Lord, *The Plenary Inspiration of the Holy Scriptures* (New York: M. W. Dodd, 1857), 9, 14.

39. David Dyer, *The Plenary Inspiration of the Old and New Testaments* (Boston: Tappan, 1849), 15, 16, 56.

40. See John H. Giltner, *Moses Stuart* (Atlanta: Scholars Press, 1988), 31.

41. See Giltner, *Moses Stuart*, 52–53; Frei, *Eclipse of Biblical Narrative*, 246–55.

42. See Moses Stuart, "Are the Same Principles of Interpretation to Be Applied to the Scriptures as to Other Books?" *American Biblical Repository* 2 (January 1832): 124–37; George Marsden, "Everyone One's Own Inter-

preter? The Bible, Science, and Authority in Mid-Nineteenth Century America," in *The Bible in America*, ed. Nathan O. Hatch and Mark A. Noll (New York: Oxford University Press, 1982), 79–100.

43. See John H. Giltner, "Moses Stuart" (Ph.D. diss., Yale University, 1956), 250.

44. Giltner, *Moses Stuart*, 53; Moses Stuart, *Critical History and Defence of the Old Testament Canon* (Andover, Mass.: Allen, Morrill and Wardwell, 1845), 190–93.

45. Giltner, *Moses Stuart*, 54.

46. Stuart, "Are the Same Principles of Interpretation," 129.

47. See Jerry Wayne Brown, *The Rise of Biblical Criticism in America, 1800–1870* (Middletown, Conn.: Wesleyan University Press, 1969), 140–52.

48. Theodore Parker, "The Transient and Permanent in Christianity," in *Three Prophets of Religious Liberalism*, ed. Conrad Wright (Boston: Beacon Press, 1961), 126–27.

49. Theodore Parker, *A Discourse of Matters Pertaining to Religion* (Boston: Little and Brown, 1842), 367.

50. Theodore Parker, "The Previous Question between Mr. Andrews Norton and His Alumni Moved and Handled," app. to John E. Dirks, *The Critical Theology of Theodore Parker* (New York: Columbia University Press, 1948), 140; René Wellek, *Confrontations* (Princeton, N.J.: Princeton University Press, 1965), 173, 186; Robert D. Richardson, Jr., *Myth and Literature in the American Renaissance* (Bloomington: Indiana University Press, 1978), 34–48.

51. Parker, "Previous Question," 149; "Transient and Permanent," 140, 129.

52. See Nathan O. Hatch, *The Democratization of American Christianity* (New Haven, Conn.: Yale University Press, 1989), 34–36.

53. James Warley Miles, MS sermon on Matthew 8, James Warley Miles Papers, Robert S. Small Library, College of Charleston, Charleston, South Carolina; Mitchell King diary, 1 February 1852; 18 September 1853, Mitchell King Papers, Southern Historical Collection, University of North Carolina, Chapel Hill, North Carolina. For a description of King, see E. Brooks Holifield, *The Gentlemen Theologians* (Durham, N.C.: Duke University Press, 1978), 21.

54. On Southern religion and society, see Holifield, *Gentlemen Theologians*; and Drew G. Faust, *A Sacred Circle: The Dilemma of the Intellectual in the Old South, 1840–1860* (Baltimore: Johns Hopkins University Press, 1977). For corresponding analyses of the Middle States, see Lefferts A. Loetscher, *Facing the Enlightenment and Pietism* (Westport, Conn.: Greenwood Press, 1983); and for New England, see Donald M. Scott, *From Office to Profession: The New England Ministry 1750–1850* (Philadelphia: University of Pennsylvania Press, 1978).

55. See Stanley M. Guralnik, "The American Scientist in Higher Education, 1820–1910," in *The Sciences in the American Context: New Perspectives*, ed.

Nathan Reingold (Washington, D.C.: Smithsonian Institution Press, 1979): 108–9; Louise L. Stevenson, *Scholarly Means to Evangelical Ends* (Baltimore: Johns Hopkins University Press, 1986).

56. See Henry Nash Smith, "Emerson's Problem of Vocation: A Note on 'The American Scholar,'" *New England Quarterly* 12 (1939): 59–67; Perry Miller, "Emersonian Genius and the American Democracy," *New England Quarterly* 26 (1953): 27–44; Mary K. Cayton, "'Sympathy's Electric Chain' and the American Democracy: Emerson's First Vocational Crisis," *New England Quarterly* 60 (1982): 3–24.

57. See Loetscher, *Facing the Enlightenment and Pietism*, 149.

58. On the rise of seminaries, see Glenn T. Miller, *Piety and Intellect: The Aims and Purposes of Antebellum Theological Education* (Atlanta: Scholars Press, 1990); Bruce Kuklick, *Churchmen and Philosophers* (New Haven, Conn.: Yale University Press, 1985), 86–87. For a discussion of professionalization, see Loetscher, *Facing the Enlightenment and Pietism*, 145; and Eliot Freidson, "Are Professions Necessary?" in *The Authority of Experts*, ed. Thomas L. Haskell (Bloomington: Indiana University Press, 1984), 4–5, 10.

59. See Alexandra Oleson and Sanborn C. Brown, eds., *The Pursuit of Knowledge in the Early American Republic: American Scientific and Learned Societies from Colonial Times to the Civil War* (Baltimore: Johns Hopkins University Press, 1976); and Peter D. Hall, "The Social Foundations of Professional Credibility," in Haskell, *Authority of Experts*, 114.

60. See Daniel H. Calhoun, *Professional Lives in America: Structure and Aspiration, 1750–1850* (Cambridge: Harvard University Press, 1965); and the anonymous article "Is the Religious Want of the Age Met?" *Atlantic Monthly* 5 (March 1860): 358–64.

Chapter Two: History Revealed

1. W. G. T. Shedd, "The Nature and Influence of the Historic Spirit," *Theological Essays* (New York: Scribners, 1877), 54, 64. For discussion of Shedd's career, see Cushing Strout, "Faith and History: The Mind of William G. T. Shedd," *Journal of the History of Ideas* 15 (1954): 153–62.

2. See Henry W. Bowden, *Church History in the Age of Science* (Chapel Hill: University of North Carolina Press, 1971), 7–15, 36–39.

3. Shedd, *Lectures upon the Philosophy of History* (1856; reprint, Andover, Mass.: Warren F. Draper, 1861), 10–11, 14–26, 42–43.

4. Shedd, "Nature and Influence of the Historic Spirit," 55, 61–62, 79–80, 85; *Lectures upon the Philosophy of History*, 45.

5. Shedd, "Nature and Influence of the Historic Spirit," 68–70.

6. Shedd, *Lectures upon the Philosophy of History*, 57–58, 70–74.

7. James W. Miles, *Philosophic Theology; or, Ultimate Grounds of All Religious Belief Based in Reason* (Charleston, S.C.: John Russell, 1849), 123–25.

8. Miles, *Philosophic Theology*, 125.
9. Miles, *Philosophic Theology*, 105; *Annual Oration Delivered before the Chrestomatic Society at the College of Charleston* (Charleston, S.C.: E. C. Councell, 1850), 16–21; *An Address Delivered at the Residence of the American Minister in Berlin, on the Fourth of July, 1855* (Berlin: G. Bernstein, 1855), 3–9 (quotation p. 9).
10. On romanticism's view of history, see M. H. Abrams, *Natural Supernaturalism* (New York: W. W. Norton, 1973), 56–65, 200–206.
11. Miles, *God in History: A Discourse Delivered before the Graduating Class of the College of Charleston* (Charleston, S.C.: Evans and Cogswell, 1863), 9.
12. Miles, *God in History*, 19–21.
13. Miles, *God in History*, 22–28.
14. See the reviews of *Philosophic Theology* in the *Charleston Gospel Messenger and Protestant Episcopal Register* (May 1850): 17–20; and *Southern Quarterly Review* (April 1850): 134–45.
15. Neander's review can be found in *Southern Quarterly Review* (September 1850): 259–60. The German translation made by Neander's student W. A. Lampadius was published in Leipzig in 1850. The story of the delivery of Miles's book to Neander can be found in the entry for 31 January 1850 in the diary of James Johnston Pettigrew, Pettigrew Papers, Southern Historical Collection, University of North Carolina, Chapel Hill, North Carolina.
16. Fredrika Bremer, *The Homes of the New World; Impressions of America*, 2 vols. (New York: Harper & Bros., 1854), 1:378–79; Miles to David James McCord, 24 April 1851, in James H. Easterby, ed., "Letters of James Warley Miles to David James McCord," *South Carolina Historical and Genealogical Magazine* 44 (April 1942): 189–90.
17. James W. Miles to Mrs. Thomas Young, c. spring 1854, James Warley Miles Papers, Duke University, Durham, North Carolina; James W. Miles to Robert Gourdin, 8 July 1854, Robert Gourdin Papers, Duke University, Durham, North Carolina; Francis Lieber to William Porcher Miles, 20 March 1855 and 22 May 1856, William Porcher Miles Papers, Southern Historical Collection, University of North Carolina, Chapel Hill, North Carolina. For discussion of Miles's return as librarian, see Muscoe Russell Hunter Garnett to William Porcher Miles, 25 July 1856, and Robert Gourdin to William Porcher Miles, 17 October 1856, William Porcher Miles Papers.
18. Philip Schaff, *History of the Christian Church*, rev. ed. (New York: Scribners, 1882), 50. Isaak Dorner is quoted in George Prentiss, *The Union Theological Seminary in the City of New York* (New York: A. D. Randolph, 1889), 263. For the details of Smith's early life, see *Henry Boynton Smith: His Life and Work*, ed. his wife (New York: A. C. Armstrong, 1881), 1–37.
19. For an excellent review of the historiographical literature on the *Vermit-*

tlungstheologie, see Jörg Rothermundt, *Personale Synthese* (Göttingen: Vandenhoeck and Ruprecht, 1968), 11–42. For further discussion of nineteenth-century mediating theology, see Ragnar Holte, *Die Vermittlungstheologie* (Uppsala, Sweden: Almquist, 1965); Claude Welch, *Protestant Thought in the Nineteenth Century*, 2 vols. (New Haven, Conn.: Yale University Press, 1972–85), 1:269–91; Martin Kähler, *Geschichte der protestantischen Dogmatik im 19. Jahrhundert* (Berlin: Evangelische Verlagsanstalt, 1962), 82–146; Horst Stephan and Martin Schmidt, *Geschichte der deutschen evangelischen Theologie seit dem deutschen Idealismus*, 3d ed. (Berlin: Walter de Gruyter, 1973), 228–45.

20. For discussion of the church union program, see Walter H. Conser, Jr., *Church and Confession: Conservative Theologians in Germany, England, and America, 1815–1866* (Macon, Ga.: Mercer University Press, 1984), 13–27.

21. Karl Ullmann, *Das Wesen des Christenthums* 3d ed. (Hamburg: Friedrich Perthes, 1849), 5–11. The concern with Christology, as Claude Welch has written, "came to the center of the stage of Protestant theology in the middle third of the nineteenth century." Welch, *Protestant Thought*, 1:145.

22. Ullmann, *Das Wesen des Christenthums*, 86,130.

23. For a discussion of the Awakening, see Conser, *Church and Confession*, 27–38; Friedrich W. Kantzenbach, *Die Erweckungsbewegung* (Neuendettelsau, Germany: Freimund Verlag, 1957).

24. For discussion of Neander's life and work, see Philip Schaff, *August Neander* (Gotha, Germany: Friedrich Perthes, 1886); Adelbert Wiegand, *August Neanders Leben* (Erfurt, Germany: Fr. Bartholomaeus, 1889); Kähler, *Geschichte der protestantischen Dogmatik*, 119–21; Stephan and Schmidt, *Geschichte der evangelischen Theologie*, 134–37.

25. See August Neander, *General History of the Christian Religion and Church*, trans. from the 2d ed. by Joseph Torrey, 4 vols. (Boston: Crocker and Brewer, 1852), preface to the 1st ed. and pp. 1–3. For discussion of this work in the context of Neander's life and writings, see Kurt-Victor Selge, "August Neander—ein getaufter Hamburger Jude der Emanzipations- und Restaurationzeit als erster Berliner Kirchenhistoriker (1813–1850)," in *450 Jahre Evangelische Theologie in Berlin*, ed. Gerhard Beiser and Christof Gestrich (Göttingen: Vandenhoeck and Ruprecht, 1989), 233–76. For an assessment of the influence of Plato and Greek philosophy and literature generally, see the letter of Neander to Adelberth v. Chamisso, undated c. 1806–8, August Neander Papers, Deutsche Staatsbibliothek Preussischer Kulturbesitz, Berlin.

26. For discussion of Tholuck's career, see Leopold Witte, *Das Leben D. Friedrich August Gottreu Tholucks*, 2 vols. (Bielefeld, Germany: Velhagen, 1884–86); Stephan and Schmidt, *Geschichte der evangelischen Theologie*, 137–39.

27. Philip Schaff, "Autobiographical Reminiscences," Philip Schaff Papers,

Evangelical and Reformed Historical Society, Lancaster Theological Seminary, Lancaster, Pennsylvania; August Tholuck, *Die Glaubenswür-digkeit der evangelischen Geschichte* (Hamburg: Friedrich Perthes, 1837), 2–3, 54, 92, 440. For a comparable overall assessment of Tholuck, see Hans-Walter Krumwiede, "August G. Tholuck," in *Gestalten der Kirchengeschichte*, ed. Martin Greschat, 12 vols. (Stuttgart: Kohlhammer, 1985), 9/1: 281–92.

28. For discussion of Smith's years in Germany, see *Life*, ed. his wife, 39–84. Smith's remarks to Tholuck are contained in a letter from Smith to Tholuck, 24 December 1838, Tholuck Papers, Katechetisches Oberseminar, Naumburg, Germany.

29. See *Life*, ed. his wife, 49, 74.

30. Smith, "The Relations of Faith and Philosophy," in *Faith and Philosophy: Discourses and Essays*, ed. Henry B. Smith (Edinburgh: T. T. Clark, 1878), 35–38.

31. Smith, "The Relations of Faith and Philosophy," 5, 12–16, 24–27.

32. Smith, "The Relations of Faith and Philosophy," 21, 32–35.

33. Smith, "Nature and Worth of the Science of Church History," *Faith and Philosophy: Discourses and Essays*, 52.

34. Smith, "Nature and Worth," 61–66; "The Idea of Christian Theology as a System," *Faith and Philosophy: Discourses and Essays*, 132.

35. See Sydney E. Ahlstrom, *The American Protestant Encounter with World Religions* (Beloit, Wisc.: Beloit College, 1962); Carl T. Jackson, *The Oriental Religions and American Thought: Nineteenth-century explorations* (Westport, Conn.: Greenwood Press, 1981); and for discussion of later developments, see Welch, *Protestant Thought in the Nineteenth Century*, 2:104–45.

36. Horace Bushnell, *Nature and the Supernatural*, 5th ed. (1858, reprint, New York: Charles Scribner, 1863), 13–21.

37. Smith, "The Idea of Christian Theology as a System," *Faith and Philosophy: Discourses and Essays*, 131–34.

38. James W. Miles to Mrs. T. Young, 21 August 1864, Miles Papers.

39. James W. Miles to Mrs. T. Young, 21 August 1864, Miles Papers.

40. Philip Schaff, *What Is Church History?* (Philadelphia: Lippincott, 1846), 36–40.

41. Schaff's description of his university studies is found in his unpublished "Autobiographical Reminiscences." Detailed biographical information can be found in David S. Schaff, *The Life of Philip Schaff* (New York: Scribners, 1897); and George H. Shriver, *Philip Schaff* (Macon, Ga.: Mercer University Press, 1987).

42. Schaff, *What Is Church History*, 79.

43. Schaff, *What Is Church History*, 26.

44. Bowden, *Church History in the Age of Science*, 31; Schaff, *America: A Sketch of Its Political, Social, and Religious Character*, ed. Perry Miller (Cambridge: Harvard University Press, 1961), 27–28.

45. Schaff, *What Is Church History*, 4.
46. Schaff, *What Is Church History*, 9, 38.
47. Schaff, *What Is Church History*, 28, 39–41.
48. Perry Miller's comments are found in his editorial introduction to *America* xvii; Schaff, "Prolegomena zur Kirchengeschichte der Vereinigten Staaten, *Der Deutsche Kirchenfreund* 1 (December 1848): 357.
49. Schaff, *America*, 25, 191.
50. See H. Richard Niebuhr, *The Kingdom of God in America* (New York: Harper & Row, 1937); Ernest Lee Tuveson, *Redeemer Nation: The Idea of America's Millennial Role* (Chicago: University of Chicago Press, 1968); and Conrad Cherry, ed., *God's New Israel: Religious Interpretations of American Destiny* (Englewood Cliffs, N.J.: Prentice-Hall, 1971).
51. Schaff, *What Is Church History*, 91–92; Schaff, *America*, 195.
52. Schaff, *America*, 80–81.
53. Schaff, *America*, 191, 214–15, 221–22.

Chapter Three: Biblicism Reaffirmed

1. A. A. Hodge, *The Life of Charles Hodge* (New York: Scribners, 1880), 65. Other biographical studies of Hodge include John Oliver Nelson, "Charles Hodge: Nestor of Orthodoxy," in *Lives of Eighteen from Princeton*, ed. Willard Thorp (Princeton, N.J.: Princeton University Press, 1946); and Leonard J. Trinterud, "Charles Hodge," in *Sons of the Prophets*, ed. Hugh T. Kerr (Princeton, N.J.: Princeton University Press, 1963).
2. Charles Hodge, *A Dissertation on the Importance of Biblical Literature* (Trenton, N.J.: George Sherman, 1822), 43; Charles Hodge to Hugh Hodge, 29 August 1826, Hodge Papers, Princeton University Library, Princeton, New Jersey.
3. Edward Robinson to Charles Hodge, 5 December 1826, Hodge Papers, Princeton University Library; Thomas A. Olbricht, "Charles Hodge as an American New Testament Interpreter," *Journal of Presbyterian History* 57 (Summer 1979): 117–33.
4. See Jurgen Herbst, *The German Historical School in American Scholarship: A Study in the Transfer of Culture* (Ithaca: Cornell University Press, 1965), 13–19; Bruce Sinclair, "Americans Abroad: Science and Cultural Nationalism in the Early Nineteenth Century," in *The Sciences in the American Context: New Perspectives*, ed. Nathan Reingold (Washington, D.C.: Smithsonian Institution Press, 1979), 35–53.
5. Sydney E. Ahlstrom, *A Religious History of the American People* (New Haven, Conn.: Yale University Press, 1972), 599; Carl Diehl, *Americans and German Scholarship, 1770–1870* (New Haven, Conn.: Yale University Press, 1978), 155–58.
6. For detailed discussion of Charles Hodge's stay in Europe see Hodge, *Life*, 104–201.

7. Archibald Alexander to Charles Hodge, 27 July 1827, Hodge Papers, Princeton University Library.

8. Edward Robinson to Charles Hodge, 5 December 1826; Charles Hodge to Sarah Hodge, 11 March 1827, Hodge Papers, Princeton University Library. Charles Hodge to August Tholuck, 25 February 1828, August Tholuck Papers, Katechetisches Oberseminar, Naumburg, Germany.

9. Charles Hodge to Archibald Alexander, 19 September 1827, Hodge Papers, Princeton University Library. Hodge's low opinion of the condition of German philosophy did not soften in later years. Surveying the range of philosophical options in nineteenth-century Germany, Hodge quipped that it was difficult to find any two men occupying the same position. "Had these men to act together," he wrote, "Babel would be a scene of order in comparison with a convocation of German theologians and philosophers." See Hodge's comments in "Ruckert's Commentary on Romans," *Princeton Review* (January 1836): 43. For discussion of the context and significance of Witherspoon's presidency, see Mark Noll, *Princeton and the Republic, 1768–1822* (Princeton, N.J.: Princeton University Press, 1989).

10. See the entry for 6 March 1827 in Hodge's manuscript Journal of European Travels and his notes on Tholuck's lectures in Charles Hodge Papers, Princeton Theological Seminary, Princeton, New Jersey.

11. Charles Hodge to Archibald Alexander, 4 April 1828; Charles Hodge to his mother, 6 April 1828, Hodge Papers, Princeton University Library.

12. Charles Hodge, "The Nature and Method of Theology," MS lectures, Hodge Papers, Princeton Theological Seminary.

13. For a discussion of Common Sense philosophy and its influences in America, see Terence Martin, *The Instructed Vision* (Bloomington: Indiana University Press, 1961); Theodore Dwight Bozeman, *Protestants in an Age of Science* (Chapel Hill: University of North Carolina Press, 1977); D. H. Meyer, *The Instructed Conscience* (Philadelphia: University of Pennsylvania Press, 1972); Mark Noll, "Common Sense Traditions and American Evangelical Thought," *American Quarterly* 37 (Summer 1985): 217–38.

14. Nelson, "Charles Hodge," 197, 206.

15. Hodge, "Nature and Method of Theology," Hodge Papers, Princeton Theological Seminary.

16. See Hodge, "Nature and Method of Theology," Hodge Papers, Princeton Theological Seminary; "Inspiration," *Princeton Review* 29 (October 1857): 669.

17. Hodge, *Systematic Theology*, 3 vols. (New York: Scribners, 1872), 1:163–64.

18. The standard biography of Thornwell is Benjamin Palmer, *The Life and Letters of James Henley Thornwell* (Richmond, Va.: Whitter and Shepperson, 1875). More recent studies of Thornwell include James O. Farmer, *The Metaphysical Confederacy: James Henley Thornwell and the Synthesis of*

Southern Values (Macon, Ga.: Mercer University Press, 1986); E. Brooks Holifield, *The Gentlemen Theologians* (Durham, N.C.: Duke University Press, 1978); and Theodore Dwight Bozeman, *Protestants in an Age of Science: The Baconian Ideal and Antebellum American Religious Thought* (Chapel Hill: University of North Carolina Press, 1977).

19. For discussion of Thornwell's early life and collegiate career, see Palmer, *Life and Letters*, 1–83. The description of Thornwell's physical appearance is found on page 53.

20. Palmer, *Life and Letters*, 127, 175–79, 457; Daniel Walker Hollis, *The University of South Carolina* (Columbia: University of South Carolina Press, 1951), 1:160–76.

21. Thornwell, "Inaugural Discourse," in *The Collected Writings of James Henley Thornwell*, ed. John B. Adger, 4 vols. (Richmond, Va.: Presbyterian Committee of Publication, 1871–73), 1:578–79; "Address to Clariosophic and Euphradian Societies," 3 December 1839, James Henley Thornwell Papers, South Caroliniana Library, University of South Carolina, Columbia, South Carolina.

22. See Holifield, *Gentlemen Theologians*, 73, 120; Palmer, *Life and Letters*, 411; Farmer, *Metaphysical Confederacy*, 149; Bozeman, *Protestants in an Age of Science*, 30.

23. Thornwell, *Collected Works*, 3:275–76.

24. Thornwell, "Address to Clariosophic and Euphradian Societies, 3 December 1839, Thornwell Papers; Thornwell to General Gillespie, 13 August 1834; Thornwell to Alexander H. Pegues, 1 October 1834, Thornwell Papers, University of South Carolina.

25. For details of Robinson's life, see Henry B. Smith and Roswell D. Hitchcock, *The Life, Writings, and Character of Edward Robinson* (New York: Anson Randolph, 1863).

26. Timothy Dwight to August Tholuck, 26 May 1826, Tholuck Papers, Katechetisches Oberseminar, Naumburg; Smith and Hitchcock, *Life*, 48–51.

27. See Robinson to Tholuck, 6 March 1828, 20 January 1831, Tholuck Papers, Katechetisches Oberseminar; Smith and Hitchcock, *Life*, 52.

28. Edward Robinson to August Tholuck, 6 March 1828, Tholuck Papers, Katechetisches Oberseminar.

29. For a concise and insightful analysis of romanticism, see René Wellek, "The Concept of Romanticism in Literary History," reprinted in *Concepts of Criticism*, ed. Stephen Nichols, Jr. (New Haven, Conn.: Yale University Press, 1963), 160–67. On Neander, see Philip Schaff, *August Neander* (Gotha, Germany: Friedrich Perthes, 1886); and Adelbert Wiegand, *August Neanders Leben* (Erfurt, Germany: Fr. Bartholomaeus, 1889); on Carl Ritter, see G. Kramer, *Carl Ritter, ein Lebensbild* (Halle, Germany: Waisenhaus Buchhandlung, 1864); and W. L. Gage, *The Life of Carl Ritter* (New York: Scribners, 1867).

30. Robinson, "Philology and Lexicography of the New Testament," *Biblical Repository* (January 1834): 156.
31. See William H. Goetzmann, "Paradigm Lost," in *The Sciences in the American Context: New Perspectives*, ed. Nathan Reingold (Washington, D.C.: Smithsonian Institution Press, 1979), 21–34.
32. Robinson, *The Bible and Its Literature* (New York: Office of the American Bible Repository, 1841), 23, 36.
33. Robinson provides a characteristic acknowledgment of the significance of his work for "science in the new world," in Edward Robinson to E. W. Hengstenberg, 29 August 1840, E. W. Hengstenberg Papers, Staatsbibliothek Preussischer Kulturbesitz, Berlin, Germany. For an overview of early American interest in the Middle East, see David H. Finnie, *Pioneers East: The Early American Experience in the Middle East* (Cambridge: Harvard University Press, 1967). For discussion of the exploration of Palestine and Robinson's contribution, see H. V. Hilprecht, *Explorations in Bible Lands during the Nineteenth Century* (Philadelphia: A. J. Holman, 1903); and William F. Albright, *The Archaeology of Palestine* (reprint, Gloucester, Mass.: Peter Smith, 1971). Albright quotes Titus Tobler on page 25 and further cites the special issue in 1939 of the *Journal of Biblical Literature* marking the centenary of Robinson's first trip to Palestine and praising his work. Robinson's own reflections are scattered throughout the narrative of his *Biblical Researches in Palestine, Mount Sinai, and Arabia Petraea*, 3 vols. (Boston: Crocker and Brewster, 1841).
34. Robinson, *Biblical Researches*, 1:371–77, 501–3; Albrecht Alt, "Edward Robinson and the Historical Geography of Palestine," *Journal of Biblical Literature* 57 (1939); 373–77; Edward Robinson to Carl Ritter, 31 December 1840, Carl Ritter Papers, Deutsche Staatsbibliothek Preussischer Kulturbesitz, Berlin, Germany.
35. Robinson, *The Bible and Its Literature*, 40.

Chapter Four: Language Reinterpreted

1. Samuel Taylor Coleridge, *Aids to Reflection . . . Together with a Preliminary Essay*. Ed. James Marsh (Burlington, Vt.: Chauncey Goodrich, 1829), vi, viii.
2. *The Remains of the Rev. James Marsh, D.D., with a Memoir of His Life*, ed. Joseph Torrey (Boston: Crocker and Brewer, 1843), is still a standard source on Marsh's life. For other treatments, see Marjorie H. Nicholson, "James Marsh and the Vermont Transcendentalists," *The Philosophic Review* 34 (January 1925): 28–50; John Dewey, "James Marsh and American Philosophy," *Journal of the History of Ideas* 2 (April 1941): 131–50; A. C. McGiffert, Jr., "James Marsh (1794–1842): Philosophical Theologian, Evangelical Liberal," *Church History* 38 (December 1969): 437–58; Peter

Carafiol, *Transcendent Reason: James Marsh and the Forms of Romantic Thought* (Tallahassee: University Presses of Florida, 1982).

3. Marsh, "Ancient and Modern Poetry," *North American Review* 22 (1822): 94–131.

4. Marsh, "Review of Stuart on the Epistle to the Hebrews," *Quarterly Christian Spectator* 1 (March 1829): 115, 116, 117.

5. Marsh, "Review of Stuart," 119, 121.

6. Marsh, "Review of Stuart, 119.

7. Torrey, *Remains of Marsh*, 44–48.

8. Marsh, *Aids*, xiii, xx.

9. Marsh, *Aids*, xxi, xxii.

10. Marsh, *Aids*, xxxi.

11. Marsh, *Aids*, xl, xlii. See also Walter H. Conser, Jr., "James Marsh and the Germans," *New England Quarterly* 59 (June 1986): 259–66.

12. Marsh, *Aids*, xlix.

13. See James Marsh to Samuel Taylor Coleridge, 24 February 1830, qtd. in John J. Duffy, ed. *Coleridge's American Disciples: The Selected Correspondence of James Marsh* (Amherst: University of Massachusetts Press, 1973), 108–10; James Marsh to August Tholuck, 4 September 1830, August Tholuck Papers, Katechetisches Oberseminar, Naumburg, Germany; James Marsh to Richard Dana, 21 August 1832, qtd. in Ronald V. Wells, *Three Christian Transcendentalists* (New York: Columbia University Press, 1943), 160–62.

14. Noah Porter, "Coleridge and His American Disciples," *Bibliotheca Sacra* 4 (1847): 163.

15. For biographical details of Shedd's life, see the short notices in *The Dictionary of American Biography* (1963 ed.), 9:56–57; and George L. Prentiss, *The Union Theological Seminary* (New York, 1899); as well as the article by Cushing Strout, "Faith and History: The Mind of William G. T. Shedd," *Journal of the History of Ideas* 15 (1954): 153–62.

16. Shedd, "The Method and Influence of Theological Studies," *Theological Essays* (New York: Scribners, 1877), 39ff. This lecture was first delivered in 1845. For discussion of Romantic aesthetics, see M. H. Abrams, *The Mirror and the Lamp* (New York: Oxford University Press, 1953).

17. Shedd, "The Relation of Language and Style to Thought," *Literary Essays* (New York: Scribners, 1878), 149–55; James Marsh, "Stuart on the Epistle to the Hebrews," 115–16. On neoclassicism in America, see William Charvat, *The Origins of American Critical Thought, 1810–1835* (New York: A. S. Brown, 1961). For a review of the growth of linguistics, see Holger Pedersen, *The Discovery of Language: Linguistic Science in the Nineteenth Century* (Bloomington: Indiana University Press, 1967); as well as the broader study by Robert D. Richardson, Jr., *Myth and Literature in the American Renaissance* (Bloomington: Indiana University Press, 1978).

18. Shedd, "Relation of Language," 153.
19. Shedd, "Relation of Language," 166–73; "The True Nature of the Beautiful and Its Relation to Culture," *Literary Essays*, 26.
20. Shedd, "Relation of Language," 158.
21. Robert N. Gourdin to William Porcher Miles, 17 October 1856, William Porcher Miles Papers, Southern Historical Collection, University of North Carolina, Chapel Hill, North Carolina. See Miles's own description of himself as a "dolt," in Miles to Mrs. T. J. Young, undated, ca. 1856, James Warley Miles Papers, Duke University, Durham, North Carolina.
22. James Waddell to James S. Miles, 13 and 20 March 1834, William Porcher Miles Papers, Southern Historical Collection. For biographical details concerning Miles, see George Williams, *The Reverend James Warley Miles* (Charleston, S.C.: Dalcho Historical Society, 1954); and Ralph Luker, *A Southern Tradition in Theology and Social Criticism, 1830–1930* (New York: Edwin Mellen Press, 1984).
23. Miles, *Farewell Sermon* (Charleston, S.C.: B. B. Hussey, 1843), 11. The letter of Miles on his interest in missionary work is printed in the *Charleston Gospel Messenger* (May 1843): 59.
24. For discussion of the Southgate mission station, see Charles T. Bridgeman, "Mediterranean Missions of the Episcopal Church from 1828–1898," *Historical Magazine of the Protestant Episcopal Church* 31 (June 1962): 95–125; for Miles's reflections on the state of the South, see "The Turkish Language," *Southern Quarterly Review* 13 (January 1848): 70. Broader analysis of the context of Southern intellectual life is provided in Drew G. Faust, *A Sacred Circle: The Dilemma of the Intellectual in the Old South* (Baltimore: Johns Hopkins University Press, 1977).
25. Miles, "Lieber, Nordheimer, and Donaldson on the Philosophy of Language," *Southern Quarterly Review* 20 (October 1851): 392–93, 403. See chap. 5: "Religion and the Science of Society," for discussion of Miles's view of Southern slavery.
26. Miles, *Student of Philology* (Charleston, S.C.: John Russell, 1853), 18, 38. For an assessment of the state of scientific philology, see Hans Aarsleff, *The Study of Language in England, 1760–1860* (Princeton, N.J.: Princeton University Press, 1967).
27. Miles to Mrs. T. J. Young, undated, ca. 1857, Miles Papers, Duke University.
28. Miles to Mrs. T. J. Young, 28 November 1864, Miles Papers, Duke University.
29. Miles to Mrs. T. J. Young, 28 June 1864, Miles Papers, Duke University.
30. Miles to Mrs. T. J. Young, 23 July 1864, Miles Papers, Duke University.
31. Miles to Mrs. T. J. Young, 11 June 1864, Miles Papers, Duke University.
32. Miles to Mrs. T. J. Young, 10 December 1864, Miles Papers, Duke University.

33. Charles Feidelson, Jr., *Symbolism and American Literature* (Chicago: University of Chicago Press, 1953), 131; James Marsh to Richard H. Dana, 14 March 1838; and James Marsh to Henry J. Raymond, 1 March 1841, qtd. in Ronald V. Wells, *Three Christian Transcendentalists* (New York: Columbia University Press, 1943), 163, 167.

34. Miles, "The Philosophy of the Beautiful," *Southern Quarterly Review* 14 (October 1849): 134.

35. Miles, "Address before the Charleston Bible Society," MS lecture, January 1874, Miles Papers, College of Charleston, Charleston, South Carolina. The same theme can be found in Miles's earlier work, *Philosophic Theology*, published in 1849, and thus illustrates the continuity in Miles's thought.

36. See Charvat, *American Critical Thought*, 22; Mary Bushnell Cheney, *The Life and Letters of Horace Bushnell* (New York: Harper and Bros.: 1880), 209.

37. Cheney, *Life*, 32; Noah Porter, "Horace Bushnell," *New Englander* 37 (1877): 157–69.

38. See Cheney, *Life*, 35–66; and the study by Barbara Cross, *Horace Bushnell* (Chicago: University of Chicago Press, 1958).

39. Bushnell, "Natural Science and Moral Philosophy," MS lecture, Bushnell Papers, Yale Divinity School Library, Yale University, New Haven, Connecticut.

40. Bushnell, *Nature and the Supernatural*, 5th ed. (New York: Scribners, 1863), 20. The chapters of this book were first presented as the Dudleian Lectures at Harvard University in 1852.

41. Bushnell, "There Is a Moral Governor," MS sermon, Bushnell Papers, Yale University.

42. See Cheney, *Life*, 208–9, 499.

43. For Bushnell's hopes that his publications would win him a post at Harvard Divinity School or one of the other major seminaries, see Cross, *Horace Bushnell*, 84. For contemporary reviews of Bushnell's discussion of language, see David N. Lord, "Dr. Bushnell's Dissertation on Language," *Theological and Literary Journal* 2 (July 1849): 61–131; [Charles Hodge], "Bushnell's Discourses," *Princeton Review* 21 (April 1849): 259–98. For more recent appraisals, see Donald A. Crosby, *Horace Bushnell's Theory of Language* (The Hague: Mouton, 1975); Conrad Cherry, *Nature and Religious Imagination: From Edwards to Bushnell* (Philadelphia: Fortress Press, 1980); David L. Smith, *Symbolism and Growth: The Religious Thought of Horace Bushnell* (Chico, Calif.: Scholars Press, 1981); Philip E. Gura, *The Wisdom of Words: Language, Theology, and Literature in the New England Renaissance* (Middletown, Conn.: Wesleyan University Press, 1981); James O. Duke, *Horace Bushnell on the Vitality of Biblical Language* (Chico, Calif.: Scholars Press, 1984).

44. Bushnell, *God in Christ, Three Discourses . . . with a Preliminary Dissertation on Language* (Hartford, Conn.: Brown and Parsons, 1849), 12, 13, 21–27; Crosby, *Bushnell's Theory of Language*, 233.

45. Josiah W. Gibbs, *Philological Studies* (New Haven, Conn.: Durrie and Peck, 1857), 18. For mention of Humboldt and Tooke, see Bushnell, *Preliminary Dissertation*, 19, 27.

46. Bushnell, *Preliminary Dissertation*, 30. For discussion of the function and meaning of typology, see Ursula Brumm, *American Thought and Religious Typology* (New Brunswick, N.J.: Rutgers University Press, 1970); and Sacvan Bercovitch, ed., *Typology and Early American Literature* (Amherst: University of Massachusetts Press, 1972). For commentary on Bushnell's use, see David Smith, *Symbolism and Growth*, 16.

47. Bushnell, *Preliminary Dissertation*, 38–40.

48. Bushnell, *Preliminary Dissertation*, 48–49, 85, 78, 93.

49. Bushnell, *Preliminary Dissertation*, 92, 80–81, 88–89.

Chapter Five: Religion and the Science of Society

1. See D. H. Meyer, *The Instructed Conscience* (Philadelphia: University of Pennsylvania Press, 1972); and Thomas L. Haskell, *The Emergence of Professional Social Science: The American Social Science Association and the Nineteenth-Century Crisis of Authority* (Urbana: University of Illinois Press, 1977).

2. Charles Hodge to Hugh Hodge, 19 September 1832; Charles Hodge to F. A. G. Tholuck, 9 February 1831, Hodge Reports, Princeton University Library, Princeton, New Jersey.

3. Charles Hodge to F. A. G. Tholuck, 14 November 1827, August Tholuck Papers, Katechetisches Oberseminar, Naumburg, Germany; Charles Hodge to Hugh Hodge, 1 August 1837, Hodge Papers, Princeton University Library.

4. For a discussion of prescriptive politics, see Daniel Walker Howe, *The Political Culture of the Whigs* (Chicago: University of Chicago Press, 1979). For Hodge's various political views, see A. A. Hodge, *The Life of Charles Hodge* (New York: Scribners, 1880), 218, 346, 348; and Charles Hodge's essay "The American Quarterly Review on Sunday Mails," *Princeton Review* (January 1831): 89, 127.

5. For Hodge's view of social contract theory, see "Sermon on Romans 13:1," Charles Hodge Papers, Princeton Theological Seminary, Princeton, New Jersey; Charles Hodge to Hugh Hodge, 23 December 1833, Hodge Papers, Princeton University Library.

6. For a discussion of the American school of anthropology, see William Stanton, *The Leopard's Spots* (Chicago: University of Chicago Press, 1960);

Reginald Horsman, *Josiah Nott* (Baton Rouge: Louisiana State University Press, 1987); Robert E. Bieder, *Science Encounters the Indian, 1820–1880* (Norman: University of Oklahoma Press, 1986).

7. See Hodge, "Slavery," *Princeton Review* 8 (April 1836): 277, 285; Charles Hodge to Hugh Hodge, 18 February 1861, Hodge Papers, Princeton University Library.

8. For Hodge's views, see "Slavery," *Princeton Review* 270; Hodge, "The Princeton Review on the State of the Country," *Princeton Review* 33 (January 1861): 1–36; Charles Hodge to Hugh Hodge, quoted in A. Hodge, *Life*, 466. Lewis Tappan's inquiry is found in Lewis Tappan to Charles Hodge, 25 November 1849, Hodge Papers, Princeton University Library. For further discussion of the content and reception of proslavery arguments, see William Sumner Jenkins, *Proslavery Thought in the Old South* (Chapel Hill: University of North Carolina, 1935); Drew G. Faust, ed., *The Ideology of Slavery* (Baton Rouge: Louisiana State University Press, 1981); Bertram Wyatt-Brown, "From Piety to Fantasy: Proslavery's Troubled Evolution," in *Yankee Saints and Southern Sinners*, ed. Bertram Wyatt-Brown (Baton Rouge: Louisiana State University Press, 1985); Larry E. Tise, *Proslavery* (Athens: University of Georgia Press, 1987).

9. James Henley Thornwell, *The Collected Writings of James Henley Thornwell*, ed. John B. Adger, 4 vols. (Richmond, Va.: Presbyterian Committee of Publication, 1871–73), 4:403, 385–87, 392. For Thornwell's characterization of abolitionism, see his journal entry of 19 May 1841, James Henley Thornwell Papers, South Caroliniana Library, University of South Carolina, Columbia, South Carolina.

10. Thornwell, *Collected Writings*, 4:405–6, 414.

11. Thornwell, *Collected Writings*, 4:433–34, 420–423.

12. Thornwell to his wife, 2 July 1841; Thornwell to James Gillespie, 19 November 1861, Thornwell Papers, University of South Carolina.

13. See Thornwell, *National Sins: A Fast-Day Sermon* (Columbia: Guardian Press, 1860); *The State of the Country*, in Palmer, *Thornwell's Life and Letters*, 591–610. For a discussion of antifederalism, see the classic and still relevant essay by Cecelia M. Kenyon, "Men of Little Faith: The Anti-Federalists on the Nature of Representative Government," *William and Mary Quarterly*, 3d ser. 12 (1955): 3–43; as well as the more recent article by Richard E. Ellis, "The Persistence of Antifederalism after 1789," in *Beyond Confederation*, ed. Richard Beeman et al. (Chapel Hill: University of North Carolina Press, 1988), 295–314.

14. See Thornwell to his wife, 28 June 1862, Anderson-Thornwell Papers, Southern Historical Collection, University of North Carolina, Chapel Hill, North Carolina; and Thornwell, *Collected Works*, 4:446–64. In a recent article William W. Freehling has explored Thornwell's reflections

on emancipation of the slaves. It is clear, however, that Thornwell remained committed to slavery. See William H. Freehling, "James Henley Thornwell's Mysterious Antislavery Moment," *Journal of Southern History* 57 (August 1991): 383–406.

15. See Hodge, "The Princeton Review on the State of the Country and the Church," *Princeton Review* 37 (October 1865): 627–57. W. G. T. Shedd, though he grounded his comments more in an interpretation of biblical history than scriptural exegesis, joined Hodge in condemning Southern secession. See Shedd's address of 1862, "The Union and the War," reprinted in *Orthodoxy and Heterodoxy* (New York: Scribners, 1893), 267–97.

16. Schaff, *American Nationality* (Chambersburg, Pa.: Kieffer, 1856), 14.

17. Schaff's self-description is contained in his unpublished "Autobiographical Reminiscences," Philip Schaff Papers, Evangelical and Reformed Historical Society, Lancaster Theological Seminary, Lancaster, Pennsylvania. The phrase *Phenix grave* is quoted from Philip Schaff, in *America*, ed. Perry Miller (Cambridge: Harvard University Press, 1961), 51.

18. Schaff, *America*, 45, 183.

19. For a discussion of romantic racial nationalism, see Reginald Horsman, *Race and Manifest Destiny* (Cambridge: Harvard University Press, 1981), 158–86.

20. Schaff, *Anglo-Germanism, or, The Significance of the German Nationality* (Chambersburg, Pa.: Kieffer, 1846), 16–17.

21. Schaff, *What Is Church History?* (Philadelphia: Lippincott, 1846), 38–39.

22. For a discussion of romanticism, see René Wellek, "The Concept of Romanticism in Literary History," reprinted in *Concepts of Criticism*, ed. Stephen Nichols, Jr. (New Haven, Conn.: Yale University Press, 1963), 160–67; Maurice Mandelbaum, *History, Man, and Reason* (Baltimore: Johns Hopkins University Press, 1974), 41–44; M. H. Abrams, *The Mirror and the Lamp* (New York, 1958), 202–5. For a thorough tracing of the background of Schaff's thought, see Klaus Penzel, "Church History and the Ecumenical Quest: A Study of the German Background and Thought of Philip Schaff" (Th.D. diss, Union Theological Seminary, 1962).

23. Schaff, *American Nationality*, 13–14.

24. Schaff, *Systematic Benevolence: A Sermon* (Mercersburg, Pa.: 1851), 25. For a discussion of paternalism, see David Moore, *The Politics of Deference* (New York: Barnes and Noble, 1976).

25. Schaff, *America*, 217, 6–7.

26. Schaff, *America*, 7, 44. For a discussion of the themes of civilization and Christianization in the rhetoric of American missionaries, see William R. Hutchison, *Errand to the World* (Chicago: University of Chicago Press, 1987).

27. Schaff, *Slavery and the Bible* (Chambersburg, Pa.: Kieffer, 1861), 24–32.

28. Schaff, *Slavery and the Bible*, 31–32. For a broader assessment, see the discussion in Leon Litwack, *North of Slavery* (Chicago: University of Chicago Press, 1961); and George Fredrickson, *The Black Image in the White Mind* (New York: Harper and Row, 1971).

29. Schaff, *America*, 6. See James Moorhead, *American Apocalypse* (New Haven, Conn.: Yale University Press, 1978), for analysis of Northern Protestant attitudes toward the war.

30. Schaff, *Der Bürgerkrieg und das christliche Leben in Nord Amerika* (Berlin: Wiegand and Grieben, 1866), 17–18, 25.

31. Miles, *The Relation between the Races of the South* (Charleston: Evans and Cogswell, 1861), 18.

32. Miles, *Relation between the Races*, 17–19.

33. Miles to Francis Lieber, undated letter, circa 1853, Francis Lieber Papers, The Huntington Library, San Marino, California.

34. Miles, *Relation between the Races*, 4, 8.

35. See *Relation between the Races*, 9–15, quotation on p. 9.

36. Miles, *Relation between the Races*, 18.

37. Miles to Mrs. Thomas Young, 6 February 1865, James Warley Miles Papers, Duke University, Durham, North Carolina. For further discussion of Jefferson Davis's proposal, see Robert F. Durden, *The Gray and the Black* (Baton Rouge: Louisiana State University Press, 1972).

38. Miles, *God in History* (Charleston: Evans and Cogswell, 1863), 24; Miles to Mrs. Young, undated letter, circa 1864, Miles Papers, Duke University Library.

39. See James W. Silver, *Confederate Morale and Church Propaganda* (1957; reprint, New York: W. W. Norton, 1967), 25–41; and Gardiner H. Shattuck, Jr., *A Shield and Hiding Place* (Macon, Ga.: Mercer University Press, 1987), 35–50.

40. Miles to Mrs. Young, 7 January 1865, Miles Papers, Duke University.

41. Miles to Mrs. Young, 7 July 1865, Miles Papers, Duke University. See also Silver, *Confederate Morale*, 37; and Shattuck, *Shield*, 41–42.

42. Miles, *A Discourse Delivered . . . before the Washington Light Infantry* (Charleston: Evans and Cogswell, 1874), 10.

43. Miles, *Annual Oration Delivered at the Commencement of the Chrestomathic Society* (Charleston: Evans and Cogswell, 1874), 6.

44. See John J. Duffy, ed., *Coleridge's American Disciples: The Selected Correspondence of James Marsh* (Amherst: University of Massachusetts Press, 1973), 27.

45. On Wilhelm von Humboldt and the meaning of *Bildung*, see W. H. Bruford, *The German Tradition of Self-Cultivation* (New York: Cambridge University Press, 1975).

46. Lewis S. Feuer, "James Marsh and the Conservative Transcendentalist Philosophy: A Political Interpretation," *New England Quarterly* 31

(March 1958): 3–31; Joseph Torrey, ed., *The Remains of the Rev. James Marsh* (Boston: Crocker and Brewster, 1843), 15, 28, 68.

47. See Lawrence A. Cremin, *American Education: The National Experience, 1783–1876* (New York: Harper and Row, 1980), 272; Franz Schnabel, *Deutsche Geschichte im Neuenzehnten Jahrhundert*, 2d ed., 4 vols. (Freiburg: Herder Verlag, 1951), 1:291, 408–13.

48. See David F. Allmendinger, Jr., "New England Students and the Revolution in Higher Education, 1800–1900," in *The Social History of Education*, ed. B. Edward McClellan and William J. Reese (Urbana: University of Illinois Press, 1988), 65–71.

49. See Marsh, *An Exposition of the System of Instruction in the University of Vermont* (Burlington, Vt.: Chauncey Goodrich, 1829).

50. Torrey, *Remains of Marsh*, 560.

51. Torrey, *Remains of Marsh*, 559, 562.

52. Torrey, *Remains of Marsh*, 569–71.

53. Torrey, *Remains of Marsh*, 562, 69–71.

54. Torrey, *Remains of Marsh*, 18–19, 44–47, 126–27; Duffy, *Coleridge's American Disciples*, 178–88.

55. See J. Bartlett Brebner, *Canada: A Modern History* (Ann Arbor: University of Michigan Press, 1970), 217–23, 235–40.

56. Duffy, *Coleridge's American Disciples*, 194–99, 204–7.

57. See Marsh to Henry J. Raymond, 1 March 1841, quoted in Ronald V. Wells, *Three Christian Transcendentalists* (New York: Columbia University Press, 1943), 166–67.

58. Bushnell, *A Discourse on the Moral Tendencies and Results of Human History* (New York: M. Y. Beach, 1843), 29.

59. See Bushnell, *Politics under the Law of God* (Hartford, Conn.: E. Hunt, 1844). Daniel Walker Howe analyzes Bushnell's views in "The Social Science of Horace Bushnell," *Journal of American History* 70 (September 1983): 305–22.

60. Bushnell, *Barbarism the First Danger* (New York: American Home Missionary Society, 1847), 7, 20.

61. Bushnell, *Barbarism*, 20. See also Bushnell's address, "The True Wealth or Weal of Nations," first published in 1837 and reprinted in *Work and Play* (New York: Scribners, 1864), 45.

62. Bushnell, *A Discourse on the Slavery Question* (Hartford, Conn.: Case, 1839), 6–7.

63. Quoted in Mary Bushnell Cheney, *Life and Letters of Horace Bushnell* (New York: Harper and Bros., 1880), 411.

64. Bushnell, *Discourse on Slavery*, 11–12.

65. Bushnell, *Discourse on Slavery*, 13.

66. Bushnell, "Popular Government by Divine Right," reprinted in *Building Eras in Religion* (New York: Scribners, 1910), 287–88.

67. Bushnell, "Popular Government," 315–18.

68. Bushnell, "Our Obligations to the Dead" (1865), reprinted in *Building Eras in Religion*, 355.

Epilogue

1. See Neal C. Gillespie, *Charles Darwin and the Problem of Creation* (Chicago: University of Chicago Press, 1979), 8–12.
2. See Jay Martin, *Harvest of Change: American Literature, 1865–1914* (Englewood Cliffs, N.J.: Prentice-Hall, 1967); Henry W. Bowden, *Church History in the Age of Science* (Chapel Hill: University of North Carolina, 1971).
3. See James O. Duke, *Horace Bushnell on the Vitality of Biblical Language* (Chico, Calif.: Scholars Press, 1984), 91–93; Robert Morgan, *Biblical Interpretation* (New York: Oxford University Press, 1988), 74–75.
4. See George H. Daniels, *Science in American Society: A Social History* (New York: Alfred A. Knopf, 1971), 272–76.
5. See Gillespie, *Charles Darwin*, 12–16.
6. Henry Ward Beecher, *Lectures on Preaching* (New York: J. B. Ford, 1872), 88.
7. See Edwards A. Park, "Connection between Theological Study and Pulpit Eloquence," *American Biblical Repository* 10 (July 1837): 169–91; and "The Theology of the Intellect and That of the Feelings," *Bibliotheca Sacra* 7 (1850): 533–69. For discussion of changes in the late nineteenth-century Protestant ministry and especially the increasingly prominent role of personality as a factor, see Robert S. Michaelsen, "The Protestant Ministry in America, 1850–1950," in *The Ministry in Historical Perspective*, ed. H. Richard Niebuhr and Daniel D. Williams (San Francisco: Harper and Row, 1983), 250–88; E. Brooks Holifield, *A History of Pastoral Care in America* (Nashville: Abingdon Press, 1983), 174.
8. William Newton Clarke, *An Outline of Christian Theology* (New York: Scribners, 1901), 18–19. For general discussion of this shift in Protestant theology, see Cynthia Russett, *Darwin in America* (San Francisco: W. H. Freeman, 1976), 38–43.
9. See David Hull, *Darwin and His Critics: The Reception of Darwin's Theory of Evolution by the Scientific Community* (Cambridge: Harvard University Press, 1973); Peter J. Bowler, *The Eclipse of Darwinism: Anti-Darwinian Evolution Theories in the Decades around 1900* (Baltimore: Johns Hopkins University Press, 1983), 10–14; Jon H. Roberts, *Darwinism and the Divine in America* (Madison: University of Wisconsin Press, 1988), 121–22.
10. Bowler, *Eclipse of Darwinism*, 118–40.
11. Horace Bushnell, "Science and Religion," *Putnam's Magazine* 1 (March 1868): 267, 269.

12. Bushnell, "Science and Religion," 271. For additional discussion of Bushnell's response, see Thomas P. Thigpen, "On the Origin of Theses: An Exploration of Horace Bushnell's Rejection of Darwinism," *Church History* 57 (December 1988): 499–513.

13. Charles Hodge, *What Is Darwinism?* (New York: Scribners, 1874), 26–27.

14. Hodge, *What Is Darwinism*, 141, 144, 173–77; Roberts, *Darwinism and the Divine*, 41–43.

15. Sydney Ahlstrom coined the phrase *harmonial piety;* see his *A Religious History of the American People* (New Haven, Conn.: Yale University Press, 1972), 1019. For William James's evaluation, see his *Varieties of Religious Experience* (New York: Random House, 1902), 92–94, 106–7, 116–20. For further analysis of this response, see Stephen Gottschalk, *The Emergence of Christian Science in American Religious Life* (Berkeley: University of California Press, 1973); Robert C. Fuller, *Alternative Medicine and American Religious Life* (New York: Oxford University Press, 1989); and Catherine L. Albanese, *Nature Religion in America* (Chicago: University of Chicago Press, 1990), 117–52.

16. See David A. Hollinger, "Justification by Verification: The Scientific Challenge to the Moral Authority of Christianity in Modern America," in *Religion and Twentieth-Century American Intellectual Life*, ed. Michael J. Lacey (New York: Cambridge University Press, 1989), 116–35.

17. Washington Gladden, *How Much Is Left of the Old Doctrines?* (Boston: Houghton Mifflin, 1900), 16. For an insightful examination of modernism, see William R. Hutchison, *The Modernist Impulse in American Protestantism* (Cambridge: Harvard University Press, 1976).

18. Henry Ward Beecher, *Evolution and Religion* (New York: J. B. Ford, 1885), 46; Lyman Abbott, *The Theology of an Evolutionist* (Boston: Houghton Mifflin, 1897), 75–77.

19. See Roberts, *Darwinism and the Divine*, 117–26.

20. William Hutchison, *Modernist Impulse*, 48; Washington Gladden, *Recollections* (Boston: Houghton Mifflin, 1909), 119. Further invocations of the liberating spirit of Bushnell can be seen in Theodore Munger's manifesto "The New Theology," in his volume *The Freedom of Faith* (Boston: Houghton Mifflin, 1884), 3–44; and his essay, "Evolution and Faith," in *The Appeal to Life* (Boston: Houghton Mifflin, 1887), 209–43; as well as Newman Smyth's book, *Old Faiths in New Light* (New York: Scribners, 1879).

21. See George M. Marsden, *Fundamentalism and American Culture* (New York: Oxford University Press, 1980), 4.

22. Marsden, *Fundamentalism and American Culture*, 19, 213–21.

23. See Marsden, *Fundamentalism and American Culture*, 55–62; and Ernest R. Sandeen, *The Roots of Fundamentalism* (Chicago: University of Chicago Press, 1970). For discussion of the continuation and transformation of this understanding of science into the twentieth century and its signifi-

cance for the rise of twentieth-century creationism, see Ronald Numbers, *The Creationists* (New York: Alfred A. Knopf, 1992).

24. Noah Porter, "The Collapse of Faith," *Princeton Review* (March 1882): 165; Arthur M. Schlesinger, Sr., "A Critical Period in American Protestantism, 1875–1900," *Massachusetts Historical Society Proceedings* 64 (1932): 523–48.

Bibliography

I. Manuscripts

Anderson [James]–Thornwell [James Henley]. Papers. Southern Historical Collection, University of North Carolina, Chapel Hill, North Carolina.

Bushnell, Horace. Papers. Yale Divinity School Library, Yale University, New Haven, Connecticut.

Gourdin, Robert. Papers. Duke University, Durham, North Carolina.

Hengstenberg, Ernst. Papers. Staatsbibliothek Preussischer Kulturbesitz, Potsdamerstrasse, Berlin, Germany.

Hodge, Charles. Papers. Princeton Theological Seminary, Princeton, New Jersey.

———. Papers. Princeton University Library, Princeton, New Jersey.

King, Mitchell. Papers. Southern Historical Collection, University of North Carolina, Chapel Hill, North Carolina.

Lieber, Francis. Papers. The Huntington Library, San Marino, California.

Miles, James Warley. Papers. College of Charleston, Charleston, South Carolina.

———. Papers. Duke University, Durham, North Carolina.

Miles, William Porcher. Papers. Southern Historical Collection, University of North Carolina, Chapel Hill, North Carolina.

Neander, August. Papers. Deutsche Staatsbibliothek Preussischer Kulturbesitz, Unter den Linden, Berlin, Germany.

Pettigrew, James Johnston. Papers. Southern Historical Collection, University of North Carolina, Chapel Hill, North Carolina.

Ritter, Carl. Papers. Deutsche Staatsbibliothek Preussischer Kulturbesitz, Unter den Linden, Berlin, Germany.

Schaff, Philip. Papers. Evangelical and Reformed Historical Society, Lancaster Theological Seminary, Lancaster, Pennsylvania.

Tholuck, August. Papers. Katechetisches Oberseminar, Naumburg, Germany.

Thornwell, James Henley. Papers. South Carolinian Library, University of South Carolina, Columbia, South Carolina.

II. Printed Sources

Aarsleff, Hans. *The Study of Language in England, 1760–1860.* Princeton: Princeton University Press, 1967.

Abbott, Lyman. *The Theology of an Evolutionist*. Boston: Houghton Mifflin, 1897.

Abrams, M. H. *The Mirror and the Lamp*. New York: Oxford University Press, 1953.

———. *Natural Supernaturalism*. New York: W. W. Norton, 1973.

Adger, John B., ed. *The Collected Writings of James Henley Thornwell*. 4 vols. Richmond: Presbyterian Committee of Publications, 1871–73.

Ahlstrom, Sydney E. *The American Protestant Encounter with World Religions*. Beloit, Wisc.: Beloit College, 1962.

———. *A Religious History of the American People*. New Haven, Conn.: Yale University Press, 1972.

Albanese, Catherine L. *Nature Religion in America*. Chicago: University of Chicago Press, 1990.

Albright, William F. *The Archaeology of Palestine*. Reprint. Gloucester, Mass.: Peter Smith, 1971.

Allmendinger, David F., Jr. "New England Students and the Revolution in Higher Education, 1800–1900." In McClellan and Reese, *The Social History of Education*, 65–71.

"The Argument for Natural Religion." *Christian Examiner* 19 (1835): 137–62.

Bartlett, Irving R. "The Romantic Theology of Horace Bushnell." Ph.D. diss., Brown University, 1952.

Beecher, Henry Ward. *Lectures of Preaching*. New York: J. B. Ford, 1872.

———. *Evolution and Religion*. New York: J. B. Ford, 1885.

Beeman, Richard, et al., eds. *Beyond Confederation*. Chapel Hill: University of North Carolina Press, 1988.

Beiser, Gerhard, and Christof Gestrich, eds. *450 Jahre Evangelische Theologie in Berlin*. Göttingen: Vandenhoeck and Ruprecht, 1989.

Bercovitch, Sacvan, ed. *Typology and Early American Literature*. Amherst: University of Massachusetts Press, 1972.

Bieder, Robert. *Science Encounters the Indian, 1820–1880*. Norman: University of Oklahoma Press, 1986.

Bowden, Henry W. *Church History in the Age of Science*. Chapel Hill: University of North Carolina Press, 1971.

Bowler, Peter. *The Eclipse of Darwinism: Anti-Darwinian Evolution Theories in the Decades around 1900*. Baltimore: Johns Hopkins University Press, 1983.

———. *Evolution: The History of an Idea*. Berkeley: University of California Press, 1984.

Bozeman, Theodore Dwight. *Protestants in an Age of Science: The Baconian Ideal and Antebellum American Religious Thought*. Chapel Hill: University of North Carolina Press, 1977.

Brebner, J. Bartlett. *Canada: A Modern History*. Ann Arbor: University of Michigan Press, 1970.

Bremer, Fredrika. *The Homes of the New World; Impressions of America.* 2 vols. New York: Harper and Bros., 1854.

Bridgeman, Charles T. "Mediterranean Missions of the Episcopal Church from 1828–1898." *Historical Magazine of the Protestant Episcopal Church* 31 (1962): 95–125.

Brooke, John Headley. *Science and Religion.* Cambridge: Cambridge University Press, 1991.

Brown, Ira. "The Higher Criticism Comes to America, 1880–1900." *Journal of the Presbyterian Historical Society* 38 (1960): 193–212.

Brown, Jerry Wayne. *The Rise of Biblical Criticism in America, 1800–1870.* Middletown, Conn.: Wesleyan University Press, 1969.

Bruford, W. H. *The German Tradition of Self-Cultivation.* New York: Cambridge University Press, 1975.

Brumm, Ursula. *American Thought and Religious Typology.* New Brunswick, N.J.: Rutgers University Press, 1970.

Bushnell, Horace. *A Discourse on the Slavery Question.* Hartford, Conn.: Case, 1839.

———. *A Discourse on the Moral Tendencies and Results of Human History.* New York: M. Y. Beach, 1843.

———. *Politics under the Law of God.* Hartford, Conn.: E. Hunt, 1844.

———. *Barbarism the First Danger.* New York: American Home Missionary Society, 1847.

———. *God in Christ, Three Discourses . . . with a Preliminary Dissertation on Language.* Hartford, Conn.: Brown and Parsons, 1849.

———. *Nature and the Supernatural.* 5th ed. 1858. Reprint. New York: Scribners, 1863.

———. *Work and Play.* New York: Scribners, 1864.

———. "Science and Religion." *Putnam's Magazine* 1 (1868): 265–75.

———. *Building Eras in Religion.* New York: Scribners, 1910.

Butterfield, Herbert. *The Origins of Modern Science, 1300–1800.* Rev. ed. New York: Free Press, 1965.

Calhoun, Daniel. *Professional Lives in America.* Cambridge: Harvard University Press, 1965.

Carafiol, Peter. *Transcendent Reason: James Marsh and the Forms of Romantic Thought.* Tallahassee: University Presses of Florida, 1982.

Cayton, Mary K. "'Sympathy's Electric Chain' and the American Democracy: Emerson's First Vocational Crisis." *New England Quarterly* 60 (1982): 3–24.

Charvat, William. *The Origins of American Critical Thought, 1810–1835.* New York: A. S. Brown, 1961.

Cheney, Mary Bushnell. *The Life and Letters of Horace Bushnell.* New York: Harper and Bros., 1880.

Cherry, Conrad, ed. *God's New Israel: Religious Interpretations of American Destiny.* Englewood Cliffs, N.J.: Prentice Hall, 1971.

———. *Nature and Religious Imagination: From Edwards to Bushnell.* Philadelphia: Fortress Press, 1980.

Clarke, William Newton. *An Outline of Christian Theology.* New York: Scribners, 1901.

Cohen, I. Bernard. *Revolution in Science.* Cambridge: Harvard University Press, 1985.

Coleridge, Samuel Taylor. *Aids to Reflections . . . Together with a Preliminary Essay.* Ed. James Marsh. Burlington, Vt.: Chauncey Goodrich, 1829.

Conser, Walter H., Jr. *Church and Confession: Conservative Theologians in Germany, England, and America, 1815–1866.* Macon, Ga.: Mercer University Press, 1984.

———. "James Marsh and the Germans." *New England Quarterly* 59 (1986): 259–66.

Cremin, Lawrence. *American Education: The National Experience, 1783–1876.* New York: Harper and Row, 1980.

Crosby, Donald A. *Horace Bushnell's Theory of Language.* The Hague: Mouton, 1975.

Cross, Barbara. *Horace Bushnell.* Chicago: University of Chicago Press, 1958.

Dana, John Jay. "The Claims of the Natural Sciences on the Christian Ministry." *Bibliotheca Sacra* 6 (1849): 461–71.

Daniels, George H. *American Science in the Age of Jackson.* New York: Columbia University Press, 1968.

———. *Science in American Society: A Social History.* New York: Alfred A. Knopf, 1971.

DeJong, John A. "American Attitudes toward Evolution before Darwin." Ph.D. diss., State University of Iowa, 1962.

Dewey, John. "James Marsh and American Philosophy." *Journal of the History of Ideas* 2 (1941): 131–50.

Diehl, Carl. *Americans and German Scholarship, 1770–1870.* New Haven: Yale University Press, 1978.

Dillenberger, John. *Protestant Thought and Natural Science.* Nashville: Abingdon Press, 1960.

Dirks, John E. *The Critical Theology of Theodore Parker.* New York: Columbia University Press, 1948.

Draper, John William. *History of the Conflict between Religion and Science.* New York: D. Appleton, 1874.

Duffy, John J., ed. *Coleridge's American Disciples: The Selected Correspondence of James Marsh.* Amherst: University of Massachusetts Press, 1973.

Duke, James O. *Horace Bushnell on the Vitality of Biblical Language.* Chico, Calif.: Scholars Press, 1984.

Dupree, A. Hunter. *Science in the Federal Government.* Rev. ed. Baltimore: Johns Hopkins University Press, 1986.

Durden, Robert F. *The Gray and the Black.* Baton Rouge: Louisiana State University Press, 1972.

Dyer, David. *The Plenary Inspiration of the Old and New Testaments.* Boston: Tappan, 1849.

Easterby, James H., ed. "Letters of James Warley Miles to David James McCord." *South Carolina Historical and Genealogical Magazine* 43 (1942): 185–93.

Ellis, Richard E. "The Persistence of Antifederalism after 1789." In Beeman et al., *Beyond Confederation,* 295–314.

Farmer, James O. *The Metaphysical Confederacy: James Henley Thornwell and the Synthesis of Southern Values.* Macon, Ga.: Mercer University Press, 1986.

Faust, Drew G. *A Sacred Circle.* Baltimore: Johns Hopkins University Press, 1977.

———, ed. *The Ideology of Slavery.* Baton Rouge: Louisiana State University Press, 1981.

Feidelson, Charles, Jr. *Symbolism and American Literature.* Chicago: University of Chicago Press, 1953.

Feuer, Lewis S. "James Marsh and the Conservative Transcendentalist Philosophy: A Political Interpretation." *New England Quarterly* 31 (1958): 3–31.

Finnie, David H. *Pioneers East: The Early American Experience in the Middle East.* Cambridge: Harvard University Press, 1967.

Fredrickson, George. *The Black Image in the White Mind.* New York: Harper and Row, 1971.

Freehling, William H. "James Henley Thornwell's Mysterious Antislavery Moment." *Journal of Southern History* 57 (1991): 383–406.

Frei, Hans. *The Eclipse of Biblical Narrative.* New Haven, Conn.: Yale University Press, 1974.

Friedson, Eliot. "Are Professions Necessary." In Haskell, *Authority of Experts,* 3–27.

Fuller, Robert C. *Alternative Medicine and American Religious Life.* New York: Oxford University Press, 1989.

Gage, W. L. *The Life of Carl Ritter.* New York: Scribners, 1867.

Gaustad, Edwin S., ed. *The Rise of Adventism.* New York: Harper and Row, 1974.

Gibbs, Josiah W. *Philological Studies.* New Haven, Conn.: Durrie and Peck, 1857.

Gillespie, Neal C. *Charles Darwin and the Problem of Creation.* Chicago: University of Chicago Press, 1979.

Giltner, John. "Moses Stuart." Ph.D. diss., Yale University, 1956.

———. *Moses Stuart.* Atlanta: Scholars Press, 1988.

Gladden, Washington. *How Much Is Left of the Old Doctrines?* Boston: Houghton Mifflin, 1900.

———. *Recollections.* Boston: Houghton Mifflin, 1909.

Glass, Bentley, et al., eds. *Forerunners of Darwin, 1745–1859.* Baltimore: Johns Hopkins Press, 1959.

Glick, Wendell. "Bishop Paley in America." *New England Quarterly* 27 (1954): 347–54.

Goetzmann, William H. "Paradigm Lost." In Reingold, *Sciences in the American Context,* 21–34.

Gottschalk, Stephen. *The Emergence of Christian Science in American Religious Life.* Berkeley: University of California Press, 1973.

Gould, Stephen Jay. "Eternal Metaphors of Palaeontology." In Hallam, *Patterns of Evolution,* 1–26.

———. *The Mismeasure of Man.* New York: W. W. Norton, 1981.

Grant, Edward. "Science and Theology in the Middle Ages." In Lindberg and Numbers, *God in Nature,* 49–75.

Greene, John C. *The Death of Adam: Evolution and Its Impact on Western Thought.* Ames: Iowa State University Press, 1959.

———. *American Science in the Age of Jefferson.* Ames: Iowa State University Press, 1984.

———. "Science and Religion." In Gaustad, *Rise of Adventism,* 50–69.

Greene, Mott T. *Geology in the Nineteenth Century.* Ithaca: Cornell University Press, 1982.

Gura, Philip E. *The Wisdom of Words: Language, Theology and Literature in the New England Renaissance.* Middletown, Conn.: Wesleyan University Press, 1981.

Guralnik, Stanley M. "The American Scientist in Higher Education, 1810–1910." In Reingold, *Sciences in the American Context,* 99–141.

Haber, Francis. *The Age of the World.* Baltimore: Johns Hopkins Press, 1959.

Hall, Peter D. "The Social Foundations of Professional Credibility." In Haskell, *Authority of Experts,* 107–41.

Hallam, A., ed. *Patterns of Evolution.* Amsterdam: Elsevier, 1977.

———. *Great Geological Controversies.* New York: Oxford University Press, 1983.

Harris, Samuel. "The Demands of Infidelity Satisfied by Christianity." *Bibliotheca Sacra* 13 (1856): 272–314.

Haskell, Thomas. *The Emergence of Professional Social Sciences.* Urbana: University of Illinois Press, 1977.

———, ed. *The Authority of Experts.* Bloomington: Indiana University Press, 1984.

Hatch, Nathan. *The Democratization of American Christianity.* New Haven, Conn.: Yale University Press, 1989.

Hatch, Nathan, and Mark Noll, eds. *The Bible in America.* New York: Oxford University Press, 1982.

Herbst, Jurgen. *The German Historical School in American Scholarship.* Ithaca: Cornell University Press, 1965.

Hilprecht, H. V. *Explorations in Bible Lands during the Nineteenth Century.* Philadelphia: A. J. Holman, 1903.

Hindle, Brooke. *The Pursuit of Science in Revolutionary America, 1775–1789.* Chapel Hill: University of North Carolina Press, 1956.

Hitchcock, Edward. *The Highest Uses of Learning.* Amherst: J. S. Adams, 1845.

———. *The Religion of Geology and Its Connected Sciences.* Rev. ed. Boston: Phillips, Sampson, 1859.

———. *Reminiscences of Amherst College.* Northampton, Mass.: Bridgman and Childs, 1863.

Hodge, A. A. *The Life of Charles Hodge.* New York: Scribners, 1880.

Hodge, Charles. *A Dissertation on the Importance of Biblical Literature.* Trenton, N.J.: George Sherman, 1822.

———. "Bushnell's Discourses." *Princeton Review* 21 (1849): 259–98.

———. *Systematic Theology.* 3 vols. New York: Scribners, 1872.

———. *What Is Darwinism?* New York: Scribners, 1874.

Holifield, E. Brooks. *The Gentlemen Theologians.* Durham, N.C.: Duke University Press, 1978.

———. *A History of Pastoral Care in America.* Nashville: Abingdon Press, 1983.

Hollinger, David A. "T. S. Kuhn's Theory of Science and Its Implications for History." *American Historical Review* 78 (1973): 370–93.

———. "Justification by Verification: The Scientific Challenge to the Moral Authority of Christianity in Modern America." In Lacey, *Religion and Twentieth-Century American Intellectual Life,* 116–135.

Hollis, Daniel Walker. *The University of South Carolina.* 2 vols. Columbia: University of South Carolina Press, 1951–56.

Holte, Ragner. *Die Vermittlungstheologie.* Uppsala, Sweden: Almquist, 1965.

Hood, Fred J. *Reformed America: The Middle and Southern States, 1783–1837.* University: University of Alabama Press, 1980.

Horsman, Reginald. *Race and Manifest Destiny.* Cambridge: Harvard University Press, 1981.

———. *Josiah Nott.* Baton Rouge: Louisiana State University Press, 1987.

Hovenkamp, Herbert. *Science and Religion in America: 1800–1860.* Philadelphia: University of Pennsylvania Press, 1978.

Howe, Daniel Walker. *The Political Culture of the Whigs.* Chicago: University of Chicago Press, 1979.

———. "The Social Science of Horace Bushnell." *Journal of American History* 70 (1983): 305–22.

Hull, David. *Darwin and His Critics: The Reception of Darwin's Theory of Evolution by the Scientific Community.* Cambridge: Harvard University Press, 1973.

Hutchison, William. *The Modernist Impulse in American Protestantism.* Cambridge: Harvard University Press, 1976.

———. *Errand to the World.* Chicago: University of Chicago Press, 1987.

Hutton, James. *Theory of the Earth.* 2 vols. Edinburgh: Cadell and Davies, 1795.

"Is the Religious Want of the Age Met?" *Atlantic Monthly* 5 (1860): 358–64.

Jackson, Carl T. *The Oriental Religions and American Thought: Nineteenth-Century Explorations.* Westport, Conn.: Greenwood Press, 1981.

James, William. *Varieties of Religious Experience.* New York: Random House, 1902.

Jenkins, William Sumner. *Proslavery Thought in the Old South.* Chapel Hill: University of North Carolina Press, 1935.

Johnson, William Alexander. *Nature and the Supernatural in the Theology of Horace Bushnell.* Lund: Gleerup, 1963.

Kähler, Martin. *Geschichte der protestantischen Dogmatik im 19. Jahrhundert.* Berlin: Evangelische Verlagsanstalt, 1962.

Kantzenbach, Friedrich W. *Die Erweckungsbewegung.* Neuendettelsau, Germany: Freimund Verlag, 1957.

Kenyon, Cecelia M. "Men of Little Faith: The Anti-Federalists on the Nature of Representative Government." *William and Mary Quarterly* 12 (1955): 3–43.

Kerr, Hugh T., ed. *Sons of the Prophets.* Princeton, N.J.: Princeton University Press, 1963.

Koyré, Alexander. *From the Closed World to the Infinite Universe.* Baltimore: Johns Hopkins University Press, 1957.

Kramer, G. *Carl Ritter, ein Lebensbild.* Halle: Waisenhaus Buchhandlung, 1864.

Kuhn, Thomas S. *The Structure of Scientific Revolutions.* 2d ed. Chicago: University of Chicago Press, 1970.

Kümmel, Werner. *The New Testament: The History of the Investigation of Its Problems.* Nashville: Abingdon Press, 1972.

Kuklick, Bruce. *Churchmen and Philosophers.* New Haven, Conn.: Yale University Press, 1985.

Lacey, Michael J., ed. *Religion and Twentieth-Century American Intellectual Life.* New York: Cambridge University Press, 1989.

"Life of Sir Isaac Newton," *Christian Examiner* 12 (1832): 277–98.

Lindberg, David C., and Ronald L. Numbers, eds. *God and Nature.* Berkeley: University of California Press, 1986.

Litwack, Leon. *North of Slavery.* Chicago: University of Chicago Press, 1961.

Loetscher, Lefferts. *Facing the Enlightenment and Pietism.* Westport, Conn.: Greenwood Press, 1983.

Lord, David. "Dr. Bushnell's Dissertation on Language." *Theological and Literary Journal* 2 (1849): 61–131.

Lord, Eleazar. *The Plenary Inspiration of the Holy Scriptures.* New York: M. W. Dodd, 1857.

Lovejoy, Arthur. *The Great Chain of Being.* Rev. ed. New York: Harper and Row, 1960.

Luker, Ralph. *A Southern Tradition in Theology and Social Criticism, 1830–1930.* New York: Edwin Mellen Press, 1984.

McClellan, B. Edward, and William J. Reese, eds. *The Social History of Education*. Urbana: University of Illinois Press, 1988.

McElligott, John F. "Before Darwin: Religion and Science as Presented in American Magazines, 1830–1860." Ph.D. diss., New York University, 1973.

McGiffert, A. C., Jr. "James Marsh (1794–1842): Philosophical Theologian, Evangelical Liberal." *Church History* 38 (1969): 437–58.

McLoughlin, William G. *The Meaning of Henry Ward Beecher.* New York: Alfred A. Knopf, 1970.

McLoughlin, William G., and Walter H. Conser, Jr. "'The First Man Was Red'—Cherokee Responses to the Debate over Indian Origins, 1760–1860." *American Quarterly* 41 (1989): 243–64.

Mandelbaum, Maurice. *History, Man, and Reason.* Baltimore: Johns Hopkins University Press, 1974.

Marsden, George. *The Evangelical Mind and the New School Presbyterian Experience.* New Haven, Conn.: Yale University Press, 1970.

———. *Fundamentalism and American Culture.* New York: Oxford University Press, 1980.

———. "Everyone One's Own Interpreter? The Bible, Science, and Authority in Mid-Nineteenth-Century America." In Hatch and Noll, *Bible in America*, 79–100.

Marsh, James. "Ancient and Modern Poetry." *North American Review* 22 (1822): 94–131.

———. *An Exposition of the System of Instruction in the University of Vermont.* Burlington, Vt.: Chauncey Goodrich, 1829.

———. "Review of Stuart on the Epistle to the Hebrews." *Quarterly Christian Spectator* 1 (1829): 112–49.

———. *The Remains of the Rev. James Marsh, D.D., with a Memoir of His Life.* Ed. Joseph Torrey. Boston: Crocker and Brewer, 1843.

Martin, Jay. *Harvests of Change: American Literature, 1865–1914.* Englewood Cliffs, N.J.: Prentice-Hall, 1967.

Martin, Terence. *The Instructed Vision.* Bloomington: Indiana University Press, 1961.

Mathews, Donald G. *Religion in the Old South.* (Chicago: University of Chicago Press, 1977.

Meyer, D. H. *The Instructed Conscience.* Philadelphia: University of Pennsylvania Press, 1972.

Michaelsen, Robert S. "The Protestant Ministry in America, 1850–1950." In Niebuhr and Williams, *Ministry in Historical Perspective*, 250–88.

Miles, James Warley. *Farewell Sermon.* Charleston, S.C.: B. B. Hussey, 1843.

———. *Philosophic Theology; or, Ultimate Grounds of All Religious Belief Based in Reason.* Charleston, S.C.: John Russell, 1849.

———. *Annual Oration Delivered before the Chrestomatic Society of the College of Charleston.* Charleston, S.C.: E. C. Councell, 1850.

————. *Student of Philology.* Charleston, S.C.: John Russell, 1853.

————. *An Address Delivered at the Residence of the American Minister in Berlin, on the Fourth of July, 1855.* Berlin: G. Bernstein, 1855.

————. *The Relation between the Races of the South.* Charleston, S.C.: Evans and Cogswell, 1861.

————. *God in History: A Discourse Delivered before the Graduating Class of the College of Charleston.* Charleston, S.C.: Evans and Cogswell, 1863.

————. *Annual Oration Delivered at the Commencement of the Chrestomatic Society.* Charleston, S.C.: Evans and Cogswell, 1874.

————. *A Discourse Delivered . . . before the Washington Light Infantry.* Charleston, S.C.: Evans and Cogswell, 1874.

Miller, Glenn T. *Piety and Intellect: The Aims and Purposes of Antebellum Theological Education.* Atlanta: Scholars Press, 1990.

Miller, Perry. "Emersonian Genius and the American Democracy." *New England Quarterly* 26 (1953): 27–44.

Morgan, Robert. *Biblical Interpretation.* New York: Oxford University Press, 1988.

Moore, David. *The Politics of Deference.* New York: Barnes and Noble, 1976.

Moore, James R. The Post-Darwinian Controversies. Cambridge: Cambridge University Press, 1979.

Moorhead, James. *American Apocalypse.* New Haven, Conn.: Yale University Press, 1978.

"Moral Aesthetics or the Goodness of God in the Ornaments of the Universe." *Princeton Review* 24 (1852): 38–52.

Muller, Richard. "Henry Boynton Smith: Christocentric Theologian." *Journal of Presbyterian History* 61 (1983): 429–44.

Munger, Theodore. *The Freedom of Faith.* Boston: Houghton Mifflin, 1884.

————. *The Appeal to Life.* Boston: Houghton Mifflin, 1887.

Murchie, David. "Charles Hodge and Jacksonian Economics." *Journal of Presbyterian History* 61 (1983): 248–56.

Muzzey, A. B. "Family Worship." *Christian Examiner* 61 (1856): 182–97.

"Natural History in Its Relation to Georgia." *DeBow's Review* 16 (1854): 354–68.

Neander, August. *General History of the Christian Religion and Church.* Trans. from the 2d ed. by Joseph Torrey. 4 vols. Boston: Crocker and Brewer, 1852.

Neill, Stephen, and Tom Wright. *The Interpretation of the New Testament.* Rev. ed. New York: Oxford University Press, 1988.

Nelson, John Oliver. "Charles Hodge: Nestor of Orthodoxy." In Thorp, *Lives of Eighteen from Princeton,* 192–211.

Nicholson, Marjorie H. "James Marsh and the Vermont Transcendentalists." *The Philosophic Review* 34 (1925): 28–50.

Niebuhr, H. Richard. *The Kingdom of God in America.* New York: Harper, 1937.

Niebuhr, H. Richard, and Daniel D. Williams, eds. *The Ministry in Historical Perspective*. San Francisco: Harper and Row, 1983.

Noll, Mark. "Common Sense Traditions and American Evangelical Thought." *American Quarterly* 37 (1985): 217–38.

———. *Princeton and the Republic, 1768–1822*. Princeton, N.J.: Princeton University Press, 1989.

Nott, Josiah. *Two Lectures on the Connection between the Biblical and Physical History of Man*. New York: Bartlett and Welford, 1849.

———. "Ancient and Scripture Chronology." *Southern Quarterly Review* 18 (1850): 385–426.

Noyes, George. "Causes of the Decline of Interest in Critical Theology." *Christian Examiner* 43 (1847): 325–44.

Numbers, Ronald. "The Creationists." In Lindberg and Numbers, *God and Nature*, 391–423.

———. *The Creationists*. New York: Alfred A. Knopf, 1992.

Numbers, Ronald, and Todd Savitt, eds. *Science and Medicine in the Old South*. Baton Rouge: Louisiana State University Press, 1989.

Olbricht, Thomas A. "Charles Hodge as an American New Testament Interpreter." *Journal of Presbyterian History* 57 (1979): 117–33.

Oleson, Alexandra, and S. Brown, eds. *The Pursuit of Knowledge in the Early American Republic*. Baltimore: Johns Hopkins University Press, 1976.

Oleson, Alexandra, and J. Voss, eds. *The Organization of Knowledge in Modern America, 1860–1920*. Baltimore: Johns Hopkins University Press, 1979.

Palmer, Benjamin. *The Life and Letters of James Henley Thornwell*. Richmond, Va.: Whitter and Shepperson, 1875.

Parker, Theodore. *A Discourse of Matters Pertaining to Religion*. Boston: Little, Brown, 1842.

———. "The Previous Question between Mr. Andrews Norton and His Alumni Moved and Handled." In Dirks, *Critical Theology of Theodore Parker*, 137–59.

———. "The Transient and Permanent in Christianity." In Wright, *Three Prophets of Religious Liberalism*, 113–49.

Parks, Edwards A. "Connection between Theological Study and Pulpit Eloquence." *American Biblical Repository* 10 (1837): 169–91.

———. "The Theology of the Intellect and That of the Feelings." *Bibliotheca Sacra* 7 (1850): 533–69.

Pedersen, Holger. *The Discovery of Language: Linguistic Science in the Nineteenth Century*. Bloomington: Indiana University Press, 1967.

Penzel, Klaus. "Church History and the Ecumenical Quest: A Study of the German Background and Thought of Philip Schaff." Ph.D. diss., Union Theological Seminary, 1962.

Petersen, Thomas. *Ham and Japheth*. Metuchen, N.J.: Scarecrow Press, 1979.

Popkin, Richard H. "Pre-Adamism in Nineteenth-Century American Thought." *Philosophia* 8 (1978–79): 205–39.

———. *Isaac La Peyrère.* Leiden, Netherlands: E. J. Brill, 1987.

Porter, Noah. "Coleridge and His American Disciples." *Bibliotheca Sacra* 4 (1847): 117–71.

———. "Horace Bushnell." *New Englander* 37 (1877): 157–69.

———. "The Collapse of Faith." *Princeton Review* 12 (1882): 164–84.

Prentiss, George. *The Union Theological Seminary in the City of New York.* New York: A. D. Randolph, 1889.

Reingold, Nathan. "Definitions and Speculations: The Professionalization of Science in America in the Nineteenth Century." In Oleson and Brown, *Pursuit of Knowledge in the Early American Republic,* 33–69.

———, ed. *The Sciences in the American Context: New Perspectives.* Washington, D.C.: Smithsonian Institution Press, 1979.

Reventlow, Henning Graf. *The Authority of the Bible and the Rise of the Modern World.* Philadelphia: Fortress Press, 1985.

Richardson, Robert D., Jr. *Myth and Language in the American Renaissance.* Bloomington: Indiana University Press, 1978.

Roberts, Jon H. *Darwinism and the Divine in America.* Madison: University of Wisconsin Press, 1988.

Robinson, Edward. "Philology and Lexicography of the New Testament." *Biblical Repository* 13 (1834): 154–82.

———. *The Bible and Its Literature.* New York: Office of the American Bible Repository, 1841.

———. *Biblical Researches in Palestine, Mount Sinai, and Arabia Petraea.* 3 vols. Boston: Crocker and Brewster, 1841.

Rogerson, John. *Old Testament Criticism in the Nineteenth Century: England and Germany.* Philadelphia: Fortress Press, 1985.

Rosenberg, Charles. *No Other Gods: On Science and American Social Thought.* Baltimore: Johns Hopkins University Press, 1976.

Rossiter, Margaret. *The Emergence of Agricultural Science.* New Haven, Conn.: Yale University Press, 1975.

Rothermundt, Jörge. *Personale Synthese.* Göttingen: Vandenhoeck and Ruprecht, 1968.

Russett, Cynthia. *Darwin in America.* San Francisco: W. H. Freeman, 1976.

Sandeen, Ernest R. *The Roots of Fundamentalism.* Chicago: University of Chicago Press, 1970.

Saum, Lewis. *The Popular Mood of Pre-Civil War America.* Westport, Conn.: Greenwood Press, 1980.

Schaff, David S. *The Life of Philip Schaff.* New York: Scribners, 1897.

Schaff, Philip. *Anglo-Germanism; or, The Significance of the German Nationality.* Chambersburg, Pa.: Kieffer, 1846.

———. *What Is Church History?* Philadelphia: Lippincott, 1846.

———. "Prolegomena zur Kirchengeschichte der Vereinigten Staaten." *Der Deutsche Kirchenfreund* 1 (1848): 257–64.

———. *Systematic Benevolence*. Mercersburg, Pa.: Rice, 1851.

———. *America: A Sketch of Its Political, Social and Religious Character.* Ed. Perry Miller. 1855. Reprint. Cambridge: Harvard University Press, 1961.

———. *American Nationality*. Chambersburg, Pa.: Kieffer, 1856.

———. *Slavery and the Bible*. Chambersburg, Pa.: Kieffer, 1861.

———. *Der Bürgerkrieg und das christliche Leben in Nord Amerika*. Berlin: Wiegard and Grieben, 1866.

———. *History of the Christian Church*. Rev. ed. New York: Scribners, 1882.

———. *August Neander*. Gotha, Germany: Friedrich Perthes, 1886.

Schlesinger, Arthur M., Sr. "A Critical Period in American Protestantism, 1875–1900." *Massachusetts Historical Society Proceedings* 64 (1932): 523–48.

Schnabel, Franz. *Deutsche Geschichte im Neuenzehnten Jahrhundert*. 4 vols. 2d ed. Freiburg, Germany: Herder Verlag, 1951.

Scott, Donald M. *From Office to Profession: The New England Ministry, 1750–1850*. Philadelphia: University of Pennsylvania Press, 1978.

———. "The Popular Lecture and the Creation of a Public in Mid-Nineteenth Century America." *Journal of American History* 66 (1980): 791–809.

Scovel, Raleigh. "Orthodoxy in Princeton: A Social and Intellectual History of Princeton Theological Seminary, 1812–1860." Ph.D. diss., University of California at Berkeley, 1970.

Selge, Kurt-Victor. "August Neander—ein getaufter Hamburger Jude der Emanzipations- und Restaurationzeit als erster Berliner Kirchen-historiker (1813–1850)." In Beiser and Gestrich, *450 Jahre Evangelische Theologie in Berlin*, 233–76.

Shattuck, Gardiner H., Jr. *A Shield and a Hiding Place*. Macon, Ga.: Mercer University Press, 1987.

Shedd, W. G. T. *Lectures upon the Philosophy of History*. 1856. Reprint. Andover, Mass.: Warren F. Draper, 1861.

———. *Theological Essays*. New York: Scribners, 1877.

———. *Literary Essays*. New York: Scribners, 1878.

———. *Orthodoxy and Heterodoxy*. New York: Scribners, 1899.

Shriver, George H. *Philip Schaff*. Macon, Ga.: Mercer University Press, 1987.

Silver, James W. *Confederate Morale and Church Propaganda*. 1957. Reprint. New York: W. W. Norton, 1967.

Sinclair, Bruce. "Americans Abroad: Science and Cultural Nationalism in the Early Nineteenth Century." In Reingold, *Sciences in the American Context*, 35–53.

Smith, David L. *Symbolism and Growth: The Religious Thought of Horace Bushnell.* Chico, Calif.: Scholars Press, 1981.

Smith, H. Shelton. "The Church and the Social Order in the Old South as Interpreted by James H. Thornwell." *Church History* 7 (1938): 115–24.

Smith, Henry Boynton. *Faith and Philosophy: Discourses and Essays.* Edinburgh: T. T. Clark, 1878.

———. *Henry Boynton Smith: His Life and Work.* Ed. his wife. New York: A. C. Armstrong, 1881.

Smith, Henry B., and Roswell D. Hitchcock. *The Life, Writings, and Character of Edward Robinson.* New York: Anson Randolph, 1863.

Smith, Henry Nash. "Emerson's Problem of Vocation: A Note on 'The American Scholar.'" *New England Quarterly* 12 (1939): 56–67.

Smyth, Newman. *New Faith in New Light.* New York: Scribners, 1879.

Stanton, William. *The Leopard's Spots.* Chicago: University of Chicago Press, 1960.

Stephan, Horst, and Martin Schmidt. *Geschichte der deutschen evangelischen Theologie seit dem deutschen Idealismus.* 3d ed. Berlin: Walter de Gruyter, 1973.

Stevenson, Louise L. *Scholarly Means to Evangelical Ends.* Baltimore: Johns Hopkins University Press, 1986.

Stoever, William K. B. "Henry Boynton Smith and the German Theology of History." *Union Seminary Quarterly Review* 24 (1968): 69–89.

Strout, Cushing. "Faith and History: The Mind of William G. T. Shedd." *Journal of the History of Ideas* 15 (1954): 153–62.

Stuart, Moses. "Are the Same Principles of Interpretation to be Applied to the Scriptures as to Other Books?" *American Biblical Repository* 2 (1832): 124–37.

———. *Critical History and Defence of the Old Testament Canon.* Andover, Mass.: Allen, Morrill and Wordwell, 1845.

Thigpen, Thomas P. "On the Origin of Theses: An Exploration of Horace Bushnell's Rejection of Darwinism." *Church History* 57 (1988): 499–513.

Tholuck, August. *Die Glaubenswürdigkeit der evangelischen Geschichte.* Hamburg, Germany: F. Perthes, 1837.

Thornwell, James Henley. *National Sins: A Fast-Day Sermon.* Columbia: Guardian Press, 1860.

———. *The State of the Country.* In Palmer, *Thornwell's Life and Letters,* 591–610.

Thorp, Willard, ed. *Lives of Eighteen from Princeton.* Princeton, N.J.: Princeton University Press, 1946.

"Thoughts on the Revelations of the Microscope." *New Englander* 5 (1847): 231–46.

Tise, Larry E. *Proslavery.* Athens: University of Georgia Press, 1987.

Trevor-Roper, H. R. *Catholics, Anglicans, and Puritans.* Chicago: University of Chicago Press, 1988.

Trinterud, Leonard J. "Charles Hodge." In Kerr, *Sons of the Prophets*, 22–38.

Tuveson, Ernest Lee. *Redeemer Nation: The Idea of America's Millennial Role.* Chicago: University of Chicago Press, 1968.

Ullmann, Karl. *Das Wesen des Christenthums.* 3d ed. Hamburg, Germany: F. Perthes, 1849.

Ussher, James. *The Annals of the World.* London: E. Tyler, 1685.

Vander Stelt, John C. *Philosophy and Scripture: A Study in Old Princeton and Westminster Theology.* Marlton, N.J.: Mack, 1978.

"Vestiges of Creation and Its Reviewers." *New Englander* 4 (1846): 113–27.

Welch, Claude. *Protestant Thought in the Nineteenth Century.* 2 vols. New Haven, Conn.: Yale University Press, 1972–85.

Wellek, René. *Concepts of Criticism.* Ed. Stephen Nichols, Jr. New Haven, Conn.: Yale University Press, 1963.

———. *Confrontations.* Princeton, N.J.: Princeton University Press, 1965.

Wells, Ronald V. *Three Christian Transcendentalists.* New York: Columbia University Press, 1943.

Westfall, Richard S. *Science and Religion in Seventeenth-Century England.* Ann Arbor: University of Michigan Press, 1973.

White, Andrew Dickson. *A History of the Warfare of Science with Theology in Christendom.* 2 vols. New York: D. Appleton, 1896.

Wiegand, Adelbert. *August Neanders Leben.* Erfurt, Germany: Fr. Bartholomaeus, 1889.

Williams, George. *The Reverend James Warley Miles.* Charleston, S.C.: Dalcho Historical Society, 1954.

Witte, Leopold. *Das Leben D. Friedrich August Gottreu Tholucks.* 2 vols. Bielefeld, Germany: Velhagen, 1884–86.

Wright, Conrad, ed. *Three Prophets of Religious Liberalism.* Boston: Beacon Press, 1961.

Wyatt-Brown, Bertram. *Yankee Saints and Southern Sinners.* Baton Rouge: Louisiana State University Press, 1985.

Index